FRENCH SCULPTURE OF THE ROMANESQUE PERIOD
ELEVENTH AND TWELFTH CENTURIES

FRENCH SCULPTURE
OF THE ROMANESQUE PERIOD
ELEVENTH AND TWELFTH
CENTURIES

by

PAUL DESCHAMPS

HACKER ART BOOKS

NEW YORK

1972

First published by Pantheon. Casa Editrice
Firenze, 1930
Reprinted by Hacker Art Books, Inc.
New York, 1972

Library of Congress Catalog Card Number: 78-143343
ISBN: 0-87817-063-4

CONTENTS

LIST OF PLATES

9 TOULOUSE, St.-Sernin. Tympanum of the Miégeville door: The Ascension of Christ. *End of* xi *or early years of* xii *century.*

10 TOULOUSE, St.-Sernin. Details of the Miégeville door: A. Base of the statue of St. James. B. Base of the statue of St. Peter. *Beginning of* xii *century* (?).

11 A-B. TOULOUSE, St.-Sernin. Miégeville door: A. Statue of St. James. B. Statue of St. Peter. *Beginning of* xii *century* (?).
C-E. LEÓN, San Isidoro. c, e. Statues on the south transept door. D. Museo San Marco: Bust found in the cloister of San Isidoro. *Beginning of* xii *century* (?).

12 CAPITALS AND ABACI IN THE STYLE OF TOULOUSE. *First half of* xii *century.*
A. TOULOUSE, St.-Sernin. West façade (after the cast in the Trocadéro).
B. St.-GAUDENS (Haute-Garonne). (After the cast in the Trocadéro).
c. SANTIAGO DE COMPOSTELA. Goldsmiths' Door.
D. SANT'ANTIMO (Tuscany).

13 MOISSAC, St.-Pierre. Bas-reliefs of the cloister pillars: A. St. Paul and St. Peter. B. St. Bartholomew. *About* 1100.

14 MOISSAC, St.-Pierre. Bas-relief of the cloister pillars. St. James and St. John. *About* 1100.

15 MOISSAC, St.-Pierre. a-b. Capitals in the cloister. *About* 1100.

16 A-C. MOISSAC, St.-Pierre. a-b. Capitals in the cloister. c. Daniel in the lions' den. *About* 1100.
D. TOULOUSE, Musée des Augustins. Capital from the cloister of La Daurade: Daniel in the lions' den. *About* 1100.

17 MOISSAC, St.-Pierre. Tympanum of the doorway (after the cast in the Trocadéro). *Between* 1100 *and* 1135.

18 MOISSAC, St.-Pierre. Pier of the doorway (after the cast in the Trocadéro). *Between* 1100 *and* 1135.

19 MOISSAC, St.-Pierre. a-b. Details of the bas-reliefs on the projection of the doorway. *Middle of* xii *century.*

20 CARENNAC (Lot). Tympanum of the doorway. *First half of* xii *century.*

21 SOUILLAC (Lot). Pier of the doorway (after the cast in the Trocadéro). *First half of* xii *century.*

22 A. SOUILLAC (Lot). Detail of an abutment of the doorway: The Prophet Isaiah. *First half of* xii *century.*
B. RODEZ, Musée de la Société des Lettres d'Aveyron. God in Majesty. *First half of* xii *century.*

23 BEAULIEU (Corrèze). Central portion of the tympanum. *Second quarter of* xii *century.*

24 BEAULIEU (Corrèze). A-B. Carvings on a pier of the doorway. *Second quarter of* XII *century.*

25 TOULOUSE, Musée des Augustins. Carvings from the door of the chapter-house of St.-Étienne. *First half of* XII *century.*

26 A. ST.-GAUDENS (Haute-Garonne). Capital. *First half of* XII *century.*
B. HAGETMAU (Landes). Capital. *First half of* XII *century.*
C-D. LESCAR (Basses-Pyrénées). Capitals. *First half of* XII *century.*

27 A. LESCAR (Basses-Pyrénées). Capitals. *First half of* XII *century.*
B-C. CASTELNAU-RIVIÈRE-BASSE (Hautes-Pyrénées). Capitals. *First half of* XII *century.*

28 CATUS (Lot). Capital: Delivery of the keys to St. Peter. *First half of* XII *century.*

29 TOULOUSE, Musée des Augustins. Capitals from the cloister of the cathedral of St.-Étienne: A. Herod and Salome. B. The Wise Virgins. *Middle of* XII *century.*

30 TOULOUSE, Musée des Augustins. Capital from the church of La Daurade: A bear-hunt (after the cast in the Trocadéro). *End of* XII *century.*

31 A. CHARLIEU (Loire). Tympanum of the doorway. *About* 1094.
B. NEUILLY-EN-DONJON (Allier). Tympanum of the doorway. *Beginning of* XII *century.*

32 A. ANZY-LE-DUC (Saône-et-Loire), Priory Church. Capital. *End of* XI *century.*
B. CHARLIEU (Loire), St.-Fortunat. Capital (the same as at Anzy-le-Duc). *End of* XI *century.*

33 CLUNY (Saône-et-Loire), Musée Ochier. Capital from the abbey church of St.-Pierre: A-B. Adam and Eve. *After* 1088, *end of* XI *or first years of* XII *century.*

34 AUTUN, Cathedral of St.-Lazare. Central portion of the tympanum of the main doorway. *About* 1120(?).

35 AUTUN, Victor Terret Collection. Fragment of the lintel of a lateral doorway of the cathedral: A-B. Eve.

36 AUTUN. Cathedral of St.-Lazare. Capitals: A. The Stoning of St. Stephen. B. The Flight into Egypt. C. Apparition to St. Mary Magdalen. D. The body of St. Vincent protected by eagles. *First half of* XII *century.*

37 VÉZELAY, Ste.-Madeleine. Tympanum of the doorway of the nave (after the cast in the Trocadéro). *About* 1130.

38 VÉZELAY, Ste.-Madeleine. Capitals: A. Miracle of St. Benedict. B. Moses and the golden calf. C. The Building of the Ark. D. St. Paul grinding the corn of the ancient Law into the fine flour of the Gospel. *Between* 1120 *and* 1138.

39 CAPITALS. *First half of* XII *century*.

A. SAULIEU (CÔTE-D'OR), ST.-ANDOCHE. Christ appearing to St. Mary Magdalen.

B-C. CHALON-SUR-SAÔNE, ST.-VINCENT. B. Christ appearing to St. Mary Magdalen. C. Capital decorated with foliage.

D. ANZY-LE-DUC (SAÔNE-ET-LOIRE). Capital ornamented with birds and foliage.

40 CAPITALS. *First half of* XII *century*.

A. MOUTIER-ST.-JEAN (CÔTE-D'OR). Vintage Scene (now in the Louvre).

B. CAMBRIDGE (MASS.). FOGG MUSEUM. Cain and Abel make their offerings.

C-D. ROMANS (ISÈRE), ST.-BARNARD. Capitals from the nave (cast in the museum at Valence): C. Annunciation. D. The weighing of souls.

41 A. MONTCEAUX-L'ETOILE (SAÔNE-ET-LOIRE). Tympanum: The Ascension. *First half of* XII *century*.

B. PERRECY-LES-FORGES (SAÔNE-ET-LOIRE). Tympanum: Christ in Majesty. On the lintel: Christ in the Garden of Olives. *First half of* XII *century*.

42 CLUNY, MUSÉE OCHIER. Capital from the choir of the Abbey Church of St.-Pierre: Spring. *Second quarter of* XII *century*.

43 CLUNY, MUSÉE OCHIER. Capitals from the choir of the Abbey Church of St.-Pierre: A. One of the liberal arts(?). B. The first tone of music. *Second quarter of* XII *century*.

44 CLUNY, MUSÉE OCHIER. Capitals from the choir of the Abbey Church of St.-Pierre: A. The third tone of music. B. The fourth tone of music. *Second quarter of* XII *century*.

45 A-C. CLUNY, MUSÉE OCHIER. Capitals from the choir of the Abbey Church of St.-Pierre: A., C. The rivers of Paradise. B. The labours of the Earth. *Second quarter of* XII *century*.

D. VÉZELAY, STE.-MADELEINE. Capital: Apiarists at work. *Between* 1120 *and* 1138.

46 PARAY-LE-MONIAL, MUSEUM. Tympanum from the church at Anzy-le-Duc (cast in the Trocadéro). *Latter half of* XII *century*.

47 A. CHARLIEU (LOIRE), ST.-FORTUNAT. Tympanum of a small door at the side of the entrance at the front of the porch. Lintel: The sacrifice of the Ancient Law. Tympanum: The Marriage at Cana. Archivolt: The Transfiguration (cast in the Trocadéro). *Middle or third quarter of* XII *century*.

B. ST.-JULIEN-DE-JONZY (SAÔNE-ET-LOIRE). Tympanum: Christ in Majesty. On the lintel: The Last Supper. *Middle or third quarter of* XII *century*.

48 A. VIENNE, Cathedral of St.-Maurice. Statue of St. Paul.
B. VIENNE, Musée St.-Pierre. Tympanum of a doorway of the church of St.-Pierre. Bas-relief: St. Peter.
C. VIENNE, Cathedral of St.-Maurice. Statue of a saint. *First half of* XII *century.*

49 A-B. VIENNE, St.-André-le-Bas. Capitals (cast of the Trocadéro Museum): A. Samson and the lion. B. Job an object of disgust to his family. *About* 1152.
C-D. VIENNE, Cathedral of St.-Maurice. Capitals: C. The Holy Women at the Tomb. D. David and Goliath.

50 THINES (Ardèche). Statues on the abutments of the doorway. *Latter half of* XII *century.*

51 AVENAS (Rhône). Altar: A. Lateral panel. B. Front. *About* 1166.

52 CAPITALS. *First half of* XII *century.*
A-C. MOZAT (Puy-de-Dôme). A-B. Figure capitals. C. Annunciation (cast in the Trocadéro Museum).
D. VOLVIC (Puy-de-Dôme). Angels.

53 CAPITALS. *First half of* XII *century.*
A-B. CLERMONT-FERRAND, Notre-Dame-du-Port. A. Combat between Virtues and Vices (cast in the Trocadéro Museum). B. Annunciation.
C-D. ST.-NECTAIRE (Puy-de-Dôme). C. Miracle of the loaves. D. The Guardians of the Sepulchre.

54 ISSOIRE, St.-Paul. Capitals: A. The Last Supper. B. The Bearing of the Cross (cast in the museum at Clermont). *First half of* XII *century.*

55 MAURIAC (Cantal). Tympanum. *First half of* XII *century.*

56 ST.-JUNIEN (Haute-Vienne). Tomb of St. Junien (northern face). *Last quarter of* XII *century.*

57 CONQUES, Ste.-Foy. Central portion of the tympanum: The Last Judgement. *Second quarter or middle of* XII *century.*

58 BOURGES, St.-Ursin. Detail of the tympanum: Fables of Aesop and hunting-scenes. *Beginning of* XII *century.*

59 ST.-RÉVÉRIEN (Nièvre). Seraph. *Middle of* XII *century.*

60 ST.-GENOU (Indre). A-B. Capitals. *First half of* XII *century.*

61 LA BERTHENOUX (Indre). A-D. Capitals. *First half of* XII *century.*

62 A-B. ST.-GENOU (Indre). Capitals. *First half of* XII *century.*
C. NEUVY-ST.-SÉPULCRE (Indre). Capital. *First half of* XII *century.*

63 A. ST.-PIERRE-LE-MOUTIER (Nièvre). Capital. *First half of* XII *century.*
B. BOMMIERS (Indre). Capital. *First half of* XII *century.*
C-D. GARGILESSE (Indre). Capitals. *First half and middle of* XII *century.*

64 ST.-BENOÎT-SUR-LOIRE (Loiret). A-C. Capitals of the choir, transept and nave. D. (Cast in the Trocadéro Museum). *End of* XI *and first half of* XII *century.*

65 ST.-AIGNAN (Loir-et-Cher). Capitals: A. Centaur shooting an arrow at a stag. B. Flight into Egypt. C. The Beast of the Apocalypse. D. Sirens. *First half of* XII *century.*

66 L'ILE-BOUCHARD (Indre-et-Loire). Capitals: A. Annunciation, Visitation and Adoration of the Magi. B. Entry into Jerusalem. C. Announcement to the Shepherds. D. Decorative capital. *First half of* XII *century.*

67 A-B. FONTEVRAULT (Maine-et-Loire). Capitals. *Third quarter of* XII *century.*
C. CUNAULT (Maine-et-Loire). Capital. *Middle of* XII *century.*

68 CHAUVIGNY (Vienne). A-D. Capitals: A. Announcement to the Shepherds. *First half of* XII *century.*

69 ANGOULÊME, Cathedral of St.-Pierre. A. Western façade. Frieze: A scene of combat (cast in the Trocadéro Museum). B. Western façade. Tympanum of a blind bay: The Apostles going out to preach the Gospel. C. Frieze of the apse (cast in the Trocadéro Museum). *First half of* XII *century.*

70 A. AULNAY (Charente-Inférieure). St.-Pierre. Window in the apse. *Third quarter of* XII *century.*
B. ST.-SULPICE-D'ARNOULT (Charente-Inférieure). West Door. *Middle of* XII *century.*

71 PÉRIGNAC (Charente-Inférieure). Detail of the west front. *Middle of* XII *century.*

72 AULNAY (Charente-Inférieure), St.-Pierre. Detail of the arch-rims on the west door. *Third quarter of* XII *century.*

73 AULNAY (Charente-Inférieure), St.-Pierre. A. Samson and Delilah. B. The Murder of Abel. C. Monsters. D. Elephants. *Third quarter of* XII *century.*

74 A. ARGENTON-CHÂTEAU (Deux-Sèvres). Detail of the arch-rims.
B. AVY (Charente-Inférieure). Detail of the arch-rims. *Third quarter of* XII *century.*

75 CIVRAY (Vienne). Detail of the arch-rims. *Third quarter of* XII *century.*

76 ST.-MICHEL-D'ENTRAIGUES (Charente). St. Michael slaying the dragon. *About* 1137.

77 POITIERS, Notre-Dame-la-Grande. Detail of the façade. *Middle of* XII *century.*

78 BAYEUX, Cathedral. Sculptures in the nave (cast in the Trocadéro Museum). *Middle of* XII *century.*

79 RUCQUEVILLE (Calvados). A-D. Capitals with figures: C. Flight into Egypt. D. Incredulity of St. Thomas. *Beginning of* XII *century.*

80 ST.-GILLES-DU-GARD. Façade: A. St. Michael slaying the dragon. B. St. James the Less and St. Paul. *Latter half of* XII *century.*

81 ST.-GILLES-DU-GARD. Façade: Details. *Latter half of* XII *century.*

82 ST.-GILLES-DU-GARD. Frieze of the façade: A. Christ purges the Temple. B. Arrest of Christ in the Garden of Olives. *Last quarter of* XII *century.*

83 ARLES, St.-Trophime. Doorway: Details. *Last quarter of* XII *century.*

84 ARLES, Cloister of St.-Trophime. North-west pillar: St. Peter, St. Trophime and St. John. Bas-relief in two tiers: Two sellers of spices, the Holy Women. *About* 1180-1190.

85 A. ARLES, Cloister of St.-Trophime. Capitals. *End of* XII *century.*
B-C. CAMBRIDGE (Mass.), Fogg Museum. Capitals from Notre-Dame-des-Doms at Avignon: B. Samson and Delilah. C. Samson pulling down the pillars of the Temple. *Latter half of* XII *century.*

86 MONTPELLIER, Musée Archéologique. High relief from St.-Guilhem-le-Désert (Hérault).

87 A-B. ST.-GUILHEM-LE-DÉSERT (Hérault). A. Fragment imitated from the antique. B. Virgin and Child.
C-D. MONTPELLIER, Musée Archéologique. Bas-reliefs from St.-Guilhem-le-Désert (Hérault).

88 ELNE. Cloister of the Cathedral. *Last quarter of* XII *century.*

89 GERONA (Catalonia), Cathedral. Bas-relief on a pillar of the cloister. *Latter half of* XII *century.*

90 A. CUIXA, Abbey of St.-Michel. Bas-reliefs now on the doorway of the abbot's lodge.
B. BOULE D'AMONT (Pyrénées-Orientales), Abbey of Serrabone. Porch. *Latter half of* XII *century.*

91 A-B. PRADES (Pyrénées-Orientales). Capitals from the cloister of the Abbey of St.-Michel at Cuixa. *Latter half of* XII *century.*
C. BOULE D'AMONT (Pyrénées-Orientales), Abbey of Serrabone, Cloister. Capital from the gallery of the first storey. *Latter half of* XII *century.*

92 BOULE D'AMONT (Pyrénées-Orientales), Abbey of Serrabone. A-C. Capitals of the porch. *Latter half of* XII *century.*

93 A. CORNEILLA-DE-CONFLENT (Pyrénées-Orientales). Tympanum. *Latter half of* xii *century.*
B. BOULE D'AMONT (Pyrénées-Orientales), Abbey of Serrabone. Capital of the porch. *Latter half of* xii *century.*

94 PAMPLONA (Navarre). A. Decorative capital. B. The Kiss of Judas. C. The Entombment. *Latter half of* xii *century.*

95 NAZARETH, Basilica of the Annunciation. Capitals supposed to have belonged to the doorway. A. Apparition of Christ to St. Thomas. B. The Raising of Tabitha. C. Legend of St. James the Greater. D. Legend of St. Matthew. *Before* 1187.

96 JERUSALEM, Museum of the Greek Patriarchate. Heads found at Nazareth, probably destined for the Basilica of the Annunciation. *Before* 1187.

THE TEXT

INTRODUCTION

THE beginning of the twelfth century saw the blossoming, in many provinces of France, of a marvellous art. The capitals crowning the internal columns of her churches, the doorways which frame the entrances, sometimes the entire surface of the western fronts, were enriched with lavish ornamentation. Large surfaces were carved with great pictures containing human figures; creatures in fantastic attitudes, quaint monsters which combined in one single body all manner of discrepant features of the animal kingdom; all the fruits of an imagination that was amazing in its fertility united to provide for the churches of France an infinite variety of decoration that was fanciful, uncommon and mysterious.

It is interesting to look for the causes to which we owe these bewildering creations. Lost sight of for five hundred years, the art of carving human figures in stone appeared again in the course of the eleventh century, though it was not until the end of the century that it was fully manifest; so that the craftsmen who then tried to call forth figures from the stone were following no precedents: it was their task to revive an art that had been for some considerable time altogether neglected.

And so it came about that they imitated the achievements of many and various civilizations, following methods that also were many and various, and sometimes even estranged from the very principles of sculpture. This is why Romanesque art is the most composite of all arts. Sculptures upon the pagan temples of Gaul, sarcophagi of the earliest Christian centuries, far-away works of Asiatic antiquity, all of them supplied matter for imitation. Mohammedan objects of art, particularly ivory caskets, were widely copied. Persian, Byzantine and Arabian fabrics, with their strange groupings of animals, supplied examples of incomparable decorative elegance which strongly attracted these craftsmen.[1]

The art of the Christian East, however, supplied yet other models, and it has been said that the iconographic programme of the Romanesque art which strove to exhibit to the faithful the truths they should believe and the supernatural personages they were to venerate, came from the churches of Palestine, Syria, Cappadocia, Byzantium[1a] and Greece, and from the Christian monasteries of Egypt, through the medium of miniatures which were copied assiduously by monks in the great abbeys of Ireland, Germany, Italy, France and Spain.)

Though this is true enough up to a certain point, we must beware of attributing an exclusive influence to these miniatures, nor must we forget that upon the soil of France there existed, in the Merovingian and Carlovingian epochs, a number of churches the interiors of which were richly decorated with hangings, mosaics, paintings and so on, while their embellishments were already impregnated by artistic ideas from the East.

There remain to us but scanty specimens of these monuments, and that is why the study of them is so neglected by historians of art; but documents exist which reveal to us their richness and their astonishing number, and it is quite plain that in France, as in Italy at Rome and at Ravenna, alongside of this influence from the East the local temperament had already shown its own character, and begun to transform these models according to its own ideas. We must not, that is to say, in our investigations into the origins of Romanesque art, ever forget the native contribution of preceding centuries.

Great hangings stretched in front of the ciboria and between the columns, made in the workshops of Sicily and doubtless also in Rome, where one found religious representations borrowed partly from eastern traditions and partly from the west; mosaics, with golden backgrounds, representing sacred personages standing upright under the arcades; frescoes covering the apses with whole series of pictures, offering to sculptors an example of figures far larger than those in a miniature — these things served as guides to the sculptors of whom we are speaking.

They found other models nearer at hand and easier of reproduction in the relief-work practised by the Carlovingians and their contemporaries: bronze doors with figures in relief, altar-fronts of metal or wood, shrines and plaques of evangelists with silver-gilt figures in repoussé, stucco figures such as had been modelled and set up in our churches since the days of Charlemagne — from all of these could be copied direct the things they tried to represent.

Everywhere is found this copying from models so diverse, and herein we recognize the reason for the inexhaustible variety of Romanesque creation. On the capitals in the crypt of St.-Bénigne at Dijon are found the bird with hooked beak as on barbarian buckles. Upon the wing of a bird on a capital at Bommes (Gironde)[2] are reproduced the embroidery knots of the very piece of material that the sculptor had before his eyes. The same ornament is to be seen on the wing of a chimera on a capital in the church at Charost (Cher). The calligraphic processes of the miniaturists are repeated in the methods by which vestments are represented in certain Romanesque sculptures, notably on the tympanum of Autun and upon the Christ of the museum at Rodez. *Plates 34, 22b* In the oval glories which surround the figures of Christ in Majesty on the tympana of doorways the sculptors have copied the round, square or lozenge-shaped forms of the uncut jewels, pastes, glass and precious stones which were placed round the divine image in goldsmiths' work. This carrying-over of a technique into something with which it really has but very slight relation explains the oddities, occasionally even the clumsinesses, that are found in certain Romanesque works.

But even though the Romanesque artists drew their inspiration from such various models, they were often able thus to achieve work of great value and even to create a style that was essentially original.

The dominant idea in this Romanesque style is a careful preservation of the decorative composition. Even the proportions of the human body must adapt themselves to the ornamentation, so that sometimes they are transformed, in case of need, beyond all recognition.

We realize this when we examine the great figures on the piers of Moissac and of Beaulieu, which are elongated out of all proper proportion in order that they may fill the entire height of each face of the pier, and the statues of angels and of virtues which reach the whole length of the arch-rims on the doorways of Saintonge. [2a]

It was a long time before sculptors ventured to depict their personages in very marked relief, and they were even more reluctant to make certain parts of the body stand out from the background. Even when they ventured to carve figures of large size, they scarcely dared to leave the surface of the rectangular slabs which they had to carve. They drew the silhouettes and carved out the stone all round them, leaving at the edges of the slabs a framework occasionally decorated with an arcade and two little columns. The artists who carved the Christian sarcophagi at Arles in the fourth century followed the same system, but they knew how to give volume to their figures in such a way that they seemed independent of the background.

Great care was taken to avoid planes of different depths, and all reliefs were adjusted to the same level, which was that of the original surface of the slab. In short, there were only two planes: the body of the personage with the head, in most cases shown in profile but sometimes facing the front with flattened features, and the main level of the stone. Everything else, the projections of the body, the shoulders, knees and feet, the folds of the draperies, was merely sketched in or lightly incised. We see this in the sculptures in the ambulatory of the choir of St.-Sernin at Toulouse, on the pillars in the cloister at Moissac and on the piers of the doors at Moissac and at Beaulieu. The arched frames and the entire bodies of the personages are reduced to the same level, while the folded arms are without relief and seem crushed against the body.

The same system is followed in the statue of St. Trophime on the doorway of St.-Trophime at Arles, which dates from the end of the twelfth century. *Plate 83* As M. Jean Laran has observed: "If we hold a plane surface in a vertical position against the statue of St. Trophime, we shall see that it will touch the mitre, the crozier, parts of the face, hands and feet, and the folds of the vestments. The points of contact are so numerous that the profile of the statue is a perfectly straight line". [2b]

Even when the sculptor did not retain the edges of the stone, the background was nevertheless uniform and the figures were placed against this background in profile; examples of this are to be found in the abutments of the doorways at Moissac and Souillac and the jambs of the doorways at Étampes. When seated figures such as Christ in Majesty were represented, the marked projection of the knees offered a difficult problem which was solved either by opening wide the legs (Museum of Rodez, tympanum of Autun), or by placing both legs on one side so that the lower part of the body was *Plate 37* seen in profile (tympanum of Vézelay).

At Beaulieu and St.-Denis the crossed arms of the Christ in Majesty are shown as a prolongation of the body; at St.-Jouin-de-Marnes and Martel they hang down by the sides, while at Conques one arm is raised and the other lowered; the hands are represented open to avoid the difficulties of showing them in relief. The nearest approach to a representation in relief is seen on the tympanum of Vézelay, where the hands stand out from the background. When it is desired to represent recumbent figures, the sculptors avoid showing one arm in front of the body. The shoulders are practically eliminated and

4

the arms placed in various positions in order to form one plane with the body (cf. the Eve on a lintel of a doorway at Autun).

Plate 35

The few successful attempts at giving volume to the figures were due to the conservation of a framework round the bodies and to the placing of the figure in a concave medallion (glories on the tympana at Carennac, Mauriac, St.-Julien-de-Jonzy, Cahors; altar at Avenas; tomb of St.-Junien and certain capitals in the apse at Cluny).

Where attempts were made to make the head, legs or arms stand out from the background, these were always on capitals, that is to say the figures were of small dimensions, but no sculptor would ever have dared to attempt this on a large figure for the abutment of a doorway or on a tympanum.

Ignorant of the laws of perspective or of the artifices of foreshortening, the sculptors placed one above the other such personages as they wished to represent standing one behind the other (tympanum of Autun, pillars of Silos).

Although these technical difficulties were undoubtedly a source of embarrassment, on the other hand they caused the sculptors to give some of their figures a kind of majestic severity. In the endeavour to create movement attitudes were exaggerated, legs were crossed to represent walking, and great use was made of the folds of the draperies. It is true that some of the figures are marred by strange contortions but they are nevertheless very attractive on account of their eminently decorative style.

The Romanesque sculptors adopted the Corinthian capital as it was understood by Gallo-Roman art, and while transforming it and covering it with figures of animals and human beings they always respected its graceful outline and proportions. But these living creatures must endure distortion if they are to conform to the construction of capitals, standing, as they do, side by side near the angles, and meeting at the point of the volute so that sometimes two bodies must be joined together and have but a single head.

Along with these decorative compositions, picturesque and varied, which occupy an important place in Romanesque style, the great religious pictures with their lofty, mystical conceptions give to certain Romanesque doorways an incomparable nobility and majesty.

Everything possible has already been said about the charm of our French sculptors' work in the thirteenth century. They imitated nature with a fidelity and with an elegance that were exquisite. All the faith of a people, all the fervour of a glowing piety, seem to live again in those touching figures so full of naive emotion and of candid grace.

But Romanesque art is of quite another sort, and if on the one hand it is less gentle and soothing, it shows on the other more vigour and boldness in the scenes represented; for did not the sculptors of the twelfth century dare to show forth on their tympana and on their capitals those tremendous visions from the Revelation of St. John, so difficult to express, before which imagination might so well have recoiled?

The interpretation of the religious sentiment in the art of the twelfth century differs entirely from that of the thirteenth. In the thirteenth century the Virgin is a young mother who gazes lovingly upon her child; the figures of God and of his Saints are serene and kindly. In the twelfth century, the Virgin reverently and solemnly sustains in her arms the Child-God who has come down upon earth to redeem sinful man; in the midst of the tympana sits a God severe and terrible presiding over the Last Judgement, and surrounded, as at Autun or Conques, by scenes in which the artists have striven to depict, down to the last dreadful detail, every imaginable torment of Hell.

The thirteenth century, better instructed, more refined, more human, will reject these materialistic and terrifying pictures, and if the Last Judgement continues to be represented it will be chiefly as an introduction to the glory and the joys of Paradise.

The researches of three great archaeologists, Count Robert de Lasteyrie, André Michel and M. Émile Mâle, two of them by the study of style and the third by the addition of his investigations into the distribution of iconographic themes, have established the essential principles by which we must seek to understand how Romanesque art was born and how it developed in France, and we believe that these principles will remain true throughout.

Attempts have been made in recent years to find fault with the conclusions of these writers and to modify considerably the chronology fixed by them: but even though it may perhaps be possible to dispute certain details here and there, we are persuaded that we should be making a serious mistake if we tried to overturn their theories as a whole.

Towards the end of the eleventh century, and in several provinces at the same time, Romanesque art escaped from the hesitation, from the gropings about, of its first beginnings; and it was in Languedoc, at Toulouse and at

6

Moissac, that appeared the earliest works on a large scale which achieved real artistic effect. Burgundy, not long afterwards, produced work not less beautiful. This has been debated, in the endeavour to give to Burgundy, or rather more precisely, to Cluny, the first place; so that while there are those who think that the art of Languedoc served as guide to that of Burgundy, others believe that it was Cluny, of which Moissac was a priory, which exercised a commanding influence upon Languedoc.

In our own opinion, neither of these two schools was subordinate to the other; but we regard them as having evolved side by side though on different lines, yet with artists whose merits were on an equality. If the abbots of Cluny beyond any doubt gave new impetus to the arts, and particularly to that of sculpture, it is none the less certain that in each area they made use of whatever talent they found there, and that they allowed to all these local craftsmen a large measure of initiative. The two great schools may have exercised a mutual influence, but that was the limit of their contact; and if Languedoc can show very ancient monuments of whose date there can be no doubt, if it seems that the workshops of Toulouse and of Moissac were the first to produce an *ensemble* of remarkable works, they were but a few years in advance of the workshops of Burgundy which very soon entered into rivalry with them; and the truth is that this question of exact precedence in point of time has almost no importance at all in our study of the artistic evolution of two schools which produced, independently one of the other, monuments of equal beauty.

CHAPTER I

THE BEGINNINGS OF ROMANESQUE SCULPTURE

AFTER the barbarian invasions, the fall of the Gallo-Roman Empire and the political anarchy which followed, many of the artistic traditions disappeared from Gaul; and yet certain of the arts, though for a time neglected, soon found their way back to a place of honour. Of all the arts which suffered eclipse, that which suffered longest was the art of monumental statuary; and in this case the eclipse continued for between five and six hundred years. It may be said that from the fifth to the tenth century, both inclusive, the sculpture of scenes containing human figures was entirely neglected in Gaul and even throughout the west. The Carolingian renaissance had no influence upon this forgotten art, since the men of taste who surrounded Charlemagne made no attempt to restore it.

Plate 2   Carvers were content to decorate plaques of marble or of stone with geometrical designs or with *motifs* of stylized vegetation which are known as "interlaces".[3] The ninth and tenth centuries were the finest period of this art, of which traces are to be found throughout the Empire of Charlemagne. In France we can show some very beautiful specimens; and if here and there the Romanesque sculptors made use of "interlaces" in their decorative work, the style of these latter readily distinguishes them from the very characteristic Carolingian "interlaces".

Documents have been quoted to prove that although the art of carving human figures in stone may have ceased to be much practised, so that sculptured monuments of the Merovingian and Carolingian periods are less numerous than those of the preceding and succeeding epochs, yet the tradition was nevertheless continued and from generation to generation sculptors handed on to each other the methods of their art.

Nothing of the sort. The documents quoted[4] are not concerned with reliefs in stone, and it is only possible to point, during this period, to rough outlines which are indeed the completest proof possible that this art had been abandoned. We may instance the bas-reliefs of the underground vault of the abbot

Plate 1 a   Mellebaude at *Poitiers* which Father de la Croix[5] has attributed to the end of the seventh or beginning of the eighth century; the figure with a halo in the ancient church of St.-Pierre-en-Citadelle at Metz,[6] which belongs to the same epoch; the bas-relief in St.-Martin at Angers which M. l'Abbé Pinier has attributed to the ninth century; that at *Charlieu* representing Daniel in the *Plate 1 b* lions' den; the three statuettes on the gable-end of the Basse-Œuvre at Beauvais;[7] the small fragment dating from the tenth century in the museum at Auxerre, on which can be seen a naked figure representing a river of Paradise — a tiny figure of less than four inches. These monuments all have figures, it is true; but some of them are engraved rather than sculptured, while the others are in very low relief.

The Merovingian and Carolingian churches, however, possessed figures in high relief, and even actually in the round, but they were executed in some other material than stone. Amongst these materials were metal and wood, the two often being combined, the wooden figure being overlaid with thin plates of gold or silver; painted stucco; and ivory, which could only be used of course for figures of small size. The embellishments of Carolingian churches consisted of memorials in goldsmiths' work ornamented with figures in repoussé relief, and these figures were to be found upon liturgical books, on the fronts of altars, reliquaries, shrines and ciboria.

Of the large number of such works recorded in various documents, but a few fragments remain to us, the chief cause of their disappearance being the precious materials of which they were made. Without counting the wars, the revolutions, and the pillaging which resulted therefrom, these monuments which in course of time may have been accounted old-fashioned would be regarded as a kind of treasure in reserve, from which, by selling the metal they contained, bishops and abbots who were in search of funds might draw as need required.

Among the most important pieces of goldsmiths' work, such as altar-fronts, which have come down to us, we can hardly cite more than that of Sant'Ambrogio at Milan, of the ninth century, the fragments of that of Aix-la-Chapelle, of the tenth century, and the golden altar-front of the cathedral of Basle, executed shortly after the Carolingian epoch, in the first quarter of the eleventh century. This monument, preserved at Paris in the Musée de Cluny, has five fairly large figures carried out in repoussé.

Carolingian artists knew also how to carve in wood, and M. Louis Bréhier[8] has published some extremely interesting studies upon these "majestés d'or",

9

wooden statues covered with metal plates, which were exhibited in the churches and carried in processions, as representative of the Virgin and the principal saints of Auvergne, where they were made. The statue of St. Foy at Conques, executed in the tenth century, is one of these infinitely precious monuments.

A document dating from the beginning of the eleventh century regarding this statue is as good a proof as we could wish for of the complete abandonment of stone as a material for the carving of figures at this period. The document in question is the account of a journey made in Auvergne by two Angevin clerics, Master Bernard of Chartres and Bernier. The former speaks of their astonishment when they saw the people of Aurillac and Conques prostrating themselves before the golden statues of St. Géraud and St. Foy exposed in the churches: "It seems wrong and absurd", he says, "to make statues in plaster, wood or bronze, except such as represent the Saviour on the cross... For the commemoration of saints by figures painted on the walls ought to be the only means of reproducing their likenesses for our eyes". [8a] Of stone statues there is not a word.

Stucco must also have been used very frequently in the Carolingian epoch and during the eleventh century.[9] Formed of a mixture of plaster and sand, or pounded marble, or even of brick dust, it lent itself much more readily than stone to the chisel of the sculptor, who could model figures in this material as readily as he could in potter's clay, and yet when it dried it became as hard as stone.

Stucco was accordingly employed for the internal decoration of churches in the form of reliefs attached to the walls, such as the purely decorative arcadings which rested upon columns the elements of which, base, capital and abacus, were all of stucco, the whole being ornamented with foliage and interlaces. Stucco ornamentation of this kind may be seen in the Carolingian church of Germigny-des-Prés (Loiret).[10] Sometimes the base and the capital were adorned with animals or even with a human figure, as is seen at Mals in the Tyrol.[11] It is quite easy to explain in this way the decorative arcading sometimes noticed in Carolingian manuscripts. Such decoration had really existed, and these bases with their crouching animals, these capitals with designs of foliage or ornamented with caryatids, these columns and arches with acanthus decoration were not merely an invention of the illuminators, who had only copied

10

what they had under their eyes; and the Romanesque sculptors, in their turn, imitated the creations of the Carolingian stucco-workers and goldsmiths.

Occasionally, in Carolingian churches, large panels of painted stucco were ornamented with human figures in relief which formed actual scenes. MM. Prou and Stückelberg have recovered from amidst the débris of the church of Disentis (Grisons) painted stucco figures of human forms.[12] The six large statues at Cividale and the ornamentation surrounding them, all being of stucco, are well known; and it is not impossible that they may have belonged to Carolingian times; in any case they are quite in accordance with the traditions of Carolingian art.[13]

Lastly, we know that Abbot Angilbert, the favourite of Charlemagne, caused to be made for his church of St.-Riquier four panels of stucco representing the Nativity, the Passion, the Resurrection and the Ascension.[14] We may suppose that when the first Romanesque sculptors wished to decorate their towers or the façades of their churches, in the open air, that is to say, where it was not possible to use stucco, they must have made panels such as that of the Stoning of St. Stephen on the porch of St.-Benoît-sur-Loire, and that these first panels carved in stone were made in imitation of the Carolingian panels of stucco.

Stucco was also in use later than Carolingian times. It may even have been employed more and more for economic reasons: gilded, it could become the exact likeness of the costly monuments of the goldsmiths.

Wood also was used to replace metal work, and we thus see, in the eleventh and twelfth centuries, ciboria decorated with stucco reliefs such as those in San Pietro di Civate[15] and in Sant'Ambrogio at Milan, and altar-fronts of sculptured wood painted like those in the museum at Vich in Catalonia.[16]

In France of the eleventh century we must notice the capitals at the end of the nave of *St.-Remy* at *Rheims* which are ornamented with stucco figures.[17] *Plate 1 c* The stucco has fallen away from the whole of one of the capitals so that it is possible to see the grooves cut by the artist to allow the stucco to adhere to the stone. Finally, still in the twelfth century, was executed in St.-Julien at Brioude a tympanum bearing a representation of the Ascension in which all the figures were stone statues, though only débris remains.[18]

11

The oft-cited texts of Raoul Glaber[18a] and of Anselme, monk of St.-Remy at Rheims,[18b] say that a few years after the year one thousand a great effort was made to restore existing churches or to build new ones. If architecture then transformed and perfected itelf, it seems as though the carving of stone were awaking from a long sleep; but it was a gradual process, and the artisans who strove to bring this art to life again made but very slow progress.

We have said that in Merovingian and Carolingian times shapeless little figures were made in stone, childish attempts which do not suggest any aesthetic idea. Most of them must have been done, as André Michel has observed, in imitation of the terracotta tiles[19] which were used as mural decorations in the oldest Christian basilicae. These rectangular tiles must have been placed side by side so as to form a horizontal frieze which broke the nakedness of the wall, or served as a decoration for the upper part; while others, in the shape of keystones, would have been used for the decoration of arches and above the doors. This tradition continued on into the eleventh century. It is very difficult to determine the approximate date of such morsels of this sort as have come down to us. Some of them may very well have been used over again in churches that are more recent, and it is quite possible that among the fragments we are about to mention certain may date from before the Romanesque epoch. Such are the little bas-reliefs, each the size of a brick, which have been built into the choir of St.-Germain at Auxerre, and upon which are seen confronted peacocks, certainly earlier than the Romanesque epoch.

Sculptured stones, made in imitation of terracotta tiles, frequently represent an animal in profile, standing out from the rectangular frame. The process must have been as follows: first of all, an outline would be drawn upon the slab, and then, round about this silhouette, the stone would be cut away, leaving the edges of the slab uncut, so as to form a frame. A figure would thus be produced in low relief; and up to a point the process was similar to that of hollow enamelling employed by goldsmiths and enamellers. An unfinished example, at Lund in Sweden, shows us exactly how the sculptor set about his work. In this series of stones ornamented with animals, the figure of one of them is merely engraved in outline, the artist not having finished it.[20]

Figures of this description, with animals or little men, are found at Chabris (Indre),[21] on the tower of St.-Pierre at Cormery, at St.-Germain-sur-

Vienne, at Restigné, at Rivière, and at Bourgueil (Indre-et-Loire), at St.-Florent (Cher), at Melle and at Airvault (Deux-Sèvres), at St.-Hilaire-le-Grand at Poitiers,[22] and at Château-Larcher (Vienne), at La Celle-Bruère (Cher), at Graville-Ste.-Honorine (Seine-Inf.),[23] at Andlau (Bas-Rhin), at St.-Paul-Trois-Châteaux (Drôme),[24] at Marcillac (Lot),[25] La Charité-sur-Loire (Nièvre),[26] and at St.-Benoît-sur-Loire (Loiret)[27] on the porch, where the sculptures have been re-employed, and where is to be seen, along with other fragments, the Stoning of St. Stephen. These fragments at St.-Benoît-sur-Loire may possibly belong to the earliest work undertaken in the construction of the porch which was begun in 1026 by Gauzlin, abbot of this monastery.

We possess, in almost perfect condition, some friezes formed of the rectangular tiles made by the Romanesque sculptors in imitation of friezes of brick tiles. Such are those at St.-Romain-le-Puy[28] and at St.-Rambert-sur-Loire (Loire),[29] at St.-Restitut (Drôme),[30] St.-Pierre-d'Ainay at Lyons, and in L'Ile-Barbe (Rhône).[31]

Here and there a sculptor, wishing to decorate portions of a façade, even while carving barbarian figures has shown some care for the composition: at Beaulieu-lès-Loches (Indre-et-Loire)[32] the triangular surface of the gable is covered with tiles ornamented with horses and men; at Jussy-Champagne (Cher), above the doorway, are sculptured human figures beneath a series of arcades; the Crucifixion is represented on the façades at Veuil (Indre), of St.-Mesme at Chinon (Indre-et-Loire),[33] and at Usson (Vienne).

The first Romanesque sculptors also employed the method of restricted cutting for their capitals, as at *Cruas* (Ardèche)[34] and at *Carennac* (Lot), but they did not, in this case, as in that of the rectangular slabs, retain the frame in relief. *Plate 3 d, e*

Having thus called attention to these barbarian fragments executed by the earliest sculptors of the eleventh century, or possibly even earlier than that by some of them, certain of the fragments being engraved merely in outline, while others detach themselves slightly from the background by a process of cutting out which gives a very insignificant relief, let us now try to discover, in the midst of the laborious efforts of the beginners, the first symptoms of the renaissance of an art which was to extend itself so marvellously during the twelfth century.

13

A study of the evolution of the capital is particularly interesting. From the opening of the eleventh century, on capitals ornamented with foliage, in which they copied rather clumsily the Corinthian capital or the composite Roman capital, the workmen sometimes tried to introduce animated figures. They would substitute for the volute at the angle of a capital the head of a bird with a hooked beak, as notably in the cloister of Charlieu; and on the faces would be engraved a head in low relief from the mouth of which issued foliage; some of the more daring even attempted an entire human body upon one of the faces of a capital.

Among the most curious examples of this budding art should be noticed the figures executed in very low relief on the upper part of the narthex in St.-Philibert at Tournus, and the series of capitals in the crypt of *St.-Bénigne*

Plate 3 a, b   at *Dijon*,[35] erected under the direction of the Abbot Guillaume de Volpiano between 1001 and 1017, where is to be seen an imitation of barbarian art, especially in the carving of a bird, which reminds one of the buckles of Merovingian times which were shaped like a bird with hooked beak. In the crypt

Plate 3 f   of *St.-Aignan* at *Orleans* (989-1029)[36] are full-length human figures, though they are heavy and deformed.

Other artists there were who fought shy of figures that were merely ornamental and without meaning, and who tried to give religious signification to

Plate 3 c   their work. At *St.-Germain-des-Prés*, for example (c. 990-1014),[37] there is a series of capitals on which are seen Christ in a glory, Adam and Eve, and so on, nearly always placing but a single figure upon each face of a capital and only later attempting to surround the capital with a connected scene in which all the personages take a part. We can see this on some capitals in the porch

Plate 5 a-c   of *St.-Benoît-sur-Loire* which undoubtedly belong to the resumption of work undertaken by the Abbot Guillaume towards 1070.[38] With these capitals of the old and celebrated abbey of Fleury must be associated those of *Le Ronceray* at *Angers*[39] which belong to the same epoch and present in their execution a close resemblance to those of St.-Benoît. Attempts have been made to date from the tenth century the panels which adorn the exterior of the sanctuary of St.-Paul-lès-Dax (Landes).[40] For our part, however, we do not believe them to be as ancient as that. If certain figures appear indeed to be extremely archaic, such as those of the Crucifixion, the Last Supper or the Kiss of Judas, we shall nevertheless recognize that in the manner of their treatment, espe-

14

cially as regards the lower parts of the faces, the chins and the necks, they bear some resemblance to the figures at St.-Benoît and at Le Ronceray: the same processes were employed in their carving.

The lintels over the entrances, so richly decorated in the twelfth century, were sometimes similarly decorated also in the earliest period of Romanesque; and it is possible, by the help of an inscription, to date precisely the lintel of the little church of *St.-Genis-des-Fontaines* (Pyrénées-Orientales).[41] It was *Plate 4a* made in the time of King Robert in 1020-1021. The lintel of the church of *St.-André-de-Sorède*, a few kilometres distant from that of St.-Genis, is cer- *Plate 4b* tainly contemporary with the lintel of the latter. On the base of the window which opens upon the façade of this church will be noticed a marble plaque *Plate 4c* ornamented with figures of cherubim which are arranged with admirable decorative sense, and form with their wings a design like that of the great flowers of heraldic lilies.

From Carolingian times the marble quarries, so numerous in Roussillon and in that other portion of the ancient Septimania which was to become the department of Hérault, were exploited in order to provide decoration for the churches.

Artists sculptured and adorned with interlaces the plaques in chancels round about the sanctuary such as those of St.-Guilhem-le-Désert.[42] They hollowed out great slabs of marble which were to serve as altar-tables, and framed them with elegantly stylized ornaments. A workshop, very probably installed at the monastery of St.-Pons-de-Thomières,[43] extracted the marble from the quarries of that district and supplied altar-tables for the churches of the neighbourhood, such as those of Quarante, Sauvian, Garriguette (Hérault), Montolieu (Aude), and for cathedrals at a distance such as Rodez, and Gerona in Catalonia. In the middle of the eleventh century was made the table for the high-altar of the cathedral of Elne, the marble for which undoubtedly came from the quarry of Arles-sur-Tech.

Towards the close of the eleventh century, the sculptors of Languedoc ornamented the edges of these altar-tables with tiny figures, as may be seen on the high-altar of *St.-Sernin* at *Toulouse,* consecrated in 1096, and upon the *Plate 6a, c* altar-table preserved in the Hospital at *Lavaur*. *Plate 6d*

But the marble-workers did not stop there, and soon they were emboldened to execute in marble great figures in relief. Of such works of large size two *en-*

15

sembles have been preserved: the seven bas-reliefs of St.-Sernin at Toulouse which stand today in the circumference of the choir of that church, and the ten bas-reliefs which cover certain panels of the great pillars in the cloister of Moissac. These two groups, in the workmanship of which exist undoubted analogies both of technique and of the particular ornaments employed, belong to the end of the eleventh century, and they represent the earliest experiments in monumental statuary.

CHAPTER II

THE SCHOOL OF LANGUEDOC

TOULOUSE, as M. Mâle has said, was the marvel of the twelfth century. In the City of the Counts, centre of a brilliant civilization which held all the arts in high honour, there was in those days one long succession of fêtes and rejoicings, marked by love of luxury and rich costumes, a passion for elegance and admiration of poets, musicians and itinerant minstrels; and it would seem indeed to have been in this Chosen Land that Romanesque art awoke from its slumbers in the closing years of the eleventh century. It may be quite true, as we ourselves have offered many proofs, that work was going on before that, but no more had been accomplished than experiments and rough outlines. It was at Toulouse that the flower burst at last from its bud, to spread its petals widely by and by, in Spain, Italy and the Ile-de-France.

No other town, perhaps, in the Romanesque epoch has supplied so rich a collection of works, though of all the multitude of such works we possess but a very small part — St.-Sernin with its marble high reliefs, its capitals and its doorways; St.-Étienne with its Apostles in the Chapter-House; and the cloister of La Daurade with the exquisite figures on its capitals. Not far from Toulouse, the Cluniac Abbey of Moissac shelters a series of sculptures which have the closest affinity with those of St.-Sernin: we refer to its cloister with the great marble figures standing rigid and mysterious in the shadows of the galleries, and to the capitals with their deep reliefs where according to the time of day the sun changes its glistening iridescence, and to its marvellous doorway, one of the most admirable creations of the art of the Middle Ages.

The church of *St.-Sernin* at *Toulouse* played a prominent part in the history of Romanesque art. It is well known that it presents points of extraordinary resemblance with three other great places of pilgrimage in the Middle Ages: the churches of Ste.-Foy at Conques, St.-Martial at Limoges and Santiago de Compostela.[44] It would appear that the work upon St.-Sernin was begun in about 1060. By 1096 the choir was finished, since a chronicle tells us that Pope Urban II, in the month of May in that year, consecrated the new church and the high altar. The mensa of this altar[45] is of some importance for the study of the beginnings of sculpture in Languedoc; and it

Plate 6a-c

has the advantage, in this connection, of being precisely dated, so that we know it to have been executed in 1096 or shortly after. An inscription which surrounds it says that the sculptor who decorated it was named Bernard Gilduin.

From a document[46] we learn that Raymond Gayzard, canon and provost of the chapter of St.-Sernin, who died in 1118, presided for a number of years over the work of construction, and that when he died the walls of the entire length of the nave had risen to the level of the high windows.

An examination of the sculptures adorning the altar-table of St.-Sernin, and the connections that can be established between them and numerous other pieces of sculpture still preserved in the great basilica, will perhaps allow us to attribute these very diverse works to the sculptor Bernard Gilduin, and in any case to date them at a period very close to 1096.

The flat surface of this mensa, hollowed like a sink, is edged with lobes of circular shape, which themselves are enclosed by a rounded moulding and by varied ornaments symmetrically arranged, such as buttons in the form of marguerites with five or six petals, and beautiful palm-leaf ornaments which here and there remind one of the fleur-de-lis. The ends of the mensa, which is very thick, consist of an upright portion with a bevel; the upright portion being covered with three rows of imbrications such as one sees on Christian sarcophagi of the first centuries of the Middle Ages; the bevelled portion having ornamentation of elegant sculpture which differs on each face and represents animated figures. The lateral sides are ornamented by figures, some of them mutilated, which seem to represent Christ, the Virgin, some Apostles, a figure which has not been identified, and a winged griffin. The greater number of these figures are busts, and they are enclosed in medallions which are joined together by leaf decorations. The front side is particularly interesting, as it is ornamented by a bust of Christ holding a book and enclosed in a round medallion which is itself placed in a square frame sustained by two angels in a horizontal position, and behind each of these angels are two others, six angels altogether, that is to say, horizontal, and seeming as though they were flying. In this representation of Christ, framed in a medallion which is held up by two angels, there is an undoubted imitation of the Gallo-Roman sarcophagi which showed a bust of the deceased in a medallion, or on a shield, sustained by two winged tutelar deities.

The fourth edge, that is to say the side at the back, represents a series of birds, facing outwards and grouped two by two, among foliage. This decoration, which is skilfully treated, seems to have been copied from some piece of oriental ivory.

The figures of this mensa have close resemblances with several fragments preserved from the magnificent *ensemble* of sculpture which formerly decorated St.-Sernin, the richness of which we may judge from the descriptions of Noguier[47] in the sixteenth century and of Catel[48] in the seventeenth.

In the very first place we must call attention to the seven large marble figures[49] which are the earliest examples surviving today of figure-sculpture of large dimensions. The marble from which they were worked came, like that of the altar-table, from the quarries of St.-Béat (Haute-Garonne); and there is no doubt that originally they belonged to a doorway which has now disappeared. They are to be found at the present time in the circumference of the choir, and they represent Christ in Majesty, — a heavy figure, thickset, with expressionless countenance — four angels and two Apostles. It is these last figures especially which prove that the artist has taken as his model some upright gravestone, of Gallo-Roman origin, which he has copied slavishly, but not without a certain skill. *Plate 6 e, f* *Plate 7 a-d*

The sculptor who was bold enough to carve these figures of fairly large dimensions reveals how difficult the task appeared to him. After the manner of those artisans who were wont to carve profiles in low relief of animals on small rectangular stones for use in friezes, he has made a very cautious use of cutting and scarcely dares to cut out the stone around his personages, whom he shows in silhouette, avoiding relief and putting everything on the same plane. The faces and arms are placed flat on the body and in some cases the artist even shows the head in profile in order to avoid too deep cutting.

This reluctance to abandon the original surface of the slab and the timidity in the modelling of the forms may be seen in numerous examples of Romanesque art during its early stages.

It is generally admitted that these great bas-reliefs belong to the second half of the eleventh century, and to the same period must be attributed certain capitals, with figure decoration, which are to be seen in the choir and the transept. Examples are not lacking of churches which received consecration before their building was completed, but as soon as the choir was finished; and that is what happened at St.-Sernin in 1096. *Plate 8 a-e*

There are some striking resemblances among these three groups of sculpture, namely the altar-table, the large reliefs and the capitals decorated with figures: such as the similarity in the design of the faces, the strong lower jaws, the prominent eyes, the large noses without any hollow at the top, the hair coming far down in front, in one of two fashions, either curly or on the other hand very long and smooth and falling on the back of the neck quite clear of the ears. Upon the bas-reliefs, as upon the altar-table, the clothing of the figures is arranged in a manner which recalls the antique procedure. The medallion in the middle of the front side of the altar, which encloses the bust of Christ, is formed of a row of pearl-shaped ornaments, and of a row of lozenges alternating with small circles; and similar ornamentation is found on the oval Glory of the bas-relief of Christ in Majesty.

One of the angels of the altar-table holds in his hand the shaft of a Maltese cross identical with those carried by the angels of the great bas-reliefs. In each of these three series of monuments the wings of the angels are designed in the same manner; one notices a large band on the upper and external portion of the wing, from which depend a number of little feathers arranged like scales. And last of all, we find on the upper surface of the mensa large buttons placed at regular intervals upon the frame, shaped like marguerites, each with five or six petals and with a small leaf between every pair of petals. These are absolutely identical with decorations on the jambs of the arches which enclose certain of the great marble figures, as well as with those of the great marble figures in the cloister of Moissac of which we shall speak later. [49a]

Plates 8f,   On the south side of the church is a door — the Miégeville Door —
9-11a, b   surmounted by a tympanum on which is sculptured the Ascension; in the figures of this tympanum and on the capitals which frame it we find the same methods of execution and the same ornaments: angels grasping the shaft terminating in a cross, as we have already seen; and the same features with prominent lower jaws, the same curly hair, the same too short necks.

            Outside the tympanum of the Miégeville Door, to right and left of the ar-
Plate 11a, b   chivolt, are seen the beautiful figures of St. James and St. Peter, standing out in fairly high relief from two great slabs; above and at the feet of these fig-
Plate 10   ures are groups of strange personages, women riding on lionesses, Simon the Magician mounted on a monster, which have, like the figures on the brackets supporting the upper cornices, a surprising life and movement.

20

These sculptures are of more skilful execution than those upon the tympanum, though it would not seem that they were done very much later; and it should be noted that the vestments of St. James and of St. Peter on the one hand and those of the Ascending Christ and of the two great angels who support him, on the other, are draped in identical fashion, forming three folds on the breast and four or five from the girdle to the bottom of the robe.

All these works are closely connected, some of them dating from the end of the eleventh century, and others being perhaps of slightly later date, though in all cases certainly earlier than 1118, which was the year of the death of the Provost Raymond who took charge of the building of the church when the choir had been finished, worked on it through long years and carried it as far as above the high windows of the nave.

We cannot leave St.-Sernin without making mention of the twin doors of the southern arm of the transept: the Porte des Comtes and the Porte des Filhols with their beautiful capitals with figure decoration;[49b] and the west front with its decorated capitals, some with ornaments stylized with rare elegance, others with lionesses curiously treated, their bodies being thin and long, their skulls flat, and their large jaws having lips that are unusually folded over so as to fall far down. We shall find these lionesses again on several monuments in the neighbourhood, and on others which were inspired by the school of Languedoc. Let us also call attention to the two beautiful figures of women, holding one a lion, and the other a ram, which came from St.-Sernin and are now preserved in the Musée des Augustins.[50] The style of these figures is that of the high reliefs over the Miégeville Door.

Resemblances between the sculptures of St.-Sernin and those of the cloister of *St.-Pierre* at *Moissac* are numerous. Let us draw attention now to some of these features which they have in common: the angels whom we saw on the altar-table of St.-Sernin, placed horizontally face to face and bearing between them a medallion on which was represented a divine figure, are found again in several examples on the abaci in the cloister at Moissac. We also remarked *Plate 16b* on the confronted birds, two by two among foliage, on a panel of the altar-table at St.-Sernin; birds, similarly grouped, will be noticed on a capital at *Plate 16a* Moissac, and they can be seen also on a large basin in the church of Gaillac (Tarn).[51] And lastly, the buttons which we saw on the jambs of the arches

21

framing certain bas-reliefs at St.-Sernin, reminding us of goldsmiths' work in which similar nails are used to fasten the metal upon the wooden core, are seen again on the bas-reliefs in the cloister at Moissac.

Several archaeologists of the present day have been far too anxious to affix dates that are far too recent to the sculptures in the cloister at Moissac, although there is a document of incontestable authority which is at hand to settle the question. We refer to the inscription [52] on one of the pillars in the cloister, which tells us that this cloister was executed in the year 1100 by the Abbot Anquetil, who was Abbot of Moissac from 1085 until 1115. It is to be remembered that this cloister, possibly the most beautiful of all Romanesque cloisters, has at the angles and in the middle of each of its sides large rectangular pillars upon which are sculptured decorated panels of marble, one with the inscription of which we are now speaking, and others either with imbrications, or else with bas-reliefs representing figures standing upright beneath a semicircular arch supported by two columns. These large figures, to the number of ten, and each of them carrying a descriptive inscription, repre-

Plates 13, 14   sent the Abbot Durand and nine Apostles. [53] This Durand, who was Bishop of Toulouse, at the same time that he was Abbot of Moissac, died in 1072. A lengthy inscription [54] preserved in the church tells us that he took part in the consecration of the building in 1063. If he was represented in a cloister, it was undoubtedly on account of the role which he played in the great abbey and of the part which he took in its erection. Compared with the impersonal figures of the Apostles, it seems as though in this representation of an abbot with full cheeks, bulging chin and thick lips we have an attempt at actual

Plates 15, 16   portraiture. Between the pillars are a number of little columns, single or in couples, supporting seventy-six richly sculptured capitals, whose decoration on the vases and the abacus consists of foliage, palm-leaf ornamentation, interlaces, birds and strange monsters, sirens, griffins, eagles with two heads, figures that were most incontestably borrowed from the oriental models supplied by stuffs or small coffers of bone or ivory, little scenes drawn from the sacred books or extracted from the life of some saint: there is here a prodigality and exuberance of decoration which is truly amazing.

There is the inscription, in its original position, and it tells us that this cloister was the work of the Abbot Anquetil; just as a chronicler of the end of the fourteenth century, Aimery de Peyrac,[55] who was Abbot of Moissac, likewise gives the honour of building this cloister to Anquetil, to whom he attributes important works of art.

In our own days, M. André Michel[56] has accepted these statements to the effect that the greater part of the sculptures in the cloister date from the time of Anquetil. "The capitals in the cloister", he says, "may date for the most part at least from the time of the Abbot Ansquitil who lived until 1115... The style of the figures there follows directly upon that of the figures on the pillars and it remains, with but a few exceptions, entirely homogeneous". We, for our part, agree with André Michel.[57] M. Mâle is even more explicit, and he considers that the decoration of the cloister was finished in the year 1100.[58] But previously some other archaeologists, Canon Pottier,[59] Ernest Rupin,[60] Auguste Anglès[61] all of whom have given special attention to Moissac, have been unwilling to leave to the work of Anquetil anything more than the great marble figures. The capitals, according to them, are of too good a style to belong to an epoch so remote; and a suggestion has been made of a restoration of the cloister somewhere between 1150 and 1160, in the course of which these capitals would have been sculptured. Alterations were certainly carried out at this period and even during the latter half of the thirteenth century, but the majority of the capitals date from the time of Anquetil.

It is perfectly true that some of these are of refined execution, whilst the great figures on the pillars seem still to be the work of an inexperienced artist. But one must make the observation that at this period of Romanesque art, when it was freeing itself from the timid early stage of experimentation and was beginning to reveal itself, and when certain artists, particularly in the neighbourhood of Toulouse, already felt themselves able to make figures come forth out of stone, it is only sculptures of small dimensions which really give the impression of being works of art. More than that, it is only in stylized friezes, in *motifs* purely decorative in which the design repeats itself and demands less of invention, that our sculptors were able to express a real beauty. But when it became a question of composing, or of grouping a scene round the vase of a capital, how at such times does one recognize their inexperience! It has not been sufficiently remarked that while certain personages on the capitals are heavy and ill-proportioned, such as the capital of Daniel or that of *Plate 16c* the Magi, on the abaci of these same capitals, on the other hand, roses and

23

other floral ornaments are so harmoniously outlined as to give the impression of an art already come to full development.

It is because all this has not been sufficiently noticed, that it has seemed possible to allow an interval of more than half a century between the great bas-reliefs and the capitals in the cloister of Moissac. The sculptors responsible for the inferior figures of the Apostles on the pillars may very well at the same time have carried out the capitals of the Magi, of the Shepherds, or of Daniel, with their coarse and stumpy figures, the small scale of which minimizes the effect of their faults; but it seems surprising at a first glance that those same sculptors were also capable of carving the elegant palm-leaf ornamentation on the abaci and certain of the capitals decorated only with floral ornaments, and also the frieze of confronted birds of the altar of St.-Sernin. It needs but to be supposed that certain stages in the progress of the art of sculpture were passed over more rapidly than others. A study of the epigraphic characters goes to prove that the majority of the capitals dates from the time of Anquetil. We find the same characters throughout with but very little variation, in the great inscription of 1100, on the bas-reliefs of the pillars and on the capitals, and these characters undoubtedly exhibit the forms that were customary at the beginning of the twelfth century.

If Moissac possesses the most complete Romanesque cloister, the richest in sculpture, the most impressive by reason of its many associations and of the spirit of solemn calm and serenity which it inspires with its clear lighting, its exuberance as of luxuriant vegetation in a beautiful garden, its fairyland of colours which give darker reflections to the marbles but cause the capitals to glow like great roses that have fully opened out, the famous Cluniac priory possesses also a doorway which is one of the most magnificent examples of sculptured and illuminated stone conceived by the twelfth century; "illuminated", we say, because the great figures on this doorway were once painted and gilded.

Plate 17 The tympanum [62] represents the vision of Christ on the Day of Judgement, as described in the Revelation of St. John. According to M. Mâle,[63] this work is a reproduction in stone of a painting in a manuscript from the Abbey of St.-Sever containing a commentary on the Apocalypse written by Beatus. The pages which this great savant has devoted to this monument are among the most striking in his beautiful book on religious art in the twelfth century. He

24

has endeavoured to show that this doorway played a considerable part in the evolution of monumental sculpture, and that it served as a model for a large number of French doorways.

The Christ, bearded and crowned, garbed in ample draperies, larger in size than the other figures, is solemnly enthroned in the midst of the Symbols of the Evangelists: the Man, the Eagle, the Ox and a Lion with the characteristic features of which we have already spoken. Two angels, somewhat long of body, stand upright on either side of this central group. Around them and beneath them, in three tiers, are the Elders of the Apocalypse, small in size, seated in various attitudes and holding in their hands their "harps and golden vials full of odours", raising or turning their heads to gaze upon the Majesty of God. Some of them have the long beard with two points that will so often appear during the twelfth century upon the faces of Prophets and Elders of the Apocalypse, notably at La Charité-sur-Loire, at Anzy-le-Duc, and on the Portail Royal of Chartres. Upon the lintel[63a] is a frieze of extreme elegance composed of a number of circular elements with protruding centres bulging outward; and from this centre issue palm-leaf ornaments which increase in size with their distance from the centre, other palmettes being used to garnish the spaces between these roses. At the ends, two strange animals, of which only the foreparts can be seen, seem to be coming out from the abutments.

The pier, on its outward face, is decorated with three groups of lionesses, *Plate 18* intercrossed, and rearing one upon the other, so as to form a marvel of decorative composition. standing out from a background of rosework very similar to that upon the lintel. On the lateral faces of the pier are two upright figures which seem to be bearing up the lintel, like Atlantes. They occupy the whole height of the pier, and their bodies are extended out of all proportion. The rear face of the pier is filled by those same imbrications and scales which are found on certain pillars in the cloister, and in them we have an indication that the execution of the doorway cannot have been very much later than that of the cloister. On the abutments of the doorway, in high relief, are figures in the grand style of Isaiah and of St. Peter, their bodies being taller than nature, and their attitudes flowing and full of movement.

Such is this marvellous doorway of Moissac, which must have been even more impressive still in the days when its figures glowed in all the glory of their living colouring.

25

In this truly supernatural statue of Christ, grave and majestic in the middle of the tympanum, in these human figures of various sizes according to their hieratic dignity but whose different proportions fit in so well with the general arrangement of the whole, in the elegant decoration of the archivolt and of the frieze of the lintel, in this pier with its lionesses rampant in hieratic attitudes and with the two outlined figures stretched so strangely upon its lateral faces, Romanesque art has realized with incomparable talent all that was most original in its conceptions. And however unusual and strange this creation may appear it does not offend by any excessive oddity. It belongs to the number of those Romanesque works which surprise, whether by their almost childish naiveté, as in certain capitals in Auvergne or in the Last Judgement at Autun, or by their eccentricity, as do the figures of men, animals and monsters on the pier of Souillac. On the tympanum at Moissac the figures are grave and calm, the composition is well arranged, sober, harmonious: the craftsman has known how to express with admirable restraint the amazing recitation of the Apocalyptic Vision.[63b]

According to M. Mâle,[64] this doorway was executed before 1115, the date of the death of Abbot Anquetil to whom it is attributed by the chronicler Aimery de Peyrac. He adds that in all probability the Moissac sculptures were finished before 1125. M. André Michel[65] has remarked upon the statue of Abbot Roger, who died about 1135, over the doorway, and he thinks that if the decoration of the doorway was begun in the time of Anquetil it was completed only by his successor. The unanimity of the opinions of these two savants is striking.

There is a tradition that this doorway was originally on the west, but that when an alteration was decided later in the entrances to the church it was transported, stone by stone, to its present position on the south.

Plate 19   Upon the abutments of the porch outside the doorway are large panels covered with bas-reliefs. On the left of the spectator are represented Avarice and Luxury, the feasting of the Wicked Rich Man and the Death of Lazarus, whose sores, caused by his leprosy, the dogs are licking: near to his head we notice his leper's rattle. An angel comes to carry his soul away, and on one side is Abraham receiving that soul into his bosom. On the right are scenes of the Annunciation and of the Visitation, the latter having been restored, the Adoration of the Magi and the Flight into Egypt. These sculptures are later than

26

those of the doorway, and would seem to have been executed somewhere about the middle of the twelfth century, doubtless when the task of removing the doorway was undertaken.

To the doorway of Moissac are related those of Carennac,[66] Souillac (Lot) and of Beaulieu (Corrèze).

At *Carennac*, Christ appears throned in the midst of his Apostles, who are *Plate 20* arranged in two tiers; and we have here what is evidently a copy of the altar-fronts of goldsmiths' work which were so common in the twelfth century and earlier. On the Glory surrounding the figure of the Christ are imitations of the precious stones and coloured glass which used to be set in metal. The horizontal and vertical bands which divide the scene into several compartments take the place of the transverse pieces of wood upon which were fastened the plates of gold or silver-gilt.

Of the doorway of *Souillac*,[67] there remain today only a few fragments which *Plates 21, 22 a* are preserved inside the church: but one can see, from the style of the Prophets Isaiah and Jeremiah, that it is identical with that of the Isaiah and the *Plate 22 a* St. Peter whom we saw on the abutments of the doorway at Moissac. These distorted figures have a strange grace and seem to be dancing; but their queer attitudes and the draperies rolled round their bodies and gathered up at the bottom may have been intended to give the impression of movement. On one of the fragments are lionesses, intercrossed and devouring a bull, and closely resembling the lionesses on the pier at Moissac. An important group consists of a representation of the Legend of Theophilus, the deacon who obtained the help of the devil by selling his soul to him, but was saved by his devotion to the Virgin. The work is stiff and expressionless and the attitudes awkward. The most curious detail of the doorway at Souillac is the pier, where are grouped in the most incoherent fashion human beings mixed up with the bodies of fantastic beasts which seem to be curling themselves round them. The eye loses itself in the confusion, in this tangle of creatures devouring each other. On the left lateral face, however, a scene from the Old Testament, the Sacrifice of Isaac, is represented. The church of Souillac is known to have been completed in 1130, and the doorway may have been a little earlier than that date.

Resemblances between the doorway of *Beaulieu* and those of Moissac and *Plate 23* Souillac are numerous. We find, on the abutments, two human figures in

27

Plate 24 high relief; the projections are ornamented, as at Moissac, with bas-reliefs arranged under arcades. On the pier, Atlantes sustain the lintel as on the pier at Moissac, but on the lateral faces appear not one personage but two, one of them supporting the other upon his shoulders, and they are in consequence of more normal proportions than at Moissac.

The doorway at Beaulieu[68] is far less artistic and less skilfully composed than that at Moissac; and the stone, which is of poorer quality, has moreover been eaten away in the lower parts. It treats of the Last Judgement, and is undoubtedly among the most ancient representations of a scene which was constantly presented in the twelfth and still more in the thirteenth century. Christ, in front of the Cross, extends his arms and shows his wounds. Around him, and of smaller size, are grouped angels, two of whom are blowing trumpets. Apostles are also there, and lower down are the dead coming forth from their tombs. Lower still, in two tiers, are monstrous animals devouring the damned, and the Apocalyptic Beast upon a background of rose ornament which is far inferior to that of the doorway at Moissac.

M. Mâle[69] has shown how profound was the influence of the work of Languedoc upon monumental sculpture and how craftsmen from Languedoc must have come, round about 1135, to work in the great yard attached to the Abbey of St.-Denis, of which Suger had taken charge. He has also remarked on the close relationship betwen the Beaulieu Judgement and that of St.-Denis. Towards the middle of the twelfth century the artistic genius which put forth such magnificent flowers in northern France, at Chartres, at Le Mans, at Angers, at St.-Loup-de-Naud, at Provins, at Bourges, was inspired by the theme of the Apocalyptic Vision as it was first conceived at Moissac and at Carennac.

The necessity of showing the relation between St.-Sernin of Toulouse and Moissac has caused us to leave Toulouse itself for the moment; but we now return thither to deal with the cathedral of St.-Étienne and the church of La Daurade which were abundantly decorated in the twelfth century, although only fragments of this decoration have come down to us.

In St.-Étienne[70] some Romanesque capitals in the style of St.-Sernin were re-used in the thirteenth century; but the most important remains of this church, of Romanesque origin, are to be found today in the Musée des Augustins. These include, first of all, the high reliefs of the Twelve Apostles which

Plate 25

flanked the door of the chapter-house.[71] They form eight groups arranged beneath arcades, four of single Apostles, and four of Apostles by two and two, who appear to be conversing each with the other. Two of them, of a workmanship rather more refined than the others, bear the signature of the sculptor Gilabertus. Several of these Apostles have their legs crossed, a posture which was much in favour with the school of Languedoc. These figures exhibit a suppleness of attitude, a variety of movement, and their garments have an elegance, a studied refinement, which oblige us to attribute them to a period later than that of the works of St.-Sernin.

There remain only a few capitals of the cloister, which was demolished in 1813; and on them are represented the Legend of Mary the Egyptian, the Wise and Foolish Virgins, the Adoration of the Magi, and the Beheading of *Plate 29b* John the Baptist.[72] This capital of St. John the Baptist is particularly celebrated,[73] and it would be difficult to find anything more elegant and delicate than the little fragile body of Salome, whose chin Herod is stroking. *Plate 29a*

The series of capitals of the priory of La Daurade[74] is more considerable, some thirty of them being preserved in the Musée des Augustins at Toulouse. Work must have long gone on in this cloister which, like that of St.-Étienne, was demolished in 1813; and some of its capitals must have belonged to the earliest Languedoc period. The stiff and heavy figure of Daniel among the *Plate 16d* lions is evidently contemporary with the similar work at Moissac which represents the same subject, and offers a most striking resemblance to it.

The series of capitals representing the later episodes in the life of Christ, on the contrary, is of skilful execution, presenting scenes that are full of movement and even of agitation, such as that of the Kiss of Judas, in which the artist has successfully rendered the confusion amid which the envoys of the High Priest throw themselves upon Jesus, or that in which St. Peter and St. John hear of the Resurrection and hasten to the Sepulchre.

A last phase of Romanesque art at Toulouse manifests itself, probably towards the end of the twelfth century, in capitals which came from La Daurade and are also now preserved in the Musée des Augustins. One of these, justly celebrated, tells in six scenes the History of Job. Upon another is a Bear *Plate 30* Hunt,[75] in which the artist with remarkable ingenuity has grouped his figures in medallions set in foliage.

The style of the workshops of Toulouse and of Moissac is found throughout Languedoc and neighbouring regions, in Rouergue and Quercy; it may be seen in the great church of Ste.-Foy at Conques, where it mingles with influences from Auvergne, at Collonges (Corrèze),[76] in the cathedral of Cahors[77] of which the beautiful tympanum of the Ascension was certainly not executed until during the third quarter of the twelfth century, in the admirable tympanum of the Last Judgement at Martel (Lot),[78] and on the magnificent

Plate 28 capitals of Catus (Lot).

Plate 22 b　　At *Rodez*, however, in the Musée de la Société des Lettres de l'Aveyron, is preserved a fragment of a tympanum representing Christ in Majesty, which is supposed to have come from the cathedral, and is a work of an exceptional type. The concentric folds of the vestments are to be noticed, recalling as they do the calligraphic processes of illuminators by whom the artist was inspired; and it is even more curious to see how the artist has followed the traditions of the goldsmiths who decorated shrines and altar-frontals: the rough portions of the stone, which appear on the neck, on the edges of the sleeves, at the girdle, on the hems of the mantle, on the mandorla, and upon the Alpha and Omega must have been incrusted with pieces of glass or with strips of metal.

　　It is not any more possible to trace resemblances between the art of Toulouse and the beautiful capitals of the chapter-house of St.-Caprais at Agen.[79]

Plate 26 a　　At *St.-Gaudens* (Haute-Garonne), on the contrary, at Lescure (Tarn), at
Plates 26 c, d, 27 a-c Alet (Aude), *Castelnau-Rivière-Basse* (Hautes-Pyrénées), *Lescar* (Basses-Pyrénées)
Plate 26 b and as far as *Hagetmau* and St.-Sever (Landes) capitals and abaci are found whose ornamentation derives directly from the art of Toulouse and of Moissac. It will be enough to compare the monsters holding a man in their claws
Plates 26, 27 at St.-Sernin in Toulouse, at Lescar and Castelnau-Rivière-Basse. With the capitals of Castelnau-Rivière-Basse, according to Mlle Magdeleine Ferry,[80] who knows so admirably the Romanesque art of the extreme south-west of France, must be related a group of capitals in the churches built in the valley of the Adour or not far from that river; the Abbey of La Reule, and the churches of St.-Sever-de-Rustan, Mazères (Hautes-Pyréneés), Aignan, Nogaro and Tasque (Gers). The influence of Toulouse and of Moissac is also seen at St.-Bertrand-de-Comminges and less clearly at Valcabrère (Haute-Garonne).
Plate 11 c-e　　The art of Toulouse spread afar to San Isidoro at León, and in Santiago de Compostela imitations were made of the great figures of the Miégeville door.[81]

Even at Silos, where an excellent master created works that had a marked personal touch, the influence of Toulouse remains visible.[82]

The same palm-leaf decoration is to be found on the abaci at St.-Sernin of Toulouse, at St.-Gaudens (Haute-Garonne), at Lescure (Tarn), at Alet (Aude), at Conques (Aveyron), at Compostela and at Sant'Antimo, in Tuscany,[83] which was a priory of Cluny.

Plate 12 a, b

Plate 12 c, d

CHAPTER III

THE SCHOOL OF BURGUNDY

BURGUNDY, like Languedoc, possesses marvellous monuments of the Romanesque epoch. It was there that the monastic life spread itself, there that was built the tremendous abbey church of Cluny. The Cluniac Order set up its priories in every part of France; and everywhere, at the bidding of its great abbots, St. Hugues, Peter the Venerable, its monks extended their fruitful doctrine of art: embellish the House of the Lord, make the churches places where the soul may be lifted heavenward by beauty, let the artist who decorates the sanctuary and the benefactor who by his offerings enriches it with costly gifts, count themselves alike workers well-pleasing to God. In such surroundings of glowing fervour, art was to make a magnificent advance.

Plate 3 a, b We have already indicated the earliest efforts towards figure-sculpture on the capitals of the beginning of the eleventh century in the crypt of St.-Bénigne at Dijon.[84] Here as elsewhere progress was slow; and we must wait for the second half of the eleventh century before we can hope to see the appearance of works less rude. The tympana of Mont-St.-Vincent[85] and Fleury-la-Montagne (Saône-et-Loire),[86] with their figures still barbarian, are perhaps of this period. Of finer execution is the tympanum of the old doorway of the church
Plate 31 a in the Cluniac priory of *Charlieu* which must date from a time earlier than the consecration somewhere about 1094.[87] On the lintel are small figures of Apostles seated beneath arcades, and above them the Christ in Majesty appears in a glory sustained by two angels. These three figures on the tympanum are in very low relief, but their design is correct.

This *motif* was afterwards to become popular in Romanesque art, and there is no doubt that it appears here, sculptured in stone, almost for the first time; and if the artist who ventured upon its execution has succeeded fairly well that is because he had often had before his eyes a model in the great frescoes painted in the apses of churches or on the altar-fronts of goldsmiths' work. Some capitals decorated with human figures and with monsters, of extremely archaic aspect, can also be seen in this church at Charlieu, of which only the first bay of the nave now remains, and in front of which was added a porch towards the end of the Romanesque epoch.

Plate 32 a, b

At *Anzy-le-Duc*,[88] certain capitals have such a resemblance to those at Charlieu that it is almost impossible to distinguish them one from another: see, for example the figure of a man crouching between two lions at the angle of a capital, leopards with paws placed upon a human head, twisted scrolls the design of which reminds one of shells; these same capitals are found also at Vézelay in the last bays of the nave, and we may notice also the capital with shell-like scrolls at Souvigny (Allier).[89]

We are here dealing with an early phase of Burgundian sculpture in which the art is poor in form and poor in expression.

Before discussing the great *ensembles*, let us touch upon certain pieces of an exceptional character which are almost unknown: we mean the figures carved in high relief on the angles at the top of the northern tower of the façade of the church of St.-Philibert at Tournus. According to M. Virey this part of the building would belong to the beginning of the twelfth century.

Four great edifices contained the most beautiful *ensembles* of Romanesque art in Burgundy: the immense Abbey of Cluny, with its vast nave, its two transepts, its towers; St.-Bénigne at Dijon; St.-Lazare at Autun; and La Madeleine at Vézelay.

Of the church of Cluny, so foolishly destroyed at the beginning of the nineteenth century, there remains only the south side of the great transept. In the museum of the town some capitals can be seen which came from the circumference of the choir. St.-Bénigne has preserved its Romanesque crypt, and two tympana which came from this church are to be found in the archaeological museum of Dijon. The church of Vézelay, stripped of its great entrance doorway, restored by Viollet-le-Duc, still possesses its magnificent doorway opening upon the nave and the greater part of its capitals. The cathedral of Autun is almost intact.

The foolish destruction of the abbey church of *Cluny* is an irreparable loss. It has been thought that there existed a "Cluniac" art of sculpture, that from this abbey went forth artists who repeated in various places the creations of the great monastery, and that the great doorway which adorned its entrance served as model for other sculptured doors, though this is an hypothesis which it would be difficult to verify. In the absence of a master, how shall we distinguish his disciples? In our opinion, there was no "Cluniac" art, properly speaking. The monks of Cluny were assuredly great inspirers, admirable propagators of religious art, but they had the wisdom to make use on the spot, in every place where any sort of art centre existed, of whatever talent could be employed upon the construction of a priory; and when they thus encouraged the artists by allowing them to follow the inspiration of their own genius they imposed upon them no absolute formulae, though they doubtless indicated to them the general subject of their work.

The building of the church of Cluny[90] was undertaken in 1088 by St. Hugues, who died in 1109. By 1095 the choir was finished, and Pope Urban II, assisted by several bishops, consecrated the high altar and several neighbouring altars. This high altar is now preserved in the Musée Ochier at Cluny. It is a large slab about seven feet long in white marble veined in grey, and probably came from the marble-quarries in Hérault. It is carved in relief with foliated ornamentation resembling that of the high altar in St.-Sernin at Toulouse, consecrated by the same pope in May 1096.[90a]

According to certain documents, the church took between twenty and twenty-five years in building — that is to say, it was mainly the work of St. Hugues. In 1125 the huge nave of the basilica collapsed. In 1130 Pope Innocent II consecrated the church, which had been restored by Peter the Venerable who was Abbot of Cluny from 1122 to 1156.

The great doorway[91] where Christ was seen between the four evangelical symbols, accompanied by the Elders of the Apocalypse, is known to us only by certain drawings preserved in the Cabinet des Estampes and by a description of the eighteenth century. A learned American, Mr. Kenneth Conant, has recently recovered a fragment of a tympanum and a few elements of sculpture during an excavation.[92]

The most precious thing that has survived of all the decorative sculpture of Cluny is a group of capitals that was saved from destruction and is now preserved at Cluny itself in the Musée Ochier.[93] Ten of these capitals are particularly worthy of notice. They are not all of the same style; two of them are considerably more archaic than the others, and it is possible to distinguish here two stages in the development of the sculpture of Burgundy. These two capitals, with their three faces, surmounted a half-column flanking a pillar. *Plate 33* On one of them is seen the Temptation of Adam and Eve, and upon the other Abraham's sacrifice. The execution of these is unskilful, the bodies are stiff and heavy, their countenances without much expression; and everything goes to suggest that they belong to a period when sculpture was yet in its beginnings.

It seems to us that they should be assigned to that first stage of Romanesque sculpture in Burgundy which revealed itself when men set to work to carve large numbers of capitals and to ornament them with figures of human beings and animals. We have found testimony as to this first stage of the art at Charlieu, at Anzy-le-Duc and on some capitals at Vézelay 94; other similar examples are to be found at Tournus, at Bois-Ste.-Marie (Saône-et-Loire) and at Til-Châtel (Côte-d'Or). These two capitals at Cluny must have been executed in the time of St. Hugues.

The other capitals are quite different. Their technique is admirable; and the man who carved them was not only an incomparable artist but also one who was fortunate enough to live at an epoch when art, having slowly evolved, and profited by long and laborious experiments, was now developing magnificently. On two of these capitals are eight human figures, several of them *Plates 42-45 a-c* carrying musical instruments, personifying the eight tones of Gregorian music; two are decorated with female allegorical figures representing the Seasons, the Virtues and the Arts; on another we see Paradise with its rivers and its trees; the sixth undoubtedly represents the Earth and its labours; the seventh shows mutilated figures, the meaning of which it is impossible to gather; the last has only foliated ornamentation. Inscriptions explain some of the scenes represented. There are in the figures of these capitals a remarkable talent of execution and a considerable advance upon the capitals of Original Sin and of Abraham. The calm, the gravity of these figures, the facile method, so lacking in affectation, of treating the draperies in which they are clothed, the simplicity of their manner combined with the harmonious arrangement of the composition, the stalks of the foliage, delicately treated and detaching themselves from the background — all these things seem already to foreshadow Gothic sculpture.

These eight capitals surmounted the eight columns of the apse of the choir of the great church; and there has been a good deal of recent discussion as to the date of their execution. André Michel 95 was of opinion that they had been sculptured at some time round about the middle of the twelfth century. But Mr. Kingsley Porter has thought that they could not have been executed except between 1088 and 1095, that is to say before the consecration of the choir which was then finished, the capitals, according to him, having always

35

in the Middle Ages been carved before they were put into place. We know, however, that in those days many capitals were decorated after their erection. Mr. Conant is in complete agreement with Mr. Kingsley Porter on this point. M. Oursel admits that the capitals may have been sculptured after they were erected, but he thinks that they cannot have remained very long without decoration and that the date of their execution should be fixed between 1088 and 1113. Mlle Jalabert dates them between 1125 and 1130, that is to say after the collapse of the nave and before the consecration by Innocent II.[95a] This opinion closely resembles that of André Michel and we consider it quite acceptable; it was doubtless during the early part of Peter the Venerable's abbotcy that these capitals were executed.

In our opinion it is impossible that such accomplished works of art can belong to the period of the first construction at Cluny. As Mlle Jalabert has rightly remarked, these capitals, admitting that they date from about 1130 as she believes, represent a distinct advance in floral decoration when compared with other works of the period. There is no reason for ascribing to them an earlier date. Moreover many of them bear inscriptions in characters some of which were not in general use until about the middle of the century.

It will be noticed that on these capitals are figures which are identical with others at Autun and Vézelay: a bell-ringer at Cluny is to be seen likewise at Autun and Vézelay; on one of the Cluny capitals is a figure carrying a basket, *Plate 45 d* very like the capital of the apiarists at Vézelay. Now there is reason to suppose that most of the capitals at Vézelay and at Autun were executed somewhere between 1120 and 1132.

Lastly we know that St. Bernard in his Apology,[95b] written between 1123 and 1125, addressed certain reproaches to the monks of Cluny, blaming them in particular for the ridiculous and fantastic sculptures which were to be found in their church, such as animals with two heads, or with two bodies and only one head. Peter the Venerable was in constant touch with St. Bernard and had a great respect for his opinion. It is therefore permissible to suppose that when decorating the church at Cluny he recognized that the observations made by the fiery abbot of Clairvaux were justified, and that instead of allowing the sculptors to adorn the capitals with fabulous and grotesque monsters, he made them execute figures which were more calculated to elevate the mind to the contemplation of supernatural things.

Everything goes to prove that the figure capitals on the columns in the apse cannot be dated prior to the second quarter of the twelfth century, and we must insist on the difference of style to be noted between them and the two capitals representing the Original Sin and Abraham, which may belong to the end of the eleventh century or the first years of the twelfth. The acceptance of our opinion does not necessarily mean that the capitals in the choir were carved after being placed in position, for there is also the possibility that Peter the Venerable, after the disaster in 1125, may have ordered the recarving of the capitals during the work of repair.

The cathedral of *Autun*[96] was very probably conceived and undertaken by Étienne de Bagé, who occupied the episcopal see of the city from 1112 to 1139. A bull of Innocent II in 1132 tells us that Hugues II, who was Duke of Burgundy from 1102 until 1142, had given the necessary site for the building. In that same year of 1132 the Pope consecrated the new church dedicated to St. Lazare, to which in 1147 the relics of the saint were solemnly transferred. An account of this ceremony by an eyewitness allows us to conclude that at this date the interior works, as a whole, were completed. The great tympanum *Plate 34* must have been finished before the consecration. At this same date of 1132 the tympanum of the nave of Vézelay was very probably completed, and after making a fresh study of these monuments we believe that the tympanum of Autun is anterior to that of Vézelay. One has the impression that the tympanum of Vézelay, as a work of art, is more finished, more successful, of more accurate composition, and that it is therefore the later of the two, since these two portions of two different buildings, which have so many artistic features in common, must have been entrusted to the best sculptors of that period. And apart from all this, the tympanum of Autun, signed by the master Gislebertus, contains epigraphic characters which belong to the first quarter of the twelfth century.

This tympanum represents a Christ of large size presiding at the Last Judgement. On the lintel, the dead are reawakening; guardian angels on the right hand of Christ are gathering the souls of the blessed to whom St. Peter is opening the gate of the Heavenly Jerusalem. On the left, an angel and a demon are busy with the weighing of souls. There are some charming scenes: the gesture of one of the elect who hangs like a little child on to the robe of the angel that the latter may lift him to the heavens is most touching in its naiveté.

Here we may notice the tendency, so frequent with Romanesque sculptors to divide their figures into hierarchies by giving them different dimensions. The Christ is much larger than the other personages, while the apostles and angels are in their turn larger than the figures representing the souls of the dead. It is noteworthy, however, that the apostles and angels are not all of the same size, but in the opinion of the sculptor this was a necessary factor in order to fill the whole of the tympanum. Romanesque artists had a horror of empty spaces and always tried to fill out every part of the surface they had to carve, and in addition to this the decorator imagined that he needed numerous figures in order to give full expression to his conceptions. This explains those confused scenes in which the figures are piled upon one another.

Gothic artists were more restrained in their compositions, which were clearer and more spacious, and better arranged. It was this fear of empty spaces which led many artists, especially those of Burgundy, to depict the draperies with turned-up edges, as if they were raised by the wind. This may be noticed on the Autun tympanum in the figure of St. Peter. The capitals of the same church and those of Vézelay show numerous examples of the same device.

Plate 35 The lateral doors of the church were also decorated, though of this there remains but a single, infinitely precious fragment, preserved in a house at Autun. This is a piece of a lintel. The body of Eve can be seen, posed horizontally and resting upon one elbow and upon her knees. It is quite likely that upon the other half of the lintel was Adam, facing her, and in a similar attitude. What could be more original than the behaviour of this woman who is about to commit a fault, creeping behind the bushes, putting her hand to her mouth so that no one shall overhear her while she calls to Adam in a low voice, her right hand spread behind her in a gesture of dissimulation and fear, plucking the forbidden fruit without letting her eyes rest upon it?

Plate 36 In the interior of the church are many capitals with various scenes composed of graceful figures, lissom and elegant: we will mention the Flight into Egypt, the Temptation of Christ in the Wilderness, the Stoning of St. Stephen, the appearance of Christ to Mary Madgalen, etc... We notice the talent with which the artist has followed the design of the Corinthian capital and disposed his figures in the representation of the body of St. Vincent protected by two eagles which hold themselves erect at the angles of the capital where the central rose is moulded to the semblance of ornamental foliage.

The art of Autun appears again in *St.-Andoche* at *Saulieu*. This church, *Plate 39 a* which was consecrated in 1119,[97] belonged to the bishops of Autun, who were at the same time abbots of Saulieu. The same craftsmen must have worked upon both buildings; and we find when we examine them that they both contain certain scenes executed in much the same manner: both at Autun and at Saulieu, Balaam, the Flight into Egypt, and the Noli Me Tangere appear upon the capitals. In the third of these scenes, in both churches, Jesus has precisely the same pose; the vestments are treated by identical processes, with the result that they seem to flow freely, giving the wearer a light and realistic attitude as though he had just turned round and were standing quite still. There is also the same carriage of the head, which is slightly bent, just as we see it in other figures of this school, and particularly on the lintel of Perrecy-les-Forges (Saône-et-Loire). *Plate 41 b*

The church of *Vézelay*[98] may be regarded as the richest treasure of Burgundian sculture. Its construction was begun in 1096 by Abbot Artaud, and the choir was certainly finished by 1104, when the dedication took place. In 1120, on the feast of St. Mary Magdalen, a terrible fire destroyed the church and claimed many victims. A new consecration took place in 1132, and a reference in a chronicle allows us to suppose that by 1138 the work upon the more important parts of the church was at an end.[99]

In the last two bays of the nave there is a capital representing the Temptation of Adam and Eve, as well as other capitals, of which we have already spoken, with decorations or human figures. These are of a style more archaic than the rest of the ornamentation of the church and of the narthex leading into it: they were probably re-used when the building was restored and may have belonged to the epoch of Abbot Artaud.

All the other capitals in the nave and in the narthex are of one style, and must all have been executed between 1120 and 1138.[100] Their iconography is *Plate 38* extremely varied, the scenes being derived from the Old and New Testaments, or from the Lives of the Saints and Desert Fathers, such as St. Peter, St. Martin, St. Benedict, St. Paul the Hermit, St. Anthony and St. Eugénie. There are also pastoral and popular scenes. Weird monsters borrowed from the bestiaries, against which men are fighting, represent the struggle of humanity against Satan. In other instances, the sculptor has merely sought after harmonious compositions: gazelles stand erect, or birds in most lifelike and graceful manner raise their heads and peck at bunches of grapes. Some of these capitals which were in bad condition were copied and replaced by Viollet-le-Duc's sculptors.

The same great architect also rebuilt the great tympanum at the entrance, drawing his inspiration from the mutilated remains which were slowly mouldering away against one of the outside walls of the church. But the Madeleine at Vézelay has retained intact its great doorway, flanked by two lateral doors, which open from the narthex upon the nave. The large tympanum, concerning which M. Mâle has written some striking pages, shows the Descent of the Holy Ghost on the Day of Pentecost.[101] Around this are the nations of the world which were to be evangelized by the Apostles, even those fabulous peoples being represented who were supposed to dwell at the ends of the earth and to whom the imagination of the Middle Ages gave strange forms. On the pier is seen a statue of St. John the Baptist, and upon the abutments are Apostles grouped in twos and talking to each other, it would seem, with much animation. To the beauty of style which marks this vast composition must be added the profound signification of the theme which it interprets. On the southern lateral door are represented the Visitation, the Nativity, the Adoration of the Magi, while the Pilgrims of Emmaus appear on the door to the north.

Plate 37

The sculptures of the right doorway of the façade at *St.-Lazare* at *Avallon*[102] present considerable resemblances with those of the tympana of Vézelay. We find the same style, the same attitudes, the same draperies, and those very characteristic tuckings-up of the lower parts of the vestments which are seen especially in Burgundy. These sculptures of the church of St.-Lazare at Avallon also derive from the Ile-de-France, for the three portals of its western façade are adorned with column-statues the use of which in the *ensemble* of decoration seems to have originated at St.-Denis and Chartres, in which case they cannot have been executed before the middle of the twelfth century.

Plate 31 b

If it is very difficult to date the exceedingly archaic tympanum preserved in a farm-house at *Anzy-le-Duc*,[103] near the church, and that of *Neuilly-en-Donjon* (Allier),[104] the latter, with its Adoration of the Magi, so unusual with its great elongated outlines, we nevertheless have a good chance of being accurate when we assign to the middle of the first half of the century a number of sculptures belonging to the group of Autun, Saulieu, Vézelay and Avallon: such

as the capitals of *St.-Vincent* at *Chalon-sur-Saône*,[105] some capitals in the south *Plate 39 b, c*
side-aisle of *Notre-Dame* at *Beaune*, and some other capitals in the churches of
Perrecy-les-Forges, *Anzy-le-Duc* and *Montceaux-l'Étoile*[106] as well as the capitals *Plate 39 d*
coming from the abbey of Moutier-St.-Jean which were executed at the time *Plate 40 a*
of the abbot Bernard II, who died in 1133. Four of these capitals are preserved
in the Fogg Museum at Cambridge (U. S. A.).[107] They represent Cain and
Abel and scenes from the Life of Christ; another of these capitals has just
been acquired by the Louvre, and represents vintage-scenes.[107 a] At *Perrecy*,[108] *Plate 41 b*
the Christ in glory between two angels with long wings is a remarkable work;
on the lintel is seen a whole series of scenes referring to the Arrest of Christ
in the Garden of Olives and the incidents which preceded that arrest. As the
sculptor had not room for the reproduction of these scenes on the lintel itself,
he began and ended upon the walls of the porch which adjoins the doorway.

The tympanum of the façade of the church at Anzy-le-Duc[109] is somewhat
mutilated; it represents the Ascension and is a work of small dimensions,
treated soberly and with elegance. The tympanum of *Montceaux-l'Étoile* shows *Plate 41 a*
an art that is more advanced. The stone, which is dark yellow with a very
soft appearance, gives the effect of potter's clay. The little figures are delicately treated, they stand well away from the background and are, one might
say, "finished". All these figures have various and very natural attitudes: the
Apostles raise their arms towards heaven and show in a manner that is most
happily rendered their surprise and emotion. One of them stands with his
back to us, and each is in a different posture. Christ himself stands upright
in an elliptical glory, and holds his cross in his right hand'. The attitude of
the two angels is curious, yet very graceful: the artist has tried to show that
they are lifting themselves heavenward, and their backs are turned to the
mandorla which rests upon their loins and is supported by their hands.

The magnificent tympanum which comes from a door of the priory of *Anzy-* *Plate 46*
le-Duc,[110] and which after remaining for some time at Arcy is now to be
found in a museum at Paray-le-Monial, must belong to the second half of the
century. Upon it is seen, as on the tympanum of Montceaux-l'Étoile, the
Christ in a Glory which once again angels support upon their backs. In the
middle of the lintel is the Virgin, seated amongst a number of personages, and
preparing to feed the Child.

The archaeological museum of *Dijon* possesses two tympana which came

41

from the church of St.-Bénigne. One of these represents the Last Supper,[111] but the figures are stiffly arranged and the effect is monotonous. The other[112] shows Christ among the four Symbols of the Evangelists, with four angels, and is of far better execution. But it should be added that in the latter case we have a theme which was familiar to the sculptors and therefore easier to execute than one which required of them a new composition. The small tympanum of a lateral door of the church of *Til-Châtel* (Côte-d'Or)[113] would seem to be a reduced replica of this tympanum from St.-Bénigne.

Plate 47a The exuberant temperament of the Burgundian artists manifests itself in a particularly expressive fashion on the two doorways situated in front of the porch of the priory of *Charlieu* (Loire)[114] of which we have already mentioned the old doorway placed at the entrance to the nave.

This work belongs to the close of the Romanesque epoch. On the great doorway is a portion of the Apocalyptic Vision. The Christ is enthroned in a glory which two angels, in attitudes of extreme restlessness, sustain. They are accompanied by the four Symbols of the Evangelists. Upon the lintel appear the Virgin, between two angels, and the twelve Apostles. Above, on the bend of the arch, is the Lamb in very high relief, almost in the round. Beside this doorway is another small doorway, also richly decorated. Upon the lintel seem to be represented the blood-sacrifices of the ancient Law; on the tympanum, the first miracle of Christ at the marriage-feast at Cana; and, lastly, on the archivolt, the Transfiguration. All these figures are in awkward attitudes, and the general posing is one of disorder, since the very clever artist, in his desire to give movement to his figures, has gone beyond measure and produced a fantasy which is almost offensive.

The fact that the Charlieu sculpture is so deeply incised and its details carried out with astonishing care and minuteness is certainly to be attributed not only to the skill of the sculptor, but also to the stone which he used, namely the yellowish limestone, very fine and very easily worked, which came from the neighbouring quarries of St.-Maurice-lès-Châteauneuf (Saône-et-Loire).[114a] Sculptors appreciated the qualities of this stone and used it in the decoration of a large number of churches. It is quite probable that the carvings at Montceaux-l'Étoile and Anzy-le-Duc were executed in the same stone that was used at Charlieu. André Michel has found this Charlieu stone at Ambierle and at St.-Romain-le-Puy (Loire) and M. Thiollier had noticed that the capitals of the doorway of the church at Pouilly-les-Feurs (Loire) are carved in yellow limestone coming from the neighbourhood of Charlieu; they are more delicately carved than those in other parts of the same building. [114b]

The observations which we have made regarding the doorways in front of the porch at Charlieu might be repeated for the neighbouring doorway of *St.-Julien-de-Jonzy* (Saône-et-Loire),[115] which is remarkably like those of *Plate 47b* Charlieu. Here are seen the Last Supper and the Washing of the Feet. These two episodes are found again at Vandeins (Ain), at Savigny (Rhône), and on the beautiful tympanum of Bellenaves (Allier).[116] Close to St.-Julien-de-Jonzy must be mentioned the tympanum of *Semur-en-Brionnais*,[117] on which is depicted the history of St. Hilaire, a mediocre work of a second-rate artist.

The Romanesque sculptors further manifested their talent in St.-Vincent at Mâcon, at Chissey-lès-Mâcon, at Bois-Ste.-Marie, at Varennes-l'Arconce (Saône-et-Loire), on the tomb of Ste.-Magnance (Yonne),[118] in the Ain at Nantua, at St.-Paul-de-Varax[119] and in St.-André at Bagé.[120]

In the valley of the Rhône there is a mingling of the arts of Burgundy and of Provence. At *Romans* (Isère), for example, in the midst of capitals which *Plate 40c, d* are simply decorative in a strongly marked Provençal style, are to be seen two capitals with human figures[121] possessing all the characteristics of those of Autun, Saulieu and Vézelay; it seems almost certain that these capitals were brought hither from Burgundy. We have remarked upon the singular resemblances of capitals at Charlieu, Anzy-le-Duc and Vézelay, belonging to the end of the eleventh century; and we have noted in the Pyrenees, at Castelnau-Rivière-Basse and at Lescar, capitals which resemble each other in an extraordinary fashion. It appears quite probable that there existed a group of craftsmen who moved from place to place in some given region for the purpose of ornamenting its churches. But may one not also suppose that it was perhaps usual to turn out a series of capitals in some one workshop, of similar design, and to transport them to the various churches which were in course of construction? This may appear a strange hypothesis, but if it is remembered that during the sixth century marble capitals were sent from Constantinople to all parts of the world, some of which have been left at Jouarre; and that from the tenth to the eleventh century a workshop of marble-workers, perhaps at St.-Pons-de-Thomières, but at all events somewhere in the south, despatched altar-tables to localities as far distant as Ge-

43

rona, Rodez and even Cluny; and if later baptismal fonts and sepulchral stones were sent from Picardy even as far as to England, why should it not be allowable to suppose that the same practice was adopted in the case of Romanesque capitals?

On the beautiful tympana of La Charité-sur-Loire (Nièvre),[122] which were executed during the third quarter of the century, the art of Burgundy and the art of the Ile-de-France combined; but the imprint of the latter is nevertheless the stronger, and the lintel, on which are seen the Nativity and the Announcement to the Shepherds, is simply a copy of that at Chartres.[123]

We come to the transition phase of Romanesque and Gothic art in a monument the date of which is quite precise: the remains of the tomb of St. Lazare erected in the cathedral of Autun by the monk Martin somewhere between 1170 and 1189. The finest fragments, Christ on the cross, and statues of St. Andrew, St. Martha and St. Mary Madgalen, are preserved in the little Musée Lapidaire at Autun. A few pieces of sculpture are to be found in the Musée Rolin. A quantity of fragments from the architecture of this little monument is preserved in the cathedral. The Musée du Louvre has recently acquired a head, most probably that of a statue representing St. Peter, which was part of the same group but has disappeared.[124] These beautiful figures, so calm, so noble, and of such perfect proportions, are a foreshadowing of the stately and serene art which will show itself in the statues which are so shortly to ornament the doorways of our Gothic cathedrals.

CHAPTER IV

WORKSHOPS IN DAUPHINÉ AND IN THE VALLEY
OF THE RHÔNE

In Dauphiné and in the valley of the Rhône are a certain number of beautiful Romanesque works. Some of them are of an altogether original style, while others show signs of intrusion, of influences, that is to say, which came either from the school of Burgundy or from that of Provence.

The church of the Abbey of *St.-Martin-d'Ainay*[125] at Lyons, consecrated by Paschal II in 1107, possesses an *ensemble* of Romanesque decoration which is of exceptional interest, since it shows certain *motifs* in ornamental art which, though they may not belong here exclusively, have yet been carried out more successfully than anywhere else. Some models drawn from the decorative grammar of antiquity, and others borrowed from oriental ivories or Irish miniatures,[126] furnished inspiration to the great artist who presided over this ornamentation. Rows of dogs, each biting the loins of the one in front of him, he-goats and lions rearing themseves opposite to each other against the trunks of trees, form a decoration of extreme elegance. Some of the capitals represent masks from the mouths of which issue spirals of foliage. These figures are also to be found at Valence, and they were imitated at Modena.

Then, on others, are Biblical scenes the iconography of which is the more interesting in that they belong to the very first years of the twelfth century, illustrating the Sin of Adam and Eve, Cain and Abel presenting their offerings to the Lord, the Murder of Abel, St. Michael overcoming the Dragon, St. John announcing the Coming of Christ, Christ himself amidst the four Symbols of the Evangelists, the Annunciation, etc... The technique is still primitive, the artist having employed the method of restrained relief.

These figures have some resemblance to other sculptures of greater importance which can be seen in the cathedral of *St.-Maurice* at *Vienne*. There are three statues,[127] of which only one is intact, the others having their heads broken. The first, which without doubt represents St. Paul holding a book, has a face with a somewhat brutal expression; the orphrey with which the garment is trimmed is especially curious, the design of the embroidery forming a frame of foliage round a number of busts of small figures, these latter having some relation with the little figures carved on a panel of the high altar in St.-Sernin at Toulouse. The two statues with the broken heads represent St. Peter and St. John; and there can be no doubt that these three statues, now preserved in the cathedral of St.-Maurice, came from the old basilica of St.-Pierre. They are in any case from the same workshop as the seated St. Peter[128] on the tympanum of a door of this church, which used to open upon the cloister. This high relief is now to be found in a museum installed in the church, which is no longer used for religious purposes.

The very characteristic arrangement of the vestments of these four figures should be noticed, with their concentric folds to the knees and folds ending in spirals, a treatment which will continue throughout the whole of the twelfth century to be a well-marked feature of the art of this region. These works certainly belong to the first half of the twelfth century, probably to the first quarter.

The tympanum of Condrieu (Rhône)[129] and that of St.-Alban-du-Rhône noticed by M. J. David,[130] the tympana of the cathedral of Valence,[131] of the churches of Champagne (Ardèche)[132] and of Vizille (Isère),[133] the lintel of Savigny (Rhône),[134] on the last three of which the Last Supper is represented, are to be reckoned amongst the most interesting and the most important works of this region. M. Mâle has remarked in the doorway of Bourg-Argental (Loire)[135] resemblances to the doorway which has disappeared from the great Abbey of Cluny. We find, in the bends of the arches, the same little figures and the same heads in the medallions. Similar medallions are found at Avallon and at Vézelay. But though this doorway may have received a Burgundian imprint, and though, like all the monuments in the valley of the Rhône it preserves traces of classical influence borrowed from the Gallo-Roman monuments which were numerous in this region, the yet more curious fact should also be remarked that there are real column-statues undoubtedly borrowed from some doorway in the Ile-de-France, since this district it certainly was which, first at St.-Denis and then at Chartres, adopted the practice of attaching statues to the columns of the abutments, a practice which will develop more and more in the course of the Gothic period.

The very curious design of the folds of the vestments which we have noticed on the statues of St.-Maurice at Vienne[136] is found again in the middle of the twelfth century on the capitals with figures in the cathedral of *St.-Jean* at *Lyons,*[137] the cathedral of *St.-Maurice* at *Vienne* and in the church of *St.-*

André-le-Bas [138] at Vienne. The sculptures of St.-André-le-Bas are exactly dated by an inscription commemorating the construction of this church in 1152 and giving the name of the master of the work, Guillaume Martin. Here are to be seen the most beautiful and the most characteristic capitals of this school, such as the well-known ones depicting Job an object of disgust to his friends, and *Plate 49 a, b* Samson breaking the jaw of a lion, the figures having muscular power, movement and an extraordinary vigour.

The cathedral of St.-Maurice at Vienne possesses a series of capitals which *Plate 49 c, d* form a varied iconographic *ensemble*, with scenes that are rare, such as the Healing of the Paralytic, Mary Magdalene at the feet of Jesus, the Coming forth from Limbo, the Entry of Christ into Jerusalem, and the Resurrection of Lazarus. [139] To these capitals at Vienne M. Bégule has rightly related those of churches near Vienne, notably those in the church of Ternay (Isère). [140]

The beautiful doorway of *St.-Barnard* at *Romans* (Drôme) [141] has some large statues in union with pilasters, which offer some resemblance to the sculptures of St.-Gilles-du-Gard. Similar comparisons might be made on an examination of the less known statues of the doorway at *Thines* (Ardèche) which *Plate 50* are related to the sculptures of Valence, to the statues of Romans, and also to those of St.-Gilles. The artist who executed them shows a personal touch in his manner of treating the heads, with their noticeable eye-pupils, and with hair arranged in tight tresses separated from each other.

In conclusion, this district possesses one monument which is quite exceptional: the altar of the church of *Avenas* (Rhône), ornamented with sculptures *Plate 51* on three faces. The front is decorated with a Christ in Majesty surrounded by Apostles who are seated and arranged in two tiers. Upon one of the lateral faces are scenes in the Life of the Virgin; and, on the other, a crowned figure whom an inscription describes as "Rex Ludovicus" is kneeling and presenting a church to St. Vincent who stands in front of him.

There has been much discussion as to the identity of the king mentioned in this inscription, some saying that Louis le Débonnaire is intended, others that it is Louis VI or Louis VII. [142] M. Charles Perrat [143] has recently shown that this altar was erected as the result of a donation made to the church in June 1166 by King Louis VII. The style of the figures as well as the character of the inscriptions themselves would appear to confirm this assertion.

CHAPTER V

AUVERGNE, VELAY AND LIMOUSIN

IT was Auvergne which achieved, before any other region, the representation of human figures of large size not merely in low or high relief but in full round. It is true that these works were not in stone, but there was nevertheless something new and decisive for the renaissance of sculpture when these "majestés d'or" appeared, statues of wood overlaid with sheets of silver or of gold, of which M. Louis Bréhier has discovered many examples in the centre of France. [144] The oldest that is yet known would be the golden statue of the Virgin executed before 946 by the clerk Aleaume, goldsmith and architect, with the help of his brother Adam, at the cost of Étienne II, Bishop of Clermont and Abbot of Conques. The celebrated statue of St. Foy, which has survived to the present day and is preserved in the treasury of the church of Conques-en-Rouergue, is contemporary with this vanished work. M. Marcel Aubert has recently dated it approximately about the year 985. [144a]

It was more than another century before the sculptors grew bold enough to execute figures in high relief in stone. [145]

Auvergne, in consequence of the hardness of the lava, granite and arkose which were the only materials available, and little suited for the sculptor's work, achieved no great *ensembles* of sculpture on the outside of her churches, and her craftsmen were content to decorate a few framed lintels, a few doorways and porches.

In the interior of certain churches of Auvergne, on the other hand, we find important series of historiated capitals, and this was because the materials used inside were often different from those employed on the outside of the churches. M. Bréhier has noticed that the churches in the region of Clermont and the Limagne are constructed of arkose; thus the sculptures of the doorway of Notre-Dame at Clermont, of very mediocre execution, are of arkose, whilst the historiated capitals of the interior are worked in a soft limestone which was brought from Berry. [146]

We shall examine first the capitals of these churches; and we shall find that as M. Bréhier [147] has well remarked the traditions of antiquity have been maintained in this part of the country more faithfully than in other regions. This

48

is because the Gallo-Roman civilization had left a strong imprint, and because the monuments of that epoch were preserved there in large numbers so that Romanesque sculptors made constant borrowings from them. They imitated and sometimes copied exactly the Corinthian capital, as M. Bréhier has observed for a capital at Mozat.[148] The Victories armed with bucklers, the confronted genii, the wrestlers sculptured on the capitals, were borrowed from antique models. The sculptors have also chosen certain scenes from the sarcophagi of the first Christian centuries, notably those of the Multiplication of the Loaves and the History of Jonah, which are found upon sarcophagi preserved at Clermont.

The sculptors of Auvergne were always careful in their pictured capitals to keep the profile, the graceful outlines, of the Corinthian capital. Whilst in certain regions the figures are grouped with a kind of independence, without any apparent intention of conforming to fixed principles, here the disposition of the figures is subordinated to a very precise discipline, with well-marked intention of respect for the Corinthian "basket"; though the artists have not been prevented by this discipline from bestowing upon their groups a considerable amount of ease and life.

M. Bréhier's numerous observations on this matter are most interesting. It will be noticed that in capitals with few figures, though such capitals are not frequent, the figures are often found at the angles of the "basket", and their heads, which are intentionally made abnormally large, are there in order to take the place of the volute in the Corinthian capital.

Thus the sculptors have knowingly ignored proportion, and have subordinated the nature of the human body to the requirements of decoration, so that the body appears merely by way of an ornamental element. These figures are sometimes kneeling, and this was a device for strengthening the body and more especially the heads of angle figures, since it was possible to make the heads larger when the trunk was diminished in height. This can be seen on a capital at Mozat, and a pine-cone suspended to the abacus replaces the rosette of the Corinthian capital. At Mozat, moreover yet another, novelty appeared: four angels are sculptured on the faces, and the head of each of them, framed in a large nimbus, takes the place of the rosette, whilst in the angles their lifted wings outline a projection which represents the volute.

Certain churches of Auvergne possess a series of storied capitals which are extremely interesting: Notre-Dame-du-Port at Clermont-Ferrand,[149] St.-Nectaire, Mozat, being those which exhibit the most important groups.

Plate 53 a, b   The capitals of *Notre-Dame-du-Port* are celebrated, and photographs, post-cards, and the casts in the Musée du Trocadéro have made them known to a wide public, so that it is scarcely necessary to recall the scenes so full of spirit and animation: Adam and Eve driven out of Paradise, where the Deity is seen seizing the first man by the beard, while the latter in his indignation is administering a masterful kick to his spouse; the Annunciation and the Visitation, on which may be seen the signature of the sculptor Robert; Virtues armed as warriors triumphing over Vices, the donor Étienne presenting a capital to an angel etc. The figures, rugged and coarse, by reason of the nature of the stone that was used, have a vigour of expression that is remarkable.

Plate 53 c, d   The twenty-two storied capitals of the church of *St.-Nectaire*[150] are no less interesting, and they show a very varied iconography. There is the Multiplication of the Loaves, the Transfiguration, the Arrest of Christ in the Garden of Olives, the Flagellation, Christ carrying his cross, the Unbelief of St. Thomas, the Holy Women on their way to the tomb that is guarded by soldiers, the Descent of Christ into Limbo, the Destroying Angel, the Last Judgement, the Legend of St. Nectaire.

Plate 52 a-c   The sculptor who worked at *St.-Pierre* at *Mozat* (Puy-de-Dôme) was a great artist, and we will mention a very fine decorated capital with a human mask on each face, copied from a Gallo-Roman model, and the History of Jonah, inspired by a scene represented on a Christian sarcophagus. Upon other capitals he has sought to express his own vigorous personality and he has fully succeeded: let us instance the representation of the deliverance of St. Peter and more especially the visit of the Holy Women to the Tomb, in front of which an angel receives them.[151]

Plate 54   The church of *Issoire*[152] possesses a certain number of capitals of admirable workmanship. In the nave and side-aisles are some very simple capitals derived from the Corinthian capital; in place of the rosette is a head, from the mouth of which springs foliage; eagles with their wings spread are also seen, and centaurs. Some of the capitals are also adorned with religious scenes, such as the Good Shepherd carrying on his shoulders the lost sheep; but the most curious are on the columns of the choir and of the apse, some of which have been restored and all of them unhappily whitewashed. They represent

50

the Last Supper, the Holy Women at the Tomb, several episodes in the Life of Christ, and especially the Passion.

Mention must also be made of fine capitals in St.-Victor at Ennezat,[153] at *Volvic*, Artonne and Glaine-Montaigut (Puy-de-Dôme), in St.-Julien at Brioude (Haute-Loire),[154] at Besse-en-Chandesse,[155] and at Chauriat (Puy-de-Dôme), those in the two last-mentioned churches of less fine execution, with figures in low relief.

Plate 52 d

A certain number of scenes were thought very highly of by the sculptors of Auvergne, and are accordingly found in many churches: the capital of the Holy Women at the Tomb is to be seen at St.-Nectaire, at Mozat, at Issoire and in Haute-Loire at Brioude and Blesle; that of the Usurer between two demons is found at Notre-Dame-du-Port, at Ennezat, at Orcival, at Brioude, and with variations at Chauriat and St.-Nectaire. It is also to be seen at the church of Conques-en-Rouergue, the sculpture of which is so closely related to that of Auvergne. Four angels holding a streamer and representing the Evangelists are seen at Mozat, Volvic and Brioude; two angels only, personifying perhaps two Evangelists, at Notre-Dame-du-Port, at Chauriat and at Blesle. The Story of Jonah is represented at Mozat and at Orcival. Fine capitals with figures or animals, borrowed from antique or oriental models, without religious significance, naked youths, sirens, doves, storks, confronted griffins, are seen in other churches; let us mention those of the Moutier at Thiers, of Courpière (Puy-de-Dôme), of Chanteuges and of Blesle (Haute-Loire).

Separate consideration must be given to the capitals of certain churches of Auvergne situated on the Velay frontier, whose style distinguishes them from that of the rest of Auvergne. In *St.-Julien* at *Brioude* and in the churches of the department of Haute-Loire, at Blesle, at Chanteuges, at Lavaudieu, as in Notre-Dame at Le Puy and at Chamalières-sur-Loire in Velay, we see these dragons with their interlaced necks, these confronted doves turning their heads to peck at fruit, grotesque figures with grimacing countenances and protruding bellies, creatures whose exuberant fantasy makes us think inevitably of the Arab stuffs from which the Romanesque artists have borrowed so many designs. And M. Bréhier[156] has noted that these capitals of Velay are related rather to those of the Catalonian cloisters than to those of Auvergne. Relations were constant between Velay and Spain, thanks to the pilgrim-roads of Compostela, which explains these intrusions of Catalonian art influences.

126934

Monumental sculpture had but an insignificant position in Auvergne, and doorways decorated with sculptures are by no means numerous. We must distinguish, in this connection, between the monuments of Basse-Auvergne and those of Haute-Auvergne, two regions separated by the mountain chains of Mont-Dore and of Cantal. The former, Basse-Auvergne, is set towards the basin of the Loire by its rivers which flow into that stream; the latter is in communication with Limousin and Aquitaine.

We find, in Basse-Auvergne, a rather curious type of decoration which will not be noticed in Haute-Auvergne, triangular lintels ornamented with sculpture and surmounted by a relieving arch. Such lintels can be seen on the façade of the church of the powerful Abbey of Mozat (Puy-de-Dôme),[157] a dependency of Cluny; where in the middle of the lintel and larger than the other figures the Virgin in a rigid attitude holds the Child upon her knees; she is surrounded by St. Peter, St. John, and abbots with their croziers, and is receiving the homage of a kneeling figure, who is obviously a Benedictine monk; the work is but mediocre, the figures being stiff and expressionless. At Thuret (Puy-de-Dôme)[158] we see Christ in a glory between two angels, who, with their legs too short and their arms too long, are frankly ridiculous. At Chambon (Puy-de-Dôme)[159] is a Stoning of St. Stephen, the figures of which are very coarse in style. Beneath the north-east porch of the cathedral of Le Puy[160] opens a small door surmounted by a much-mutilated triangular lintel on which is represented the Last Supper. Above, on the tympanum, Christ is seen between two angels, standing out from a background of mosaic formed alternately of white stones and dark grey volcanic stones.

The same arrangement is found on the doorway of Notre-Dame-du-Port at Clermont,[161] on the lintel of which is the Adoration of the Magi, the Presentation in the Temple, and the Baptism of Christ, with Christ enthroned between two cherubim on the tympanum above. On the abutments, a couple of squat figures of Isaiah and St. John the Baptist, with two bas-reliefs over them representing the Annunciation and the Nativity. All these figures form an incongruous composition, without art and without nobility, and yet it is the most important *ensemble* produced in this region.

Let us take notice moreover of another work which has now almost disappeared: the tympanum under a porch of St.-Julien at Brioude[162] which was adorned with an Ascension. The thirteen figures which composed this scene, a work of the middle of the twelfth century, were of stucco, as we were able to ascertain from careful examination of a fragment, and a lengthy inscription from the Acts of the Apostles was engraved upon the stucco.

Triangular lintels with sculpture, such as we have seen in Basse-Auvergne, are also found in the districts watered by certain southern tributaries of the Loire, in the department of Allier at St.-Pourçain-sur-Sioule,[163] at Autry-Issard,[164] and at Meillers,[165] and in the department of Indre at Ruffec[166] and Chouday.

The great sculptures which we find in Haute-Auvergne,[167] of a far more skilful form of art, must truly be said to connect themselves with neighbouring provinces, since Nature herself has turned this region towards the valleys of the Dordogne and the Lot, so that the art of Limousin and Quercy and Aquitaine makes itself felt here.

The church of *St.-Georges* at *Ydes* (Cantal) possesses a porch the lateral walls of which are ornamented with very beautiful figures in high relief and of large size. On one side is represented the Annunciation and on the other Daniel in the Lions' Den and the angel carrying the prophet Habakkuk to Babylon with water and bread for Daniel. Now this type of porch belongs to Limousin, and at Serandon (Corrèze), a few kilometres from Ydes, at Beaulieu (Corrèze), at La Graulière (Corrèze)[168] we find the same thing, a porch having its lateral walls adorned with sculpture. At Serandon and at Beaulieu as at Ydes appears the scene of Daniel nourished by Habakkuk.

A similar arrangement of lateral walls with sculptural decoration is found at Moissac and in the northern porch of the cathedral of Cahors,[169] and it was also formerly to be found at Souillac.

Mauriac[170] offers the most beautiful tympanum in Auvergne, though its sculpture is not indigenous. And yet, as M. Bréhier has remarked, the architecture of its doorway has all the essential characteristics of the church doorways of Cantal. But the artists who executed the beautiful figures of the so much admired Ascension were not natives of Auvergne. This work is related with the works of Languedoc and Limousin, and especially with the Ascension represented in the cathedral of Cahors.

Plate 55

The same scene of the Ascension appears in two places in the department of Corrèze, on the tympanum of the church at *Collonges*,[171] dating from 1135 to 1145 according to M. René Fage, and on that of the church of St.-Cha-

53

mant[172] which the same writer considers to be a mediocre imitation of the earlier example executed in the middle of the twelfth century. In this same department of Corrèze there are churches possessing groups of historiated capitals; particularly noteworthy are Brive and Lubersac.[172a]

In Limousin, where we have noticed several doorways and porches, is to be seen a rather unusual monument which can hardly be assigned to any particular school. It is a work altogether Romanesque in appearance, as to the date of which there has been much discussion, some relying upon a chronicle of the Middle Ages which attributes it to the very earliest years of the twelfth century, while others, judging by the style of its sculpture, would place it at the end of that century. The "tomb of St. Junien",[173] a monument enclosing the stone sarcophagus which contains the remains of the holy hermit of the fifth century, is to be found in the apse of the church at *St.-Junien* (Haute-Vienne).

Plate 56

This monument is decorated with sculpture on its two larger sides and on one of the smaller, the other smaller side being formerly attached to the back of the high altar. Upon one of the large sides is the Virgin holding the Child, and placed in an almond-shaped Glory which is sustained by four angels. At the sides, in two tiers are twelve Elders of the Apocalypse, placed each under an arcade and holding their harps and vials of odours. Upon the other face, high up in the middle, is the small door through which it was possible to see the sarcophagus, and beneath this the divine Lamb in a round Glory which is sustained by two angels, while to right and left are twelve Elders arranged as in the other group. On the small side is an extremely beautiful figure of Christ in Majesty.

These sculptures are a reproduction in stone of those figures executed in repoussé by goldsmiths which from the Carolingian epoch and into the twelfth century ornamented the fronts of altars and sometimes the four sides of high altars in the most wealthy churches. This monument moreover, in its *ensemble*, resembles very closely the great shrines in enamelled work of which the goldsmiths of Limoges were in the Middle Ages the chief makers. In a study devoted to this monument we have dated the sculptures in the last quarter of the twelfth century.

54

The importance of this church[174] in the history of Romanesque architec-   *Plate 57*
ture is fully recognized. This splendid monument shows an exceptional
spaciousness and certain special characteristics which are to be found in an
identical form in three other churches, St.-Martial at Limoges, of which we
have the plans, though the church itself has been destroyed, St.-Sernin at
Toulouse, and Santiago de Compostela.

Of these four pilgrimage-churches between which certain striking resemblances exist, Ste.-Foy at Conques appears to be the most ancient, and although
attention was long ago directed to its architecture it does not seem that the
full interest of its decoration has yet been sufficiently understood.

We know that the Abbot Odolric (1030-1065) constructed a large part of
the building, and we find in the *Livre des Miracles de Sainte Foy* a passage
relating to the master of the work, Hugues, who was at work there in the time
of this abbot, and who was miraculously protected from accident while he
was using oxen for the transportation of the bases and wrought capitals from
the quarry to the church.[175] We also know that the building was pretty well
finished in the time of Abbot Bégon III (1087-1107), since the latter was concerned with the construction of the cloister.

The capitals in the apse are imperfect, and show merely floral ornaments
much stylized. In the transept are some capitals with figures badly grouped,
sculptured in the flat and bearing witness to the inefficiency of a workman
without experience. These capitals may belong to the middle and the second
half of the eleventh century. As one goes further into the nave one finds capitals of far better execution, as regards the incidents and persons which they
depict, but of which the figures are heavy and cramped: for example, amongst
others, two knights armed and carrying shields who are fighting, two figures
blowing upon ivory horns, and the rough figure of the usurer between two
demons, with his money-bag round his neck — just such a group as we have
noticed many times in the churches of Auvergne.

At the end of the north arm of the transept are the charming figures of an
Annunciation,[176] the grace and touching expression of which entitle them to
be better known. Near at hand, in the angles, are statues of the prophet Isaiah
and of St. John the Baptist.[177] These really remarkable figures appear to be

of a style more advanced than those of the façade, of which we are about to speak, and they may belong to the latter half of the twelfth century.

Against the south wall of the church, on the site of the ancient cloister, there exists a bas-relief [178] flanked on both sides by the inscription which commemorates the services rendered by the Abbot Bégon, who died in 1107. This bas-relief represents the Abbot himself by the side of Christ, who is blessing him; and as the inscription [179] is in characters that were used at the beginning of the twelfth century it is possible that both the inscription and the bas-relief were executed shortly after the abbot's death.

The great tympanum [180] of the façade at the west end exhibits with amazing abundance of detail a representation of the Last Judgement, and it is surprising that this fine piece of sculpture should not have become as famous as those of Moissac and Vézelay. It is an exceptional work which does not immediately attach itself to any school. M. Mâle and M. Bréhier [181] have nevertheless observed that it shows some connection with the Romanesque art of Auvergne.

We find here a double triangular lintel, and we remember that the churches of Basse-Auvergne frequently had lintels which were triangular in shape and adorned with sculpture. The angels bearing streamers who are seen here appear also on the capitals in Auvergne; and we notice that these angels at Conques have the same attitudes and the same physiognomy as those of Auvergne: their hair, especially, is treated in similar style, separated by a parting in the middle of the head and thrown back behind the ears: and another resemblance is found in the fact that here, as upon the lintels of Auvergne, there are inscriptions explaining the meaning of what is represented. The workshop of Clermont, which provided decoration for the choirs of Notre-Dame-du-Port and of St.-Nectaire, must have collaborated in the execution of this masterly piece of work.

The very numerous figures appear at first sight to be crowded together in disorder; and yet everything is perfectly arranged. It is a vast composition, a great page lavishly illustrated, and all its details can be clearly read. The artist has evidently attempted to introduce into his work a certain symmetry, a certain equilibrium, by contrasting scenes in which the blessed appear with others showing the wicked. Midway between the two parts of the lintel are the gateway of Heaven, where an angel is welcoming the elect, and the door of

56

Hell, in front of which is a monster with open jaws and a demon thrusting the reprobate onward. On the right, that is to say to the left of the spectator, we see the blessed gathered round Abraham and seated beneath arcades which represent the heavenly mansions, while on the opposite side are the damned, whose torments in their variety testify to the artist's exuberant imagination.

Above this first tier there is a long horizontal band filled by an inscription and forming the base of the principal part of the composition. Beneath this band, in the portions left empty by the slopes of the lintel, in two adjoining triangles, St. Foy is seen, bowing before the divine hand, while angels carefully lift the coverings of the tombs from which the risen dead are issuing, and there are also demons torturing the damned. In the midst of this splendid *ensemble* is the figure of a Christ of incomparable majesty. He is showing the wound in his side, his right hand is raised towards the elect, while the left hand is lowered on the side where are the reprobate. To his right, a procession of saints, the Virgin, an abbot, a king, with angels soaring above them, while to his left a host of armed angels seem to be stopping the cursèd, and withholding from them the vision of God, and a mob of hideous demons are grasping their victims and beginning to torture them. At the extreme top of the picture stands the cross, with angels bowing over it while they hold the lance and the nails; the sun and the moon are also there, and two angels are sounding the Last Trump. Bands of stone, covered with inscriptions, divide into compartments these various scenes and help to explain the full meaning of this vast composition. If the devils and the damned are either frightful, comic, or altogether ludicrous, if the angels and the elect, who both have the same sort of facial expression, are somewhat heavy or exhibit an air of satisfaction which is almost too beatific, if we search in vain among these faces for the supernatural glow which gives such nobility to the figures at Moissac, the Christ, on the other hand, in his attitude as in his countenance, is a magnificent personage, bearing the imprint of a sovereign majesty.

It would be interesting to fix the date of execution of the tympanum at Conques. We are of the opinion that the general tendency has been to assign a too recent construction to this work which has been dated from the latter half of the twelfth century. It must certainly be posterior to the bas-relief on the tomb of the abbot Bégon III, who died in 1107, the figures of which are much less advanced in style. But there can be no objection to the assump-

57

tion that this tympanum is contemporary with that of Moissac, or even a little older. It is true that these two works are very different in character but they are the work of two artists of equally vigorous talent; one of them, that of the Cluniac monastery, expresses the mysterious majesty of the Apocalypse and is a learned composition worthy of monks who devoted their entire lives to the study of the sacred texts; the other is a popular creation, essentially realistic, which aims at appealing to the imagination of the crowds of pilgrims who on their way to visit the tomb of St. James stopped to venerate that of St. Foy, situated amidst the stern background of the mountains of Rouergue. It is not to be altogether excluded that the Conques tympanum may have been executed about the end of the first quarter of the twelfth century. An examination of the letters forming the inscriptions does not contradict this hypothesis.

The Last Judgement which we see on the little tympanum of the church at Perse (Aveyron), a priory of Conques, appears to be a clumsy imitation of this imposing work.[181a]

CHAPTER VI

WORKSHOPS OF THE MIDDLE BASIN OF THE LOIRE

THERE is, in the middle of France, a district where Romanesque art manifested a singular fertility and in which sculpture takes on certain aspects which distinguish it from similar work in neighbouring provinces.[182] No great *ensembles* are to be found in this district, nor can we point to more than a few tympana, but on the other hand there are very many series of capitals which exhibit an art that is subtle and extremely varied and which show their sculptors to have been inspired by fantasy alone.

This district includes Bourbonnais and Berry, Orléanais and Nivernais, the valleys of the Allier, the Cher and the Indre, of the Creuse and the Vienne, and extended towards the west along the Loire to Touraine.

Here was no settled programme, no purpose on the part of the craftsmen to use their stone for dogmatic teaching: the bishop or the abbot, kindly disposed men that they were, left it to the artists to improvise as they would strange figures, people or animals, without any apparent intention of edifying the faithful. Thus there developed an art that was graceful, elegant and futile; yet full of a spirit which dissipated its talent even while showing itself worthy of a better direction; and we are reminded of the stern words of St. Bernard who grew angry when he saw the multitude of strange and meaningless sculptures which crowded into the churches and the cloisters. These reproaches of the Abbot of Cîteaux had but little effect among these fertile plains washed by the Indre, the Creuse and the Vienne, where life flowed pleasantly and peacefully.

In the valley of the Allier we find at St.-Menoux (Allier)[183] a fine bas-relief representing Christ in Majesty between the Symbols of the Evangelists.

At *Bellenaves* (Allier)[184] is a magnificent tympanum with Christ in glory sustained by two angels with tremendous wings; on the lintel are depicted the Last Supper and the Washing of the feet; the work is mutilated, but must once have been excellent. Whilst in most cases the artists who attempted to present the Last Supper succeeded only in making a monotonous row of figures in the same stiff postures, here the sculptor has been able to vary the attitudes: two of those who are sitting at the table talk together with animation and St.

59

John moves from his place to lean his head upon the bosom of Christ, while two apostles who are not yet at table are wiping their feet with most realistic movements. At Autry-Issard, Meillers, and St.-Pourçain-sur-Sioule (Allier) we see the triangular lintels that were noticed in the churches of Auvergne. At Souvigny (Allier)[185] is a curious octagonal column sculptured upon four sides, with, in superposed compartments, the Occupations of the Months, the Signs of the Zodiac, as well as strange figures which for people in the Middle Ages represented the inhabitants and the fabulous monsters of Africa and Asia. Mention should also be made of a most beautiful tympanum in the archaeological museum at Nevers, which came from the church of St.-Sauveur and represents the delivery of the keys to St. Peter.[186]

Particular attention must be given to the sculptural decoration of the vast church of the Cluniac priory of *La Charité-sur-Loire*.[187] The most important elements are the tympana of the two doorways, the admirable figures of which are products, as we have said, of the art of Ile-de-France, and doubtless were executed in the workshop of Chartres somewhere between 1150 and 1160; but as M. Marcel Aubert is making a special study of these in his book on the beginnings of Gothic Art, we shall not ourselves dwell upon these magnificent works. The church of *Donzy-le-Pré*[188] has a tympanum with a Virgin and Child between an angel and the prophet Isaiah; and as this church was a dependency of the priory of La Charité we find here also evidence of the influence of the workshop of Chartres.

Characteristics of the Gothic art springing up in the Ile-de-France at St.-Denis and at Chartres are to be noticed in still more immediate fashion at the Abbey of *Déols* (Indre),[189] where is a beautiful doorway furnished with column-statues and with a tympanum on which is a Christ in Majesty. M. Jean Hubert has shown, with careful precision, how this work is connected, in point of style, with the art of Languedoc, and in its composition with the art of Ile-de-France, so that it helps to show the important part played by the creations of Languedoc in the development of Gothic sculpture in northern France.

The influence of the Ile-de-France can be seen at *Bourges* on the lateral doorways of the cathedral, ornamented by column-statues, and in a small tympanum from the church of St.-Pierre-le-Puellier,[190] now preserved in the museum at Bourges, on which appear the death and burial of the Virgin.

Plate 58   At *Bourges* there is also the curious tympanum of *St.-Ursin* which seems to date from the first part of the Romanesque period. The decorations represent the Occupations of the Months, a favourite theme in Romanesque iconography, and there is also a hunting scene evidently imitated from some ancient sculpture, and some scenes from Aesop's fables.[191] Lastly we must mention the very beautiful figure of a *jongleur,* to which M. Focillon has recently drawn attention,[191a] which was originally in a house at Bourges and is now preserved in the museum at Lyons.

Coming to the capitals with figure and animal ornamentation which do really give to this region of the middle basin of the Loire a kind of originality, where we see that fantasy, that spirit of independence of which we have spoken, we find the numerous and varied series in the valley of the Allier, at Yzeure,[193] at Bourbon-l'Archambault,[193a] at Autry-Issard; while St.-Menoux and Souvigny, a priory of Cluny, possess very beautiful examples of the same sort which show Burgundian influence. On the borders of the Allier we must mention the sculptures of *St.-Pierre-le-Moutier* (Nièvre),[194] and further to the north in the centre of the department of Nièvre, at *St.-Révérien,* are magnificent capitals which show a rich iconography, while on the intrados of the entrance-archway there are two large and well executed figures of cherubim.

Plate 63a
Plate 59

In the department of Cher, at Neuilly-en-Dun,[195] at La Celle-Bruère, at Orsan, at Maisonnais, at St.-Amand and Lignières; in the department of Loiret at St.-Benoît-sur-Loire; in the department of Loir-et-Cher at Selles-sur-Cher,[196] at St.-Aignan,[197] in the church of St.-Lomer at Blois, at Romorantin,[198] at Montrichard;[199] in the department of Indre at St.-Genou, at La Berthenoux, at Neuvy-St.-Sépulcre, and at Gargilesse; in Vienne at Chauvigny; in Deux-Sèvres at St.-Jouin-de-Marnes and at Airvault; in the department of Indre-et-Loire in the church of St.-Ours at Loches and at Amboise, Cormery, Tavant, Bournan, and L'Ile-Bouchard, and in the department of Maine-et-Loire, finally, in the church of Le Ronceray at Angers, at Trèves-Cunault and Fontevrault, we notice certain affinities, certain curious resemblances in pieces that are of admirable workmanship, executed in stone that was doubtless especially favourable to the labours of sculptors, pieces which exhibit a boldness, almost a recklessness, as of artists who knew all the secrets and who made light of difficulties as they put new life into the ancient themes, or improvised novel

Plates 60-63

61

types with freedom, introducing sometimes into their work an amusing note, a flash of humour — all these things give an incomparable charm to work that is full of variety, full of differences, in spite of common traits which may be found all through it.

We observe on a large number of these capitals that the figures do not stand at the base of the capital but that they are placed on a sort of flange, with floral ornaments, which surrounds the bottom of the basket;[200] this arrangement being found at St.-Pierre-le-Moutier (Nièvre), at La Celle-Bruère,[201] Chalivoy-Milon and Neuilly-en-Dun (Cher), at St.-Benoît-sur-Loire (Loiret), at St.-Aignan (Loir-et-Cher), at St.-Genou, La Berthenoux, Neuvy-St.-Sépulcre (Indre), at Preuilly, Cormery and Amboise (Indre-et-Loire).

Plates 60, 61, 63

A precisely similar capital, showing birds with their necks interlaced, is found both at La Celle-Bruère and at Neuilly-en-Dun (Cher).[202] At Neuilly-en-Dun and St.-Genou are found representations of Daniel in the lions' den, and it would appear certain that one of these capitals was a copy of the other.[203] The *motif* of animals with necks interlaced is to be found particularly in the centre of France; and we notice it now at Villecelin (Cher) and at Preuilly (Indre-et-Loire). It is not, however, peculiar to this region, since we find it at Moissac, Blesle (Haute-Loire), and in Catalonia, especially at Lérida. It came, beyond doubt, from the East,[204] on ivories and Sassanian and Arab materials.

Plate 61 b

Dogs will be noticed, whose movements are full of grace, at *St.-Genou* and at *La Berthenoux*, both of which drew their ornamentation from the same workshop. Attention should be paid to the foliage with its delicate carvings which separated these animals one from the other; and similar foliage is found at *Neuvy-St.-Sépulcre;* while upon another capital at St.-Genou, as at Neuvy-St.-Sépulcre, there are small heads peeping out from between these slender stems.

Plate 62 a

The elegance of the sirens at *St.-Aignan* will also be admired, and the sharp turning of a stag, pierced by a centaur's arrow, and the skilful way in which the sculptor has encircled the capital with the rolls of the strange body of the seven-headed Beast of the Apocalypse. The monsters also in *St.-Pierre* at *Chauvigny*[205] will be noted: the man with two bodies, though only one head, and the winged animals with the body of a lion and human head.

Plate 65 d
Plate 65 a
Plate 65 c

Plate 68

If in these monuments the artists have given free rein to their imagination, at *Gargilesse*[206] on the other hand and at *Bommiers* where are represented

Plate 63 b-d

the Sacrifice of Abraham and the delivery of the keys to St. Peter, at L'Ile-Bouchard, they have conformed to the great themes of religious iconography.

At *L'Ile-Bouchard*[207] we see the Annunciation, the Visitation, the Adoration of the Magi, the Announcement to the Shepherds, the Presentation in the Temple, the Flight into Egypt, the Massacre of the Innocents, the Entry into Jerusalem, the Temptation of Christ, the Last Supper and the Crucifixion. The figures are cramped, without much expression, but the work is on a large and powerful scale, and the artist has shown his very personal talent even more plainly in the capitals decorated simply with foliage and in the strange creatures, hobgoblins, snakes twisting themselves with remarkable suppleness in and out, so as to give a striking impression of slimy bodies that have just attached themselves to the stone. The artist of L'Ile-Bouchard must also have worked at *St.-Ours* at *Loches,*[208] since some figures carved on the consoles of the choir of this church very strongly recall the heavy, cramped figures of the capitals at L'Ile-Bouchard.

Plate 66

The powerful abbey of *St.-Benoît-sur-Loire*[209] the monks of which played so important a part in the Middle Ages, and created so many considerable works, historical, literary and artistic, contains a collection of sculpture of the very highest interest.

Plate 64

In the nave is a series of capitals which though of but mediocre workmanship are interesting by reason of their iconography, since they represent the miracles of St. Benedict, whose body the monks claim is still preserved in the church.

There has been much discussion as to the date of the capitals of the porch, some of which are very archaic, with scenes of the Apocalypse, the Annunciation, the Visitation, the Flight into Egypt, confronted animals, etc.. According to some, the entire church is later than 1095, when there was a fire, which is referred to in the Miracles of St. Benedict; but a careful examination of the text obliges us to conclude that this fire did no damage to the church. According to others,[210] these capitals would date from the period of the Abbot Gauzlin who in 1026 gave orders to his chief workman for a tower which would be the boast of the whole of Gaul;[211] but it is known that Gauzlin died three years later without having accomplished this work. Moreover, the *Miracula Sancti Benedicti*[212] tell us that the Abbot Guillaume undertook, between 1070 and 1080, the complete reconstruction of the church which was all in ruins as the result both of a fire and of old age. He it was who caused it to be demolished in order that it might be replaced by a new church, and the Abbot Véran, who died in 1085, went on with the work. It is only from this epoch at the earliest that the carvings of the porch can be dated. We know that on the 20th of March, 1108, the choir and doubtless also the transept being finished, the translation of the body of St. Benedict to the choir was accomplished.

The greater number of the capitals of the false triforium of the choir probably date from before 1108; but Eugène Lefèvre-Pontalis has remarked upon a capital to the right side of the choir a representation of a monk offering a book to the Virgin, with the inscription *Hugo;* and this monk may very well be the Hugue de Sainte Marie who was author of the last book of the Miracles of St. Benoît, written about 1120.

Connections may be traced between the sculptured capitals of St.-Benoît-sur-Loire[213] and those of the churches of Berry, as for instance the leopards, standing upright and leaning their cheeks against the angle of the capital, which are found both at St.-Genou and on the porch of St.-Benoît. The latter church has resemblances also with Selles-sur-Cher, the heads of the figures carved in the sanctuary of Selles-sur-Cher being exactly like those of the Adam and Eve and the Sacrifice of Abraham capitals in the intersection of the transept at St.-Benoît.

Striking resemblances may also be noticed between certain capitals at St.-Benoît-sur-Loire and others at *St.-Aignan* (Loir-et-Cher). They represent the
Plate 65 b
Sacrifice of Abraham,[214] the Flight into Egypt,[215] the Virgin and other perso-
Plate 65 d
nages,[216] arranged under three arcades, two sirens facing each other,[217] all of which subjects are to be found in both churches, treated in an identical manner. Certain of the capitals at St.-Aignan have been clumsily scraped and restored.

Anjou possesses a certain number of churches which are abundantly decorated with sculptures.

The artists who at two periods, towards the middle of the twelfth century and again towards 1180, decorated the church of *Cunault* (Maine-et-Loire)[218]
Plate 67 c
gave proof both of fertile imagination and of complete independence, since

64

the very varied works which they created are in no way immediately connected with those of any buildings in the neighbourhood. There are certain
scenes based on Holy Scripture, but more especially some strange personages,
some figures of monsters and demons. At *Fontevrault*,[219] for example, the   *Plate 67 a, b*
sculptures of which tend to associate themselves with the art of Poitou and
Saintonge, there are actual friezes decorating the tops of the pillars flanked by
columns, in which one sees human figures, it is true, but more especially confronted creatures, animals sometimes arranged in groups of four, two of them
being mounted on the backs of the other two. These quadrupeds and birds
hidden in the leaf decoration and amid the twistings of the foliage form an
ornamentation that is very rich and of an elegant refinement.

In the church of St.-Denis-Hors at Amboise[220] and in that of the Abbey
of *St.-Lomer* at *Blois*[221] are likewise found friezes that are ornamented with
animals and human figures, stooping down or with only half their bodies showing, which seem to issue from a sort of floral flange running to the bottom
of the capitals. In spite of this richness of decoration, the general effect of the
work, which is of no very forceful execution, produces an impression rather of
confusion and monotony.

The cloister of St.-Aubin at Angers[222] has arcades which are entirely covered with sculptures, giving an extraordinary effect of exuberant decoration, but the figures are today much mutilated, and those which are in some
state of preservation are imperfect and rough: the faint outlines of David and
Goliath on the key of one of the arches, and the Virgin and Child with unre-
fined features on another keystone, suggest to us that they were the work of
an artist of but very middling ability.

The decoration of this cloister of St.-Aubin at Angers is manifestly an out-
come of the art of Poitou and of Saintonge, for we find here the armed Virtues, fighting against the Vices, as well as the Lamb attended by two angelic
thurifers, *motifs* which are very frequently reproduced upon the doorways of
churches in that region.

65

CHAPTER VII

THE SCHOOL OF POITOU, SAINTONGE AND ANGOUMOIS

IT was indeed a school which was formed by the sculptors of the regions of Poitou, Saintonge and Angoumois, and it has sharply marked characteristics which distinguish it from other regions in its creation of remarkable works in which variety of decoration accompanies beauty of individual figures and elevation of sentiment, and where the talent of the artists was put at the disposal of eminent men who composed great religious and mystical scenes such as were calculated to lift the souls of men towards the celestial regions.

This school extended over the departments of Vienne, Deux-Sèvres, Vendée, Charente and Charente-Inférieure, and its influence spread as far as Maine-et-Loire, to Angers and Fontevrault, and even to certain churches of Dordogne: to St.-Martin-de-Gurson and most of all to Bussières-Badil, where are to be seen upon the bends of the arches dogs running among the leaf decorations exactly resembling those on the façade of the cathedral of Angoulême. Its imprint is found also in the department of Gironde[223] in Ste.-Croix at Bordeaux,[224] at Blasimon,[225] at Castelvieil, the doorway of which is very like to that of Varaize (Charente-Inférieure),[226] and in Lot-et-Garonne at St.-Pierre-de-Londres. Further to the south, again, one recognizes the style of Poitou and Saintonge in the Landes at Mimizan[227] and in the Basses-Pyrénées at Ste.-Marie-d'Oloron and at Morlaas.[228]

Several archaeologists[229] have analysed in excellent publications the numerous works executed in these regions, and have shown that certain traits distinguish the sculptors of Poitou from those of Saintonge and of Angoumois; but it will be our task merely to examine these monuments as a whole and to draw attention to their general characters.

The twelfth century witnessed the erection in these parts of a considerable number of Romanesque churches; and the softness of the stone which the sculptors had at their disposal allowed their art to develop with marvellous fertility. The doorways of the churches of this region are, however, without tympana, that element of construction so favourable to the development of sculpture which was used by artists in other districts for the representation on a large scale of so many highly developed scenes. But if these sculptors

66

lacked tympana on which to work, they discovered other outlets for their talents; the interiors of certain churches were ornamented with numerous capitals with figures, but above all the principal doorway and very often the entire façade were also abundantly decorated by them.

These façades of the churches of the south-west have their strongly marked features. On the ground-level, the doorway without tympanum is flanked, in certain churches of Poitou, by two other doors, or by two blind bays in the churches of Charente, the latter being without side-aisles. The tympana of these blind bays are sometimes adorned with figures. The upper storey, however, reproduces the arrangement of the lower stage in three great arcades, that in the middle often enclosing a large window, as is frequently seen in Poitou, though sometimes on this level is found an arcading composed of small uniform arches. Occasionally there are even two rows of arcading. This system of small arcades is particularly common in Saintonge. A gable-end dominates the upper storey, and the various stages of the façade are divided by horizontal lines formed by sculptured cornices.

The semicircular doorway has several bends above its arch, and it is here especially that the artists of the south-west displayed their original work. These rims of the arches are ornamented with figures arranged symmetrically and converging towards the key of the arch which is for the most part used for the *motif* which forms the centre, the focus, the *raison d'être* of the scene: such as angels apparently flying one above the other, with the two angels who meet face to face at the top of the arch bearing in their lifted arms a round Glory on which is seen the face of Christ or the mystic Lamb; or the Virtues, in a similar arrangement, elevate above their heads the celestial crown reserved for the Elect; or the Wise Virgins bow before the bust of a Christ who is in the act of blessing them.

In such cases, the sculptor has been obliged to solve two difficult problems, one of an aesthetic and the other of a spiritual order.

The former of these problems consisted in the necessary subordination of the artist's work to the architectural limitations of the chosen position, and he has had to adapt the bodies of his figures in order that they may follow harmoniously the lines of the curve of the archivolt, and he has lengthened and stretched those bodies so that he may not make the lines of the construction too heavy, and so as to give more elegance and lightness to the entire work.

67

And moreover, observing faithfully the purpose of edification imposed by the bishop or abbot who controlled the work, the artist interpreted religious scenes with an extreme delicacy of feeling, a species of mystic fervour even while he was at the very same time seeking after variety, and with a care for balance and symmetry, a talent for composition truly remarkable.

We shall find on many doorways these angels and virtues, arranged one above the other upon the bendings of the arches: at the Abbey of Notre-Dame de la Couldre at Parthenay, at *Civray, Aulnay-de-Saintonge,* Fenioux, *Argenton-Château,* Chadenac, Pont-l'Abbé-d'Arnoult, Blasimon, in St.-Aubin at Angers etc., and if we go higher up the centuries we discover the distant model from which these figures sprang, the six superposed angels, three on either side of the bend of whom the topmost two bear the Glory surrounding the mystic Lamb — these appear in one of the earliest monuments of Romanesque sculpture, on the altar-table of St.-Sernin at Toulouse, where we see the two angels opposite each other, holding a round Glory enclosing the mystic Lamb or the divine Hand as on the abaci of the cloisters of Moissac and of Tarragona — the very angels which adorn the Romanesque frescoes and the Carolingian ivories. These same angels appear moreover on the sarcophagi of the earliest Christian centuries, and they are the representatives in religious art of the figures upon pagan sarcophagi, winged genii which held the shield upon which was shown the effigy of the dead man.[230]

Plates 72, 75
Plate 74a

These artists of Saintonge and Poitou were thus wonderful decorators who carried the symbolism of religious art to its highest summits. Taking some well-worn theme which had long been repeated to the point of monotony, developing it, enriching it, gathering together above it a group of angels bearing the emblem of the Lamb in the midst of their quivering wings, and above them again a group of Virtues armed as warriors beating down under their feet the Vices, and higher still the Wise Virgins, elegant female figures clad in the supple robes of the twelfth century and bowing before the image of the Saviour — these artists were able to transform the model of something that had often been merely secular by idealizing these great figures and giving them something of the supernatural.

Upon the doorways of Gothic buildings of the second half of the twelfth century and of the thirteenth will be seen these numerous figures rising along the curve of the arches. Suger tells us, in his account of the construction of the basilica of St.-Denis, that in order to make of this church a marvellous monument in which all the arts should have come together to glorify the House of God, he summoned specialists from all countries: goldsmiths, workers in mosaic, glass-workers, sculptors — all of these came from lands where the finest workmen were to be found.

If this abbot, in love with art, gathered together so many artists for his work, he was obliged also to adjust their talents, which without some such guidance would have produced but an inharmonious result. If it was in the workyard of St.-Denis that by the union of diverse elements was realized the Gothic doorway, which was to spread throughout the Ile-de-France and thence to radiate far and wide; if there it was they placed statues of prophets and of saints in front of the columns and set them in imposing lines at the entrance of the church: if the wonderful accomplishments of the school of Languedoc were used to show over the door a majestic Christ presiding at the Last Judgement and exhibiting the wounds of the Crucifixion, there was yet one other element quite as important which must help to perfect these splendid doorways — the figures that were to be grouped along the bends of the arches above the tympanum; and most assuredly these great figures of the archivolt originated in the works created by the sculptors of Poitou and of Saintonge.

The artists of the south-west, however, were not content just to ornament with outlines of supreme elegance the archivolts of doorways, and with overflowing fertility they covered with ornamentation not only the bays adjoining the doorway but also the upper storey, and sometimes even the entire stretch of the façade of the church.

On the jambs of the bays statues are superposed, others are set in the arcadings, each under its canopy as in a niche, and here it is needful to follow distant traditions and to recall to mind the rows of arcades which adorn the apses of old Merovingian churches[231] such as Notre-Dame de la Daurade at Toulouse, where appeared upright figures of apostles or prophets standing out from a background of gold, or sometimes with the mosaic replaced by painted fresco figures. It is even necessary, perhaps, to think also of the magnificent and numerous pieces of goldsmiths' work which adorned the Carolingian churches and those of the eleventh and twelfth centuries, but of which but a few scattered remnants have survived until today, those shrines, those reliquaries, those altar-fronts and retables which shone amid the lights surrounded by figures in silver-gilt in repoussé work, standing or seated beneath arcades.

When we look at the façades of Notre-Dame-la-Grande at Poitiers, of the *Plate 71* cathedral of Angoulême, of Ruffec or of *Pérignac,* with their superimposed arcades each enclosing between its columns a seated or standing sculptured figure, we are struck by their resemblance to the altar-fronts with their gilded reliefs. The altar is the essential monument in the church, or as a Merovingian writer expressed it: "The altar, glittering with gold and silver and precious stones, represents the heart of Christ"; and the masters of Saintonge and of Poitou, in planning out the arrangement of their imaged façades, have tried to make them a splendid adaptation of an altar frontal.

In the iconography of their doorways, the artists made use over and over again of certain favourite themes, and beneath one of the large arcades flanking the central doorway one sometimes sees a figure on horseback.[232] This is a representation of the Emperor Constantine, and we find it at Aubeterre and Châteauneuf-sur-Charente in the department of Charente, at Matha, Surgères (Charente-Inférieure), Melle (restored), Parthenay-le-Vieux, in Notre-Dame de la Couldre at Parthenay, St.-Jouin-de-Marnes in Deux-Sèvres; and at Civray (restored) in Vienne. It was formerly to be seen at Aulnay, in Ste.-Marie-des-Dames and St.-Eutrope at Saintes (Charente-Inférieure), at Chalais (Charente), Airvault (Deux-Sèvres), in Notre-Dame-la-Grande at Poitiers, in Ste.-Croix at Bordeaux and in Indre at Déols.

Upon the bends of the arches of the doorways, as we have shown, appear the Virtues, clad in armour and wearing the casque used by knights of the Middle Ages. They are armed with sword and spear with which they transfix a Vice, a monster or a demon prostrate beneath their feet, according to a poem of Prudentius, the "Contest of the Soul", which relates the struggle of the Virtues against the Vices.[233] This poem was reproduced in the miniatures of manuscripts, and we find it again upon the capitals of Auvergne.

Plate 72 In the south-west, we see this Psychomachia at *Aulnay,*[234] at Corme-Royal, Fenioux, Fontaine-d'Ozillac, Pérignac, Pont-l'Abbé-d'Arnoult, St.-Sympho-
Plate 74a rien, Varaize (Charente-Inférieure), *Argenton-Château,* Notre-Dame de la Couldre at Parthenay, Melle, St.-Pompain (Deux-Sèvres), Civray (Vienne), in St.-Aubin at Angers and in the Gironde at Blasimon and Castelvieil.

Plate 72 The Wise and Foolish Virgins[235] are represented at *Aulnay,* Chadenac, Cor-

70

me-Royal, Pérignac, Pont-l'Abbé-d'Arnoult (Charente-Inférieure), *Argenton-Château*, in Notre-Dame de la Couldre at Parthenay, at Melle, St.-Pompain (Deux-Sèvres), and at *Civray* (Vienne).

Plate 74a

Plate 75

The Elders of the Apocalypse are sculptured in greater or lesser numbers at Aulnay, Avy, St.-Symphorien, Ste.-Marie-des-Dames at Saintes, at Varaize (Charente-Inférieure) and in Notre-Dame de la Couldre at Parthenay. The Occupations of the Months[236] with some charming pastoral scenes are depicted at Aulnay, at *Argenton-Château,* at Fenioux, Cognac, *Civray,* and the Signs of the Zodiac at Aulnay and Fenioux.

Plates 74a, 75

Inscriptions, especially on the doorways of Saintonge, explain these scenes and indicate the persons in each.

The decorators were not satisfied to cover the walls round the arches of the doorways with figures and then to place statues beneath the arcades: they must also adorn the empty surfaces above the great arches or on the sides of the bays; on certain façades statues were placed, on others a series of high reliefs forming a vast scene with many figures.

At *St.-Jouin-de-Marnes* (Deux-Sèvres),[237] the sculptures on the façade of which may date from about 1140, three statues were added on either side of the high central window of the first storey. To the left of the spectator only one of these is ancient; on the right we recognize St. Peter and St. John the Evangelist, and above a graceful group of the Annunciation, in which, following an iconographic detail which originated in Palestine, the Virgin, who was spinning when the angel came to her, holds a spindle and a ball of thread. Above, beneath the gable, is the cohort of the risen souls, who surround the Virgin and implore her intercession. Higher still, a great Christ with nimbus is seated between a seraph and an angel who are of smaller size than the Christ, and are sounding trumpets. The two arms of the Saviour hang down beside his body, and, as Mlle E. Maillard has remarked, his two open hands suggest that they have only lately been detached from the great cross against which he is leaning, and thus, in the tremendous moment when Christ is about to deliver judgement his attitude recalls the drama of Calvary to which the sins of men drove him.

Other bas-reliefs also ornament this façade, among them one of Constantine, the vanquisher of paganism, and opposite him is Samson breaking the jaw of the lion.

71

These two, Samson and Constantine, the former prefiguring the victory of Christ which will be final when Constantine shall have triumphed over paganism, appear in *St.-Pierre* at *Parthenay-le-Vieux*, and in *Notre-Dame de la Couldre* at *Parthenay*.

The façade of this latter church[238] has also received splendid decoration. Its doorway is still in place, with its four arch-bendings on which are represented the Elders of the Apocalypse, armed Virtues and some angels which are perhaps the most elegant and graceful amongst all the doorways of this district upon which the same group appears.

Of the decoration of the upper storey there remain today but a few scattered fragments, some in the Musée du Louvre and others in America. These restored fragments, may well be compared with the most admirable creations of Romanesque art. Nothing more solemn and moving could be imagined than the attitude of Christ entering Jerusalem, nothing more majestic and more idealized in their enlarged proportions than the tall outlines of the crowned figures, nothing more exquisite or naively realistic than the Announcement to the Shepherds with the little shepherd girl busily shearing a sheep.

Plate 77 The façade of *Notre-Dame-la-Grande* at *Poitiers*[239] is covered with bas-reliefs of which a certain number are inspired by a liturgical drama, "The Prophets" which was wont to be performed at Christmas time.

Plate 69 The cathedral at *Angoulême*[240] underwent considerable restoration during the nineteenth century, but its façade has retained the greater part of the original decoration. This cathedral was built by Girard, Bishop of Angoulême from 1102 to 1136, who consecrated it in 1128. It is unlikely that the decoration was complete at this time. The sculptures on the façade are arranged in accordance with a clear and methodic plan. We find a representation of the Ascension combined with one of the Last Judgement, for according to the Acts of the Apostles Jesus would appear to judge the world as he was at the moment of the Ascension. In the tympana of the four blind doorways at the sides of the porch are twelve personages arranged in groups of three; according to M. Mâle[240a] they represent the twelve Apostles preaching the Gospel throughout the world. These Apostles, grouped in the same manner, are also found on the north transept door of the church at St.-Amand-de-Boixe (Charente),[240b] where the composition, attitudes and decoration of the archivolts are identical. The latter consists of dogs with thin bodies running amidst foliage. These two façades must certainly have been executed by the same workshop.

The church of St.-Pierre at Aulnay can show magnificent sulptural deco- *Plates 70a, 72, 73* ration in every part of the building. In the interior may be seen numerous capitals, some decorative, others ornamented with animal scenes and grotesques, carved by an unusually skilful hand. Among the capitals should be noted two *Plate 73* elephants and those representing the Temptation of Adam and Eve, Cain and Abel, and Delilah cutting the hair of the sleeping Samson. The façade has a doorway decorated with arch-rims on which we see in superposition *Plate 72* angels, the Virtues and Vices, the Wise and Foolish Virgins, the Occupations of the Months, and the Signs of the Zodiac. The blind arcades framing the doorway are decorated with a Christ between the Virgin and St. John and a Crucifixion of St. Peter.

On the arch-rims of the south doorway[241] we see the Elders of the Apocalypse and on the upper arch-rims animals such as the donkey playing the lyre, so frequently found during the Romanesque period, fabulous beings, chimera and winged dragons like those found on other churches, especially on the doorway of St.-Ours at Loches. The window[241a] above this doorway is adorned with another representation of the Virtues piercing the Vices with their lances. The exterior of the window of the apse has a sculptured framework consist- *Plate 70a* ing of naked personages climbing among foliage.

M. Dangibeaud has recently proved the relationship which exists between the rich decoration of St.-Pierre at Aulnay and the doorway of the church at Nuaillé-sur-Boutonne (Charente-Inférieure).[241b]

These Romanesque artists indeed created works of real beauty, of which we have already mentioned specially the supple harmony of the bodies stretched along the bends of the arches at Aulnay, Parthenay and Corme-Royal. Let notice be taken of the Virtues, lengthened out of all proportion at Blasimon (Gironde), and yet so beautiful in spite of their exaggerated shape. If our sculptors have now and then deformed the human anatomy, as did those who carved the pier at Moissac or the tympanum of Autun, it was certainly not for want of skill but because they were seeking after decorative effect. When the architectural lines with which they were dealing did not demand the stretching out of bodies, they knew very well how to give them their correct proportions, and how to place them in attitudes that were true to nature. We admire, for example, the lifelike movement of St. Michael slaying the Dragon, in *St.-Michel-d'Entraigues* (Charente),[242] a work which may date from about 1137. Occasionally the decorators of the south-west attained to the beauty of antiquity, and a high relief of an Angel, upright on a jamb of the doorway at Chadenac, with vestments gracefully draped, recalls in singular fashion an antique bas-relief of a dancer in the museum of Arles.

Plate 76

If these artists have succeeded admirably in their treatment of human figures, they were also excellent in their representations of animals: their horses on the façade of the cathedral of Angoulême, their dogs in the apse of the same building, as also the movements of the jumping dogs to be seen on the façade of Chadenac, are rendered with an exactness that is truly surprising.

Plate 69a, c

They certainly interpreted in a talented manner the models which they found in oriental fabrics and ivories. The eagles mounted on lions which we see on the capitals of *St.-Eutrope* at *Saintes*,[242a] the large winged dragon[242b] on a tympanum preserved at the archaeological museum of Angoulême, are admirable examples of decorative art.

There were also among them some delicate ornamentalists, who spread their work broadcast, as for instance on the capitals and abaci which are lengthened into friezes intersecting the lines of the blind arcades on the lower storeys of the churches of Charente.

In certain churches, of more humble character than those with which we have been dealing, where the work would be entrusted to artists of lesser ability, the bends of the arches are not ornamented with long outlines of Angels or of Virtues, but with decorative forms which are frequently sculptured on each keystone and repeated in exactly the same manner on each of the bends. Certain of these ornaments reproduce Gallo-Roman models brought from a distance and adapted, others are merely vegetable forms; acanthus leaves, the letter S floriated, palm-leaves of various shapes and arranged symmetrically, flowers with eight petals, and diamond points follow one upon the other as well as other decorative *motifs* which we must refrain from describing. And according to the talent of the individual artist these ornaments varied from one bend to another but almost always repeated from keystone to keystone on the same arch-rim, either give to the entrance a light and wonderful frame, a veritable lace-work in stone, or else, it may be, make the entire façade look monotonous and heavy.

74

Sometimes they are heads of animals, of horses or bulls which are thus repeated on all the keystones of a bend, and this is reminiscent of Norman art, these heads being found at Bayeux.

Sometimes, again, they are tiny figures which follow one another, as in *St.-Hilaire* at *Melle.*[243] The artist, in his anxiety to make his work perfect, was not content merely to carve the external face, but would also decorate the intrados, even though it could scarcely be seen. On the south door of the church of St.-Pierre at Aulnay small figures in caryatids may be seen on the intrados of the arch-rim. At *Avy* (Charente-Inférieure), where is to be seen a series *Plate 74 b* of arch-bends ornamented with as many human figures as there are keystones, the rim of the keystone corresponds with the knees of the figure, so that the legs are found to be sculptured on the under part of the stone.

The same thing is seen at *Ste.-Marie-des-Dames* at *Saintes*[243a] where the Elders of the Apocalypse are thus arranged. In this overloaded doorway, which from a distance gives an impression of great sculptural richness, but on closer exmination can only offer coarse figures, historiated arch-rims alternate with others overloaded with ornamentation and foliage. It will be noticed that on the upper arch-rim fifty-three Elders of the Apocalypse have been carved instead of the usual twenty-four, in order to fill in the fifty-three keystones which formed the rim.

Not all of these artists had a respect for symmetry, and certain of them, possibly to break the monotony, after repeating the same *motif* on one part of the arch-bends were not afraid to continue with quite a different *motif*. Thus, at *St.-Sulpice-d'Arnoult* (Charente-Inférieure) half of the space is ornamented *Plate 70 b* with birds, the rest with pine-cones; and these birds deserve special mention, so graceful are they with their heads turned as they smooth their feathers. Their sculptor had assuredly seen birds thus posing themselves in groups upon the outstanding moulding of a cornice or of an arch-rim. And the most charming trait which we have encountered among these artists of Charente, with their love of realism, is the habit they have of giving to their celestial figures the ordinary costumes of their own day, and the robes with long hanging sleeves which were then worn by fashionable persons.

Although right from the beginning of Romanesque art we find in this region figured bas-reliefs and capitals, especially in the churches of Poitiers,[243b] it would seem that art in these regions only reached its full development at a

75

later period than was the case in Languedoc and Burgundy. In any case it produced some marvellous works during the second quarter of the twelfth century, and artists from this region spread their creations profusely during the middle and into the second half of the century.

CHAPTER VIII

WORKSHOPS OF THE NORTH OF FRANCE

THE provinces in the north of France seem to have had a lesser share in the great movement of which we have been speaking than had those others which we have just cited. That movement, for the restoration of sculpture, showed itself from the close of the eleventh century and onward; but up to the time of the magnificent artistic effort which had the workshop of St.-Denis as its point of departure from about 1140, an effort which was to influence so considerably the destinies of French art, it is barely possible to speak of a school of sculpture in the Ile-de-France. If, from the beginning of the eleventh century at St.-Germain-des-Prés,[244] attempts were made to carve human figures on the capitals; and if, without any doubt, at the beginning of the twelfth century in the basilica of Ste.-Geneviève in Paris,[244a] Merovingian marble capitals were used for the representation of animated figures such as those of Daniel in the lions' den now preserved in the Musée du Louvre; if it is possible to find in the church of Le Wast (Pas-de-Calais) one of the most ancient examples of column-statues,[244b] executed before 1113, and at Carrières-St.-Denys (Seine-et-Oise)[245] a stone retable which likewise is to be seen today in the Musée du Louvre and of which the naive figures representing the Virgin, seated, with the Child, between scenes of the Annunciation and the Baptism of Christ, have some relation with those of the workshops of Burgundy — these are but isolated instances, and even though we take into consideration all that may have disappeared in the meantime it seems unlikely that any single group of works at all comparable to those we have seen in the south was ever executed.

And more than that, the figureless capitals of Morienval, one of the earliest churches in which the ogival transept is found, of about the year 1120, and those in other churches where we see capitals that have figures of barbarian character, or at any rate very mediocre, such as those at Deuil (Seine-et-Oise), small figures in caryatids at the springings of the arches as at Bury and Cambronne (Oise), or tympana with such rough figures as those of Mervilliers (Eure-et-Loir)[246] which are preserved in the Musée des Antiquités at Chartres, and those of Le Heaulme, near Chars, and of Meulan (Seine-et-Oise), prove very plainly how far behind were the sculptors of this region compared with those of the southern provinces.

In the workyards of St.-Denis and Chartres, however, artists who profited by the experience of a whole generation of sculptors in Languedoc, Burgundy and Poitou, and added to that experience their own creative talent and their own independent genius, were to make the tremendous experiment of a new art. The change of artistic conception which distinguishes Gothic from Romanesque was not accomplished in a day. It was by a long and imperceptible progress that it at last came to achievement.

M. Marcel Aubert will speak in his book, which is the chronological sequel to the present work, of the beginnings of Gothic art, the earliest manifestation of that art being found in the workshop of St.-Denis set up by Suger. The doorway of St.-Denis has lost a great part of its decoration and notably its column-statues; but the Portail Royal of Chartres, which was executed shortly after the doorway of St.-Denis, has come down to our times.

M. Mâle[247] has shown how much St.-Denis owed to the school of Languedoc, and the close relationship existing between its tympanum and that of Beaulieu. The doorway of Chartres also in a certain measure follows the traditions of the workshops of Toulouse; and by its statues with their lengthened and thinned bodies which have been exaggerated out of all proper proportion and subordinated to the dimensions of the columns with which they are united, by its capitals with their numerous figures, and by its decoration of stylized vegetation, the western façade of this cathedral belongs still to Romanesque art.

We shall not speak of it however, because in the arrangement of the statuary of this façade we discover the earliest symptoms of Gothic art.

At St.-Germain-des-Prés, at Le Mans, Étampes, Bourges, Angers, St.-Loup-de-Naud, St.-Ayoul at Provins, Notre-Dame at Corbeil, Vermenton and Senlis, M. Marcel Aubert[248] will show by what sort of transition the column-statues of these doorways detached themselves more and more during the second half of the twelfth century from the principles of Romanesque art to attach themselve more nearly to an art in which the sculptor, wishing to approach more closely to nature, and so to approximate more wholly to truth, became more sensitive and more human, abandoning the stylized figures and the hieratic and sometimes conventional attitudes adopted by Romanesque art.

78

No more than in the Ile-de-France do we find in Picardy and Champagne any traces of notable work at the beginning of the twelfth century.

In Picardy, Flanders and Artois there are still preserved a certain number of baptismal fonts[249] of the eleventh and twelfth centuries, ornamented with carvings of heads in very bold relief separated by foliage as at Chéreng (Nord), figures and animals as at Wierre-Effroy (Pas-de-Calais),[250] angels at Sélincourt (Somme),[251] whole scenes as at Airaines (Somme), at Samer and St.-Venant (Pas-de-Calais), and lastly with birds and animals, some of them borrowed from oriental models as at Evin and Vimy (Pas-de-Calais), Neuville-sous-Corbie (Somme) and Vermand (Aisne).[252] On the last-named, executed in blue earth from Tournai, we see winged and bearded quadrupeds which present striking resemblances to the Assyrian bulls. Some ivory casket imported from the East must have furnished the model.

Workshops which manufactured and exported[253] large numbers of baptismal fonts and tombstones existed in this part of the North of France; the most important were those of Marquise, near Boulogne, and of Tournai, which exported their productions by land, or still more by way of the Scheldt, not only to neighbouring districts, but also to the most distant regions. Products of these workshops are to be found in Normandy, in the Ardennes, in Champagne, and even in England, especially at Lincoln and Winchester.

At the beginning of the eleventh century, Richard, Abbot of St.-Vannes at Verdun, caused to be brought by way of the Scheldt and the Meuse some stone columns worked at Tournai, which were destined for the cloister of his abbey.[254] At the end of the twelfth century Itier, Abbot of Andres, near Boulogne-sur-Mer, also had stones brought by water from Tournai for the cloister of that abbey.[255]

As is seen in the case of St.-Vannes at Verdun, to avoid the expense of transporting unnecessary weights, the stone was cut, and sometimes even sculptured, at the place of extraction. When Guillaume de Sens undertook the works on Canterbury cathedral, he had the materials brought from Normandy, and the chronicler tells us explicitly that he gave the stonemasons and sculptors the necessary instructions to enable them to carve the stones on the spot.[256]

Normandy isolated itself, generally speaking, in geometrical decoration,[257] "broken stick" or inverted V ornaments, toothed bands and collars, and such like, and if now and then a few representations of living creatures appear, they are borrowed from the art of the carpenter which was highly honoured in this province. Such, in many Norman churches, are the heads of horses or bulls uniformly repeated and the human heads, almost identical, which reproduce themselves along the arches. At Graville-Ste.-Honorine,[258] and at St.-Georges-de-Boscherville,[259] in the crypt of La Sainte Trinité at Caen, at Meuvaines,[260] certain very rudimentary elements of sculpture with figures are found. The most important sculptured decoration belongs to the cathedral of *Bayeux*, where two capitals with figures from the middle of the transept are preserved in the lapidary museum: one of these without doubt represents the Unbelief of St. Thomas. They date, according to M. Jean Vallery-Radot, from the end of the eleventh century; and it must be supposed that if they were executed in this district where figure-sculpture was not held in honour, it was as a result of Burgundian influence due to the monks of St.-Bénigne at Dijon who were installed in 1096 at St.-Vigor in Bayeux.

Plate 79   The little church of *Rucqueville*, ten kilometres from Bayeux, possesses a series of capitals upon one of which also Christ and St. Thomas are represented. These capitals are later than those of Bayeux, but here also we must admit that the execution of works so little in harmony with Norman ideas was due to Burgundian artists.[261]

The cathedral of Bayeux still possesses a series of sculptures which strike us as extraordinary in the extreme, in spite of the many strange creations of Romanesque artists. These are ten bas-reliefs[262] placed on the jambs of the great

Plate 78   arches of the nave, some of them suggesting an imitation of figures from the Far East, griffins or dragons with wide-open mouths, great protruding eyes, the originals of which must have been found on ivories or bronzes. M. Vallery-Radot nevertheless finds in these figures an imitation also of Irish and Anglo-Saxon miniatures, impregnated though they may be with oriental ideas. Certain interlaced monsters on the south side of the nave have rightly been compared by this writer with a miniature in an Anglo-Saxon manuscript of the eleventh century preserved in the cathedral of Durham.[263] M. Vallery-Radot believes these bas-reliefs to have been sculptured in the days of Bishop Philippe d'Harcourt, shortly before a fire which took place in 1160, and that they were incorporated with the walls of the nave in the course of the restorations which followed this disaster.

Britanny,[264] which for so long remained politically independent, and isolated by its immense forests, maintained relations with neighbouring provinces only by sea and along the Loire. Her granite rocks were not suited for sculpture, and so her capitals were ornamented merely with line decoration, interlaces of rope and basket-work, and especially with the crossings and spirals which seem to have been the favourite *motifs* with artisans of Celtic race.

Representation of living figures is very rarely found upon these capitals, and one could hardly mention more than a few rough outlines of animals, together with a few human masks, flat and with very little expression, in the Abbey of Landevennec, at Loctudy and at Fouesnant.

There are some monuments however which offer more important work: the scenes with figures, for example, which surround in the form of a frieze the tops of the tall round pillars in the church of Perros-Guirec, where may be seen especially the representation of a banquet and the Sacrifice of Abraham; and the south tympanum of the church of Notre-Dame at Kernitron (Finistère). These figures are in very low relief and seem very roughly executed, but it should be remembered that the granite in which they were carved offers poor resistance to the weather and that it quickly wears away.

More interesting are the two *ensembles* on the capitals of St.-Aubin at Guérande (Loire-Inférieure) and of Merlévenez (Morbihan)[265] which have strong resemblances one to the other and were certainly executed in the same workshop. In both of these churches are seen the martyrdom of St. Lawrence and of St. Simon, the archer, the devil swallowing a man, Avarice, and so on.

A curious importation is to be noticed at the Abbey of St.-Gildas-de-Rhuis (Morbihan),[266] where, alongside capitals of granite are some capitals of soft limestone quite foreign to this part of the country. These capitals, with their vegetal ornamentation deeply incised, are of a style far superior to anything found in Brittany, and M. Roger Grand thinks that they were brought, ready sculptured, from Saintonge, and probably from the quarries of Taillebourg.

Some granite capitals show the same decoration as these imported capitals, and it would seem as though the Breton artist had tried to copy the models that came to him from Saintonge. On the external wall of the sanctuary, moreover, are three bas-reliefs of white stone of similar origin with the capitals of which we have just spoken, showing a bear, a figure carrying an axe, and two knights who are charging one towards the other.

The eastern parts of France are equally poor in sculpture with figures, and it is surprising that in Alsace and Lorraine, where abundant evidence was forthcoming of skill in ornamental sculpture, there should have been so little success in the endeavour to reproduce correctly the human figure.

As M. Georges Durand has well shown,[267] from the beginning to the end of the twelfth century the progress was almost nil, and to satisfy ourselves of this it will be enough if we compare the funerary statues of Gérard de Vaudémont, who died in 1108, and of his wife who died a few years later, which are now in the church of the Cordeliers at Nancy, with the tomb, preserved in the museum at Épinal, of Guy, Abbot of Chaumoussey, who died in 1182. Among the pieces of Romanesque sculpture executed in this district we should mention the doorway of the church at Andlau (Bas-Rhin),[268] some bas-reliefs, with quite barbarian figures, from the tympanum of Vomécourt-sur-Madon,[269] now in the museum at Épinal; those, of better execution, of Laître-sous-Amance (Meurthe-et-Moselle), and the baptismal font of Mousson (Meurthe-et-Moselle). All of the above are quite rudimentary, but a place apart must be given to the very beautiful doorway of Pompierre (Vosges)[270] which is the work of an artist of talent, upon the lintel being figured the Entry into Jerusalem, on the tympanum the Announcement to the Shepherds and the Adoration of the Magi, and above these the Massacre of the Innocents and the Flight into Egypt.

CHAPTER IX

THE SCHOOL OF PROVENCE

THE school of Provence is particularly distinguished by two splendid monuments: the façade of the church of *St.-Gilles-du-Gard* and that of the church *Plates 80-82* of *St.-Trophime* at *Arles* together with its richly-decorated cloister.

But first of all we must mention a monument of which we still possess important remains and which is certainly anterior to those just indicated. In the church of *Notre-Dame-des-Pommiers* at *Beaucaire* is preserved part of a long frieze[271] on which are represented several episodes from the Life of Christ, some of the details being of great interest for the study of mediaeval iconography. These scenes comprise Christ foretelling the denial of St. Peter, the Washing of Feet, the Last Supper (subsequently copied on the rood-screen of Modena Cathedral), the Arrest of Christ, the Flagellation, the Bearing of the Cross, the Holy Women at the Tomb, the Maries buying the spices which they intend to carry to the Tomb of Christ. The last scene, which has evidently been transposed and should have been placed before that representing the Maries at the Tomb, is also found at St.-Gilles-du-Gard, on a capital at Modena and on a pillar in the cloister of St.-Trophime at Arles. As M. Mâle has noted,[272] it is a reproduction in stone of a liturgical drama of the Resurrection, the earliest version of which dates from the tenth century and of which a manuscript has been preserved at Tours dating from the twelfth century.

While the frieze at Beaucaire, with its stiff, expressionless figures, may be dated as early as the middle of the twelfth century, we do not think that an equally remote date may be assigned to the Virgin and Child[273] to be found on the tympanum of the same church of Notre-Dame-des-Pommiers. Millin,[274] who saw it in its original position, tells us that it was accompanied by two other bas-reliefs representing respectively the Adoration of the Magi and the Angel warning Joseph to take the Virgin and the Infant Jesus to Egypt. The inscription beneath the figure of the Virgin is carved in characters which lead us to suppose that the reliefs date from the last quarter of the twelfth century. In any case we do not think that they can be prior to 1165 or 1170. The three groups on this tympanum at Beaucaire are likewise found at St.-Gilles-du-Gard[275] and on the Baptistery at Parma.[276]

83

The scenes on the frieze at Beaucaire are also found again at St.-Gilles in the same arrangement and with curious resemblances as regards the pose of the figures and details of decoration and dress.

As to the dates of St.-Gilles and of St.-Trophime at Arles, there has been much discussion. Some, arguing that Romanesque art had a preponderating influence upon the artists of the twelfth century, would assign a considerable role to the works of Provence, believing that her artists took a leading part in the great renaissance of monumental sculpture which was to spread itself over the Gothic doorways of the Ile-de-France. The sculptors of the Portail Royal at Chartres would thus have been inspired by the doorway of St.-Trophime and by the statuary in the cloister of that church.

According to M. Vöge [277] the doorway of St.-Trophime would date from about 1135 while M. Marignan assigns this work to the thirteenth century.[277a] We are content to remain in agreement with the opinions so ably put forth by Robert de Lasteyrie,[278] who considers that these great monuments should be placed at the end of the Romanesque period in the second half of the twelfth century. M. Labande,[279] who has spent many years upon their study, confirms in its main outlines the theory of Lasteyrie.

Thus Provençal art, far from being a beginning, would be rather an ending, and its essential works would be later than the great sculptural compositions of the Ile-de-France. If, at the beginning of the twelfth century, Provence produced certain pieces of sculpture, it seems that for the manifestation of the essential character and the magnificence of her work she waited until towards the middle of the century and for the two great monuments of which we have just spoken.

In an article of considerable length, Lasteyrie has attempted to assign to them exact dates; and by the use of arguments that are historical, epigraphical and iconographical, as well as by comparison with other monuments of precise date, he has come to the conclusion that if the construction of St.-Gilles was begun in 1116, as is proved by an inscription, then the decoration of the façade cannot have been undertaken before the middle of the century, and in his opinion it was executed between 1150 and 1179.[280] M. Labande would place these works in the last quarter of the twelfth century and the first quarter of the century that followed; and this is the opinion also of the most recent historian of St.-Gilles, M. Augustin Fliche,[281] who dates the *ensemble* of the sculptures on the façade between 1180 and 1240.

For the most ancient parts of the cloister of St.-Trophime at Arles, that is to say, for the north and east sides, Lasteyrie gives the date somewhere about 1180, and for the façade of the church between 1180 and 1190. M. Labande agrees with these conclusions.

At St.-Gilles as at St.-Trophime at Arles we find on the façades the pediments and columns of the temples of antiquity. The façade of St.-Gilles, extending with majestic width, consists of a large central doorway flanked by two lateral doorways of lesser size. Six great columns, of which four flank the lateral doorways, are placed in front of this façade,[282] and on the four middle columns rests a cornice supporting a frieze with bas-reliefs which are a continuation of those which decorate the lintel of the central doorway. Upon the projections of this doorway four statues, facing each other two by two, have *Plate 80b* their feet upon lions that are splendidly lifelike. On either side, two twin columns prolong the alignment of these statues, and upon their bases and those of the columns are beautiful bas-reliefs enclosed by beaded circles.

Ten other statues, four upon each side of the central doorway and one beyond each of the lateral doorways, occupy ten niches which are separated by fluted pilasters ornamented with large leaf decorations.

These fourteen statues represent the twelve Apostles and two angels strik- *Plates 80a, 81* ing down the devil. On one of them, representing St. Bartholomew, is carved the signature of one of the sculptors of this façade, a certain Brunus. The tympanum of the central doorway has been rebuilt. The side doorways have sculptured tympana and lintels, the scenes represented being: on the tympanum of the north doorway the Adoration of the Magi; on that of the south doorway, the Crucifixion; on the lintels of the three doorways and upon the frieze which frames the central lintel, various scenes from the Life of Christ. *Plate 82*

The work was not accomplished, so to say, in one piece: there were interruptions in its original construction and there have also been alterations, so that in its sculpture we can trace the signs of various influences and establish between these sculptures and other monuments some curious relations. The imprint of antique sculpture is found not only throughout the rich decoration which surrounds the statues and the bas-reliefs, but also in the way in which the faces are treated. We find also in these sculptures, and especially on the central doorway, connections with the sculpture of Languedoc: some of the large statues of apostles have upon their vestments those horizontal folds across the chest which we see in the sculptures of Toulouse, and their legs crossed, as in the case of the apostles at St.-Étienne at Toulouse.

We must notice also the close resemblance which exists between these sculptures and the works executed in northern Italy in the workshop of Benedetto Antelami during the last quarter of the century. Certain of the statues of St.-Gilles can be compared with those of David and Ezekiel in the cathedral of Borgo San Donnino where this master worked: the Adoration of the Magi at St.-Gilles strongly resembles another on a doorway of the baptistery at Parma on which Benedetto carved his name beside the date, 1196.[283]

The crouching lions seen on the central doorway of St.-Gilles are found also at St.-Trophime at Arles and in the Alps at the cathedral of Embrun, and they form one of the most noticeable characteristics of the art of northern Italy, where they appear on several doorways, so that we must regard them as borrowed from Lombard sculpture.

The cloister of St.-Trophime at Arles was begun after 1150, and was not completed until the end of the fourteenth century. The most ancient sculptures which it contains, those on the north, date from about 1180, the carvings on the east having been executed shortly after. The north side consists of three bays opening upon the courtyard through arcades, each group of these arcades being divided by four isolated pillars with large figures, the two pillars at the angles also presenting bas-reliefs.

Plate 84 Upon the pillar of the north-west angle is engraved an inscription of 1188, and this pillar also carries the statues of St. John and St. Peter with St. Trophime between them,[284] the latter being of marble and of a different make from the other two. Between the statues are bas-reliefs representing, on the one side, the sellers of spices and the Holy Women, and on the other side the Resurrection. The pillar at the north-east angle has the statues of St. Stephen, St. Matthew and St. Paul, the last being particularly noteworthy; one bas-relief shows the Ascension and another the Stoning of St. Stephen.

Plate 85a Of the capitals on these two sides, some are designed in imitation of Corinthian capitals with acanthus leaves between which, instead of the central rosette, is often found a human head; others represent, on the north side, scenes taken from the Old Testament, and on the east from the Life of Christ.

Plate 83 The façade of the church of St.-Trophime, which is of small size und con-

86

structed of material inferior to that used at St.-Gilles, does not give the impression of splendid space which we find in the latter. It has but the single doorway, instead of the three at St.-Gilles, and this, like the central doorway of St.-Gilles, is enclosed by a projection which forms a deep ledge, in the forefront of which are six columns behind which one sees on the left three statues and on the right two statues together with a bas-relief between the pilasters which are ornamented with foliage. At the turn, that is to say in front of the door, are four statues with their feet resting upon lions, and these statues face each other as at St.-Gilles.

At St.-Gilles the statues are surmounted by a frieze of magnificent foliage; but here it is a frieze of bas-reliefs showing scenes in the Childhood of Christ. Above and in front, resting on the capitals of the columns, a second frieze prolongs the lintel; on the left part of this is shown the procession of the Elect, and on the right that of the reprobate, grouped in a somewhat monotonous fashion. On the lintel the twelve Apostles are seated. On the tympanum, the figure of Christ in Majesty, surrounded by the Symbols of the Evangelists, is a work of real beauty. The ornamentation is strongly impregnated with classical art. The division into panels under the cornice behind the columns, the foliage, the rays spreading outward from the centre, the Greek patterns, all of these recall the models offered to sculptors by the antique monuments which abound in this region; but nevertheless all this sculpture, less careful than that of St.-Gilles, denotes an art in decadence and the work of craftsmen who were behind their time.

New feelings were guiding at this period the artists of the north of France, whence there gushed forth sources of inspiration quite other than those which had appeared nearly a century earlier in Languedoc and from which so many artists had drawn; and in this renewal, this longing of the sculptors to achieve work that should be more near to nature and to life, French sculpture was to transform itself, to find a new youth and then to spread in wonderful fashion.

Before leaving this south-eastern region, it will be well to mention other works which are chronologically earlier than St.-Gilles and St.-Trophime.

Let us mention the tumulary slab of the abbot of St.-Victor of Marseilles, Isarn,[285] executed in the middle of the eleventh century, which bears curious testimony to the first essays in the sculpture of stone at the beginning of Romanesque art; the figured frieze of the cathedral of Nîmes,[286] parts of which were rebuilt in the seventeenth century shows in its more ancient elements a close relationship to the friezes at St.-Gilles. It is perhaps slightly earlier in date than the latter, and represents scenes from the biblical stories of Adam and Eve and Cain and Abel.

Of the sumptuously decorated cloister of *Notre-Dame-des-Doms* at *Avignon*[287] with its columns and marble capitals, there remain but a few fragments.

Plate 85 b, c These capitals are scattered in the Musée Calvet at Avignon[288] and at Apt, while one of the most interesting is to be found today in America in the Fogg Museum of Cambridge. It represents four scenes from the life of Samson;[289] one of them shows Samson breaking the jaw of the lion, and bears a striking likeness to the same scene on a capital in St.-André-le-Bas at Vienne; another shows Samson shaking the columns of the temple and by its movement recalls certain figures on the capitals of La Daurade at Toulouse.

Other capitals from Notre-Dame-des-Doms show very close connection with the beautiful capitals of Catalonian cloisters, and we are reminded of the political bonds which in the twelfth century united Catalonia with Provence.

The sculptors who worked at St.-Ruf in Avignon rivalled those of Notre-Dame-des-Doms,[290] and we know that they went as far as Pisa in search of marble and that there they carved the columns and capitals for their cloister;[291] and here we find an explanation of the close connections which exist between these works in Provence and those of northern Italy.

Mention still needs to be made of the doorway of St.-Gabriel (Bouches-du-Rhône),[292] the capitals of St.-Sauveur at Aix,[293] of Montmajour,[294] of St.-Paul-de-Mausolée[295] and of Ste.-Marthe at Tarascon[296] and of those of the cloister of Vaison (Vaucluse).[297] The capitals at Vaison have, like some of the capitals in Notre-Dame-des-Doms, elegant leaf-ornaments winding round the "basket" and terminating in large leaves. We find the same thing in Catalonia. The mutilated tympanum above the west door of the cathedral at Die (Drôme)[298] shows a certain resemblance to the sculptures at St.-Gilles.

The present-day department of Hérault,[299] which borders upon Provence and once formed part of the ancient Septimania, also had flourishing workshops of sculpture in the eleventh and twelfth centuries, and from the tenth century in this region great slabs of marble were decorated with beautiful ornaments to serve as altar-tables, and these were sometimes sent to churches at a considerable distance.[300]

Traditions continued into Romanesque times: let us instance the tympana of St.-Pons, of the chapel of Guzargues and of Maguelonne[301] which bears the date of 1178 and is embellished by a frieze of elegant leaf-ornament very similar to a frieze sculptured under the lintel of the door of St.-Trophime.

Let us also notice the numerous capitals of St.-Pons-de-Thomières[302] scattered, at St.-Pons itself even, in private ownership, while others of them are to be found at Mazamet, in the Musée des Augustins at Toulouse and at Montpellier, and lastly in America at Cambridge (Mass.), at Boston and at New York; the capitals of Aniane,[303] of Agde, of St-Guilhem-le-Désert, and in the department of Aude, those of Rieux-Minervois.[304]

Very special attention should be given to the fragments of large size belonging to *St.-Guilhem-le-Désert*[305] which are preserved in the archaeological museum of Montpellier, and show groups of apostles sculptured upon marble panels which seem to be considerably earlier than those of St.-Gilles-du-Gard or of St.-Trophime at Arles. These groups are of good proportions and elegant in form, and even while manifesting considerable originality they also recall the art of Toulouse. *Plates 86, 87 c, d*

M. Richard Hamann has recently rescued from oblivion some other fragments, found at St.-Guilhem, which come close to the works of St.-Gilles, and show by the antique beauty of the faces as well as by the manner in which the vestments are treated, that they were copied directly from Gallo-Roman models. *Plate 87 a, b*

CHAPTER X

THE SCHOOL OF ROUSSILLON AND OF CATALONIA

WE know that the territory of Catalonia was in the eleventh and twelfth centuries attached to the Kingdom of France, but it is quite clear that the terms of vassalship of the Counts of Catalonia towards the King were very easy. The thing that matters most to us is that along the two slopes of the Pyrenees we find, on either side, works which are absolutely similar, showing that the same craftsmen laboured in our own department of Pyrénées-Orientales [306] and in the great cities of Catalonia, [307] in the churches and the monasteries of Barcelona, of Gerona, Tarragona and Lérida, at San Cugat del Vallés and at Ripoll. But while Pyrénées-Orientales has preserved only a few traces of this art, Catalonia possesses in her cloisters a series of sumptuously decorated monuments which are intact.

Let us begin with a study of those existing in our own country, where an early beginning was made in the sculpture of the human figure, and where is actually to be seen the oldest dated monument of Romanesque sculpture, the *Plate 4a* lintel of *St.-Genis-des-Fontaines,* which bears an inscription referring to the dedication of the church in 1020-1021. We have already spoken on an earlier *Plate 4b, c* page [307a] of this, as well as of the lintel of *St.-André-de Sorède,* and with these must be associated the small tympanum of Arles-sur-Tech [308] which also belongs to the eleventh century.

In the twelfth century doorways were decorated with figures or other orna- *Plate 93a* ments: the tympanum of the church of *Corneilla-de-Conflent* [309] has a Virgin and Child in a glory between two angels; at Le Boulou we see above the door a frieze of marble with scenes relating the Birth of Christ. In *St.-Michel* at *Plate 90a* *Cuixa* [310] cut into the marble in very low relief are two large figures, representing St. Peter and St. Paul, which formerly adorned the abutments of a portal. The doorway of the abbot's lodge is framed by figures and ornaments, cherubim and the Symbols of the Evangelists, exactly similar to those of the *Plates 90b, 91b* Abbey of *Serrabone* [311] where there is, in the porch, a series of most beautiful *92, 93b* capitals. The carvings of these two last monuments present so many resemblances that it seems very possible they were executed by the same artist.

At the beginning of the thirteenth century the very mediocre sculpture had still an entirely Romanesque character, as may be seen in the statues of St. Jean-le-Vieux at Perpignan,[312] in the funerary statues preserved at Arles-sur-Tech and in the cloister of the cathedral of Elne.[313]

It is, nevertheless, the capitals of a very special style which characterize the works of this district, presenting as they do analogies so striking that we are compelled to think that the same workshop was busy with most of these churches on both sides of the Pyrenees. We find, for instance, on these marble capitals animals, lions, he-goats and birds placed side by side and joined together with a single head in place of the volute at the angle. Capitals of this type can be seen in the cloister of Elne,[314] the oldest portion of which dates from the last quarter of the twelfth century, at St.-André-de-Sorède, at St.-Ge-nis-des-Fontaines, Le Boulou, Espira-de-l'Agly,[315] at Corneilla-de-Conflent and in the Abbey of *Serrabone* (commune of Boule d'Amont). *Plate 92 c*

Other capitals have large lions in profile, with their heads at the angles, as in the Abbey of *St.-Michel* at *Cuixa,* the capitals of which are now to be found at Prades and Codalet, or at *Serrabone,* St.-Martin-du-Canigou, Cous- *Plates 91 a, 92 a* touges and Elne. Human heads are also to be found in the place of the rosette between the two volutes in the cloister of *Elne,* at Corneilla-de-Conflent at *Plate 88* Villefranche-de-Conflent, *Serrabone,* and in Catalonia in the cloister of Ripoll. *Plate 92*

The capitals with vegetal decoration are very beautiful, and we mention especially those with three palm-leaf decorations the ribbons enclosing which are joined by loops, in the cloister of *Elne,* at Villefranche-de-Conflent, and *Plate 88* in Catalonia in the cloister of San Cugat del Vallés near Barcelona, and in the cloister of Ripoll.

Catalonia, as we have said, has preserved some far more considerable *ensembles* of sculpture, and it would seem that Roussillon was the poor relation of that fine school of Catalonian sculpture which may have felt in some measure the influence of the workshops of Languedoc, but of which the craftsmen nevertheless produced work of great independence and originality. We have already indicated certain resemblances that should be noticed between these works and those of Provence.

In the cloister of San Cugat del Vallés[316] near Barcelona, in the vast cloister of the cathedral at Gerona[317] and in the small cloister of San Pere de Galligans,[318] in the great cloisters of the cathedrals of Tarragona[319] and of Lérida,[320] in the cloisters of the monasteries of Ripoll,[321] of Santa Maria del

Estany,[322] of Peralada,[323] of the church of San Pau del Camp at Barcelona,[324] in the interior of the cathedral of Lérida we find many capitals admirably sculptured, decorated with figures, animals and vegetal ornaments. In the cloister of *Gerona* cathedral the pilasters are adorned with groups of figures which illustrate religious subjects and scenes connected with various trades: labourers are bringing water to make mortar, carpenters are using their planes. On a capital at San Cugat we see a man at work, and the picture is particularly interesting since it represents a sculptor actually carving a capital.

Plate 89

The most important Catalonian piece of sculpture is to be found in the bas-reliefs which over a vast superficies frame the doorway of the Abbey of *Ripoll*,[325] and which also constitute a rare and specially interesting iconography. The stories of Moses, of David and of Solomon are there set forth as though upon the magnificently illuminated page of some manuscript; and the fact is, as has been plainly shown,[326] that the sculptor was really copying from the miniature in some Bible identical with the Bible of Farfa, where the scenes represented have the closest possible analogy with those on the doorway of Ripoll, so that, as M. Mâle has said, there is no monument which better shows the influence exercised by the manuscripts upon Romanesque art.

The great school of Catalonia thus had an exchange of influences with Provence, and M. Bréhier has thought that he could trace it as far as Velay.[327] We have just seen that Catalonian artists worked in Roussillon, and we would add to this that artistic connection was maintained on both sides of the Pyrenees throughout their entire length. Mlle Madeleine Ferry,[328] who has made a study of Romanesque art in the extreme south-west of France, has noted a large number of churches in the departments of Gers[329] and Pyrénées whose tympana are adorned with the "XP" monogram, either alone or flanked by two angels, notably at Ste.-Engrâce (Basses-Pyrénées). These "XP" are found in the churches of Catalonia and in other provinces of northern Spain. The doorway of Oloron (Basses-Pyrénées) has figures which present certain relations with the well-known bas-reliefs of Silos. In the cloister of St.-Bertrand-de-Comminges (Haute-Garonne)[330] is a column flanked by statues which must be related with the statues similarly backed against a column found in the cloister of Solsona (Catalonia).[331] Upon the beautiful tympanum of Sévignac-Théze (Basses-Pyrénées)[332] is the Christ between St. Peter and St. Paul, a group which is likewise found in San Pau del Camp at Barcelona.

CHAPTER XI

THE INFLUENCE OF FRENCH SCULPTURE OUTSIDE FRANCE

THE art of France, which in the twelfth century produced so many remarkable works, extended its sphere of influence beyond her own borders.

In Switzerland, in St.-Pierre at Geneva[332a] may be traced the influence of the works of St.-Maurice at Vienne and St.-Jean at Lyons. In northern Italy[333] and in northern Spain[334] marks of her influence are found, and during the Romanesque period these two regions witnessed the rise of two great schools of sculpture which produced works of striking originality worthy to be reckoned as rivals even of the finest creations of France; but this fact should not lead us to overlook the profound influence which France exercised upon both of these schools.

M. Mâle[335] has well shown, in his studies of style and iconography, how much the school of Lombardy owed to the workshops of Toulouse, St.-Denis and Provence. It was in France that the *Drama of the Prophets* was first conceived, and the inscriptions engraved upon the banderoles of the Prophets at Cremona recall that Drama to our recollection, while the work of the master Nicholas at Ferrara and at Verona, who was working there about the middle of the century, allows us to trace reminiscences of the creations of Toulouse and of St.-Denis.[336] These relations with France are felt even more in the second half of the twelfth century, and the bas-reliefs of the rood-screen in the cathedral of Modena,[337] which represent the Last Supper, seem impregnated with the art of Beaucaire. In the last quarter of the century a very great artist, Benedetto Antelami, who worked at Parma and at Borgo San Donnino, was certainly inspired by the works at Chartres, and was in close touch with the workshops of St.-Gilles and of St.-Trophime.

We have stated elsewhere[338] the historical reasons for supposing that Christian Spain tried to imitate the works of the great school of Languedoc; but though the Spanish artists may have found their models at Toulouse and at Moissac they were something more than mere copyists and they created, in their turn, original works of extreme beauty.

If they owed much to France, the latter also borrowed from them certain decorative elements; and what France in her sculpture derives from Mohammedan art has come to her not only upon the materials, the coffers of oriental ivory which Syrian merchants brought overseas, but also by way of Christian Spain which, thanks to the immediate neighbourhood of the Arabs, adopted into her art certain features of their ornamental style.

The imprint of the art of Toulouse may be strikingly seen at Santiago de Compostela in the decoration of the Goldsmiths' Door,[339] executed about 1120, but in which certain elements of sculpture are perhaps of later date, as M. G. Gaillard has recently suggested.[340] On this same door of the church of Santiago are a few figures which remind us of those on the tympanum at Conques, and in the deambulatory there are four capitals of the Auvergnat type, representing angels holding streamers containing inscriptions, and sirens, while on one of them may be seen one of the damned being hanged by devils whose grimacing faces are identical with those of the demons on the Conques tympanum. Reminiscences of Toulouse and Conques can thus be traced at Santiago de Compostela not only in the general plan and architecture of the monument, but also in the details of its sculptural decoration. We have observed the imprint of Toulouse at San Isidoro at León where the carvings on the doors, despite the opinions to the contrary, cannot be earlier than the twelfth century. M. Gómez Moreno,[341] whose learned studies may be relied upon, admits the existence of native workshops from the end of the eleventh century in the Chapel of the Kings in San Isidoro at León, and at Fromista (province of Valencia), but he remarks that the influence of French art must have become predominant as early as the beginning of the twelfth century.

Mr. Kingsley Porter[342] has claimed that a date some years later than 1073-1076, but in any case earlier than the end of the eleventh century, must be assigned to the admirable bas-reliefs in the cloister of Silos[343] which are reckoned among the most perfect masterpieces of Romanesque art. For our part, we dispute this thesis without any qualification whatever.[344] These marvellous sculptures cannot possibly be dated earlier than the second quarter of the twelfth century, since the art of Toulouse is recalled to our remembrance by the large figures with crossed legs and by the small capitals bearing figures which sustain the arcades surrounding these bas-reliefs, as well as by the little balls which ornament them and which are found also upon the capitals of the ambulatory of St.-Sernin.

In Aragon,[345] in Asturias, in Old Castile, in Navarre, French traditions can be traced, and M. G. Gaillard, who is preparing an important work on Romanesque sculpture in Spain will quote numerous instances of this. It will therefore suffice for the present if we cite certain monuments where the style of the workshops of Languedoc is particularly noticeable: the tympanum of Armentia (Alava), the cloister of Huesca (Aragon); in perhaps less direct fashion San Juan de la Peña (Aragon) where can be found the independent work of some local workshop; in Navarre, at *Pamplona,* where the capitals have a remarkable resemblance to those of La Daurade at Toulouse; and lastly on the doorway of Sangüesa the column-statues of which indicate an imitation, beyond doubt, of the workshops of the Ile-de-France.

Plate 94

In conclusion, we would allude to the traces of this French art during the twelfth and thirteenth centuries to be found overseas and far from its native soil. It is known that after the first crusade at the beginning of the twelfth century, the Holy Land, that is to say Palestine and Syria, was peopled by a large colony of western folk, the great majority of them being French.

These conquered Mohammedan countries, after they came under Christian rule, were covered with admirable monuments, cathedrals, monasteries, castles — the latter being of gigantic size — in which were to be found very close imitations of the arts then practised in France itself.

Of the sculptural decoration of these monuments there now remains but very little, the Arabs after the evacuation of the Holy Land by France at the end of the thirteenth century having ruthlessly destroyed everything, even the marble which French artists had used for their sculptures being often employed by the Mohammedans for the making of lime.

Among the most important remains of such sculptures as have come down to us, and are so nearly related to French work that there can be no doubt they were executed either by sculptors specially brought from France or else by pilgrims who for the time being put their talents at the disposal of the great men who caused these buildings to be constructed, we must cite the two lintels of the great double doorway of *St.-Sépulcre* at *Jerusalem.*[346] That on the west, surmounting the present entrance to the basilica, is embellished by scenes from the Life of Christ[347] which took place either in Jerusalem itself or in the immediate neighbourhood, and its style recalls that of St.-Gilles and of

St.-Trophime at Arles. Here are seen the Resurrection of Lazarus, Martha and Mary and the friends of Lazarus imploring Jesus to raise him, a scene which of course should logically have come before the other. Next we see Jesus sending Peter and John to secure a place in which to celebrate the Passover, and then these two apostles dressing the lamb; two other Apostles in search of the she-ass upon which Christ was to ride; the Entry into Jerusalem; the Last Supper. The eastern lintel[348] is ornamented with leaf-decorations and figurines which recall very closely the art of Toulouse.

It was not only French artists who worked upon St.-Sépulcre, but Italian sculptors also collaborated, so that the tympanum of the Calvary porch,[349] ornamented with vine-branches or palm-leaves arranged horizontally, while it has not its like in France, is yet similar to the analogous decoration which we see on the lintels at Lucca.

In the ambulatory of St.-Sépulcre we find capitals of a Romanesque type which is near to Corinthian, such as are often found in Languedoc and Auvergne. In the north arm of the transept is a capital embellished with the Judgement of Solomon,[350] the same scene being found on a capital of St.-Maurice at Vienne.[351]

Various fragments of sculptured friezes and cornices from the neighbourhood of St.-Sépulcre are preserved in the Musée de Notre-Dame-de-France and in the Musée des Franciscains.

In the church of Ste.-Marie-la-Grande these was, opening upon the north side-aisle, a large doorway on which a few years ago there still remained portions of a sculptured tympanum; but this doorway was transformed in the course of the restoration at the end of the nineteenth century. The archivolt enclosing the tympanum still exists although restored, and there can be seen on it, as in Charente, the Occupations of the Months with inscriptions describing each month.

In the small French building which the Arabs have dedicated to the Ascension of Mahomet[352] we find capitals representing eagles surmounting lions, such as are also found in the Mosque of El Aksa,[353] which retains important traces of the architecture of the crusade period. Similar capitals are to be seen in France in St.-Eutrope at Saintes and at St.-Benoît-sur-Loire.

Fathers Vincent and Abel have found in the "Chapelle de la Prison du Repos" some embellished capitals representing Christ between angels.[354]

We must also remark upon the very fine capitals in the church of the Ascension on the Mount of Olives, two of which are ornamented with confronted griffins[355] which exhibit very evidently the style of Toulouse. At the Cénacle is a curious capital adorned with four owls, which M. Camille Enlart has compared with a capital from Nîmes preserved in the Musée Calvet at Avignon.

The Louvre has recently acquired at *Damascus* a capital[356] dating from the middle or the third quarter of the twelfth century and representing a woman holding a flower, and a knight, the Emperor Constantine, the feet of whose horse rest on the head of a vanquished foe. Camille Enlart has drawn attention to the resemblance between these figures and those on a twelfth-century capital in the cathedral at Autun[357] and on a thirteenth-century capital in the cloister of St.-Trophime at Arles,[358] both decorated with the same scenes.

This capital appears to be the work of an Avignon artist and is closely related to certain capitals from the cloister of Notre-Dame-des-Doms.

The Museum of the Greek Patriarchate at Jerusalem possesses some fine fragments of sculptures which came from the ruins of Ste.-Marie-Latine and from the Convent of St.-Jean-Baptiste.[359] Here are a hunting-scene, and embellished capitals upon which are two scenes, an angel announcing to the priest Zacharias the approaching birth of St. John the Baptist, and the Visitation, with figures that recall the Romanesque art of Burgundy; a springer from a marble coving with a single figure in very high relief and of very fine execution representing the Virgin in the scene of the Annunciation;[360] this latter figure reminds us of that on the Portail Royal at Chartres, and it belongs to the third quarter of the twelfth century. This museum also has two heads that came from Nazareth, of which we are about to speak.

In some excavations undertaken in 1908 at *Nazareth* on the site of the Basilica of the Annunciation, the Rev. Father Prosper Viaud discovered five historiated capitals[361] which are comparable with the purest marvels of Romanesque art. These capitals were found in a hollow formed by a sort of paving-stone, in which it had evidently been the intention to hide them. They must have belonged to the doorway of the basilica; one, larger than the others, must have been that of the pier. The faces of these capitals are hollowed out into niches, and the figures are arranged beneath arcades adorned by architectural decorations as on the capitals of the Portail Royal at Chartres.

In the style of the figures one notices very close relation with the art of Bur-

Plate 95

97

gundy. A devil has hair standing on end exactly as have the devils on the capitals at Autun and Vézelay. The nimbi of some of the figures are ornamented with small balls pierced with holes, as are the nimbi of figures on the tympana at Charlieu (Loire) and St.-Julien-de-Jonzy (Saône-et-Loire). On these two monuments, as on the capitals at Nazareth, we find the same movement, the same remarkable vivacity of the personages, the same draperies falling in numerous folds, the curves of which are studied with the utmost care for detail; a work, in short, of unusual delicacy which reminds us of works enchased on precious metals.

It is worthy of note that on the capitals in Nazareth we find, as in Burgundian works of sculpture, far more prominence than in other French provinces given to the tucking-up of the lower borders of the vestments, and to the excessive spreading-out of the body in order to fill in empty spaces.

It should further be noted that the nimbi of the personages on the capitals at Nazareth are very broad, as at Montceaux-l'Étoile, La Charité-sur-Loire and Donzy-le-Pré. It was assuredly a sculptor from France who executed these admirable works which have survived to our own day in an extraordinary state of preservation. The stone in which they were carved is a very fine limestone which comes from a quarry quite close to Nazareth, very similar to the limestone employed by the Romanesque sculptors of Burgundy.

The scenes which decorate these capitals have received various interpretations, but we are content to accept the explanation lately given by Camille Enlart. Upon the large capital is represented Faith leading an apostle who is being attacked by demons. As for the other capitals, on the first is seen the Unbelief of St. Thomas, and upon another the miraculous Draught of Fishes and the Raising of Tabitha. A third is devoted to the legend of St. Bartholomew and to that of St. James the Greater. The fourth capital illustrates the legend of St. Matthew.

Plate 96 In 1867, in the lower town of Nazareth,[362] two large bearded heads connected to two adjoining faces of the same cube of stone were discovered. These are now preserved at the Greek Patriarchate of Jerusalem, and they are undoubtedly the work of the same artist who carved the capitals.

M. Enlart thinks that they must have belonged to the statuary decorating the doorway and that these statues must have resembled those on the doorway at Morlaas (Basses-Pyrénées); that is to say that they covered both faces of an abut-

98

ment. They were perhaps intended for such a purpose but we are of the opinion that they were never placed in position. We may notice that both the heads, the carving of which has been completely finished, seem to have been hewn from a rough block, and this would appear to denote an unfinished work. In 1183 the Mahommedans arrived at the gates of Nazareth and captured the city in 1187 after the disastrous battle of Hattin which led to the taking of Jerusalem. If we admit that the five capitals, in such a perfect state of preservation that it seems impossible that they can have been exposed for any long period to the open air, were intentionally concealed, it seems permissible to suppose that the same fate befell these two heads, hewn from a shapeless block of stone, and that the decoration of the doorway of the basilica at Nazareth had not yet been terminated when the enemy arrived at the gates, when the artist saved these works, so precious for us now, on which he was actually working at the time.

CONCLUSION

In the course of our study we have traced the development of Romanesque sculpture from those early days when inexperienced sculptors were laboriously struggling to restore a completely forgotten art and were copying models of the most varied nature, some of them far removed from the technique of carving in stone, such as those provided by the arts of drawing and relief, ancient and contemporary works, native and foreign creations, miniatures, frescoes, embroidered fabrics, steles and sarcophagi, stamped bricks, ivory tablets, works in cast-iron, bas-reliefs in stucco and altar-fronts with figures in goldsmiths' work.

We have seen how they gradually recovered their knowledge of technique, succeeding after many efforts in surrounding the "baskets" of the capitals with groups of personages, executing figures in very low relief on slabs of large dimensions, and little by little venturing to decorate the broad surfaces of tympana with complicated, mystical scenes and even, in the western provinces, covering the entire façades of their churches with sculptures.

Their iconographic conceptions present an infinite number of variations. Their mystical ideas were stern and disquieting. They hesitated before the problem of the life to come, and represented God as a grave and solemn deity presiding over the fateful events of the end of the world. They were haunted by fantastic visions of the Apocalypse which they tried to interpret in sculpture.

But while some of these sculptors were reluctant to approach the problem of future life, others cared little for such profound considerations and allowed their chisels to follow the phantasies of their dreams. Hence those strange figures to which it is useless to attempt to assign any religious significance: fantastic beings, chimera, sirens, serpents, dragons, griffins, legendary animals and fabulous monsters, in the production of which the artists gave full rein to their exuberant phantasy. Some of these figures amuse us by reason of the satiric spirit which they reveal; others are merely grotesque and ridiculous, and it is not difficult to comprehend St. Bernard's indignation when he was confronted with such representations.

Other artists reveal a more delicate temperament in the execution of elegant and gracious figures such as the lightly-poised angels of the Ascension on the tympana of Burgundy and those on the doorways of Saintonge, ascending in pairs towards the summit of the arch-rim to support with their joined hands the celestial crown; or those symbols of heavenly justice, the Wise and Foolish Virgins, supple as Greek dancers, or the armed Virtues, elegant as the ancient Amazons in their costumes of knights of the Christian Faith. Occasionally they depict the alluring charm of woman, as, for example, on a certain capital at Toulouse, in that charming figure of Salome whose face Herod is caressing.

The provinces of Languedoc, Burgundy, Auvergne, Charente and Poitou, in accordance with the temperament of their artists and the resources of the materials provided by their soil, produced magnificent monuments of which we have endeavoured to distinguish the most essential characteristics.

While in Provence the traditions of Romanesque art outlived the end of the twelfth century, a new art appeared before the middle of the century to the north of the Loire, and especially in the Ile-de-France, though even there certain principles of Romanesque art survived for a considerable time. To complete our study we ought to have shown how the west door at St.-Denis and the Portail Royal at Chartres, in which appear the first symptoms of Gothic art, as in their replicas at Le Mans, Étampes, Bourges, Corbeil, Provins, Avallon, etc., still retain certain essential elements of Romanesque art in their hieratic, exaggeratedly lengthy figures placed against the columns from which they were carved, their historiated arch-rims, their capitals adorned with personages and their stylized decoration.

We have not touched upon this subject because these doorways in their *ensemble* belong to Gothic art, which is outside our province and will be treated by M. Marcel Aubert.

During the second half of the twelfth century we can follow the gradual rise of Gothic art which will soon rid itself of the conventional and artificial elements in Romanesque sculpture. The doorways are henceforward decorated with real statues in thoughtful and restrained attitudes. The striving after eccentricity and extravagant appearances gradually gives way to an attempt at harmony and sobre composition, with an ideal of beauty the sources of which are to be found in Nature. This effort to imitate nature gradually extends to the human figures and the representations of plants and flowers.[363] Historiated capitals will be banished from the church-interiors, to be replaced by capitals ornamented with foliage, not stylized according to the formulae followed for centuries, but directly imitated from the models gathered in the meadows and forests of Champagne and the Ile-de-France. This is by no means the least attractive feature of that gentle and restful art which was born at the end of the twelfth and at the beginning of the thirteenth century at St.-Denis and Chartres, and reached its full development at Senlis and Paris, at Amiens and Rheims.

BIBLIOGRAPHY

GENERAL WORKS

ANDRÉ MICHEL, *La Sculpture romane* (in France), in *Histoire de l'Art*, Paris, A. Colin, quarto, Vol. I, part 2 (1905), pp. 588-669, and Bibliography, pp. 708-710.

DENISE JALABERT, *La Sculpture romane*, Paris, Stock, n. d., duodecimo. This little book forms an excellent résumé of André Michel's doctrine.

VÖGE, *Die Anfänge des monumentalen Stiles im Mittelalter*, Strasburg 1894, octavo.

R. DE LASTEYRIE, *Études sur la Sculpture française au Moyen âge*, 145 pages, 22 plates, in *Monuments et Mémoires publiés par l'Académie des Inscriptions et Belles-Lettres* (Fondation Piot), Vol. VIII, 1902. Part of this work is devoted to a reply to that of Vöge.

R. DE LASTEYRIE, *L'Architecture religieuse en France à l'époque romane*, Paris, A. Picard, 1912, quarto. New edition published and completed by Marcel Aubert, Paris, A. Picard, 1929, quarto.

LOUIS BRÉHIER, *L'Art chrétien, son développement iconographique des origines à nos jours*, Paris, Laurens, 1928, royal octavo.

ÉMILE MÂLE, *L'Art religieux du XIIe siècle en France*, Paris, A. Colin, second edition, quarto, 1924, IV + 460 pages and 253 engravings. This very beautiful book has been the subject of numerous commentaries. See especially: J.-A. BRUTAILS, *L'origine de l'iconographie au moyen âge, à propos d'un livre récent* (Bibliothèque de l'École des Chartes, Vol. LXXXV, 1924). - L. BRÉHIER, in *Revue d'Auvergne*, 1923, p. 49 ff. - MICHEL ANDRIEU, *Les Origines de l'Iconographie médiévale*, in *Revue des Sciences religieuses*, published at Strasburg, fourth year, No. 2, April 1924, pp. 349-373. - PAUL DESCHAMPS, in *Bulletin Monumental*, 1923, p. 487 ff.

MARCEL AUBERT, *La Sculpture Française du moyen âge et de la Renaissance*, Paris and Brussels, G. Van Oest, 1926, 60 pages and 64 plates. This work gives a brief, but excellent description of the evolution of French sculpture.

PRINCIPAL COLLECTIONS OF PHOTOGRAPHS

PAUL VITRY and GASTON BRIÈRE, *Documents de Sculpture française du moyen âge*, Paris, D. A. Longuet, 1906, folio. A collection of 140 plates, containing 940 representations of statuary and ornamentation.

CAMILLE MARTIN, *L'Art roman en France*, 3 albums, royal folio; each album containing 80 plates, Paris, Eggimann, 1910-1914.

Paul Léon, *Encyclopédie des styles*, first series: *L'Art Roman*, a historical and archaeological notice containing 93 documents after those of the archives of the Commission des Monuments historiques, Paris, R. Ducher, n. d., folio.

A. Kingsley Porter, *Romanesque Sculpture of the Pilgrimage Roads*, 10 volumes, octavo, of which one containing the text (385 pages), and nine albums containing 1527 photographs. Volumes II, IV, VII, VIII, IX and X contain photographs of French monuments. This is the most important work on Romanesque sculpture in France which exists at the present day.

Jules Roussel, *La Sculpture Française, époque romane*, Paris, Éditions Albert Morancé, (1928), 1 volume, quarto, 35 pages and 50 plates (after the casts in the Musée de Sculpture comparée at the Trocadéro).

Marcel Aubert, *L'Art français à l'époque romane, Architecture et Sculpture*, Volume I: *Ile-de-France, Champagne, Alsace, Normandy, Valley of the Loire*, 1929, royal folio, 16 pages, 60 plates. This volume is the first of a series of four albums in which the above-mentioned work by Camille Martin is completed, amplified and rearranged.

Jules Baum, *L'Architecture romane en France*, Paris, Hachette, quarto, 1913, 19 pages and 313 illustrations.

NOTES

1] Émile Mâle, *Les influences arabes dans l'art roman*, in *Revue des Deux-Mondes*, 15th November 1923.

1a] Louis Bréhier, *Études sur l'Histoire de la Sculpture Byzantine*, in *Nouvelles archives des Missions scientifiques...*, new series, part 3, Paris 1911, pp. 19-105, plates and figures. - *Nouvelles Recherches sur l'Histoire de la Sculpture Byzantine*, *ibid.*, 1913, part 9, pp. 1-66, plates and figures.

2] J.-A. Brutails, *L'Archéologie du moyen âge et ses méthodes*, Paris, A. Picard, 1900, plate 1, p. 62. - Paul Deschamps, *Étude sur la renaissance de la sculpture en France à l'époque romane*, in *Bulletin Monumental*, 1925, p. 74.

2a] Louis Bréhier, *L'homme dans la Sculpture romane*, Paris, Librairie de France, n. d., quarto, 44 pages, 10 figures and 52 plates. - H. Focillon, *Apôtres et Jongleurs, étude de mouvement*, in *Revue de l'Art*, 1929, pp. 18-19.

2b] Jean Laran, *Recherches sur les proportions de la statuaire française du XIIe siècle*, in *Revue Archéologique*, 1907, I, p. 436; 1908, I, p. 331; 1909, II, pp. 74-216; special edition (1909), p. 68.

3] R. Cattaneo, *L'Architecture en Italie du VIe au XIe siècle*, translated into French by Le Monnier, Venice 1891, royal octavo, 329 pages. - R. de Lasteyrie, *L'Architecture à l'époque romane*, pp. 203-223. - E. A. Stückelberg, *Langobardische Plastik*, first edition, Zurich 1896; second edition, Kempten and Munich 1909. - L. de Farcy, *Entrelacs carolingiens de l'Anjou*, in *Bulletin Monumental*, 1906, pp. 82-90. - Maurice Prou, *Chancel carolingien orné d'entrelacs à Schaennis* (canton of St. Gall) in *Mémoires de l'Académie des Inscriptions et Belles-Lettres* (Fondation Piot), Vol. XXXIX (1912), pp. 123-138. - Paul Deschamps, *Dalles carolingiennes incrustées dans le clocher de la Charité-sur-Loire*, in *Bulletin Monumental*, 1920, pp. 223-230.

4] Paul Deschamps, *Étude sur la renaissance de la sculpture en France à l'époque romane*, *Bulletin Monumental*, 1925, pp. 14-17.

5] *L'Hypogée-Martyrium de Poitiers*, 1883.

6] *Congrès archéologique de France*, held at Metz, Strasburg and Colmar in 1920, p. 48.

7] Angers: *Guide du Congrès archéologique de France*, held at Angers and Saumur in 1910, p. 194.
Charlieu: Thiollier, *L'Art roman à Charlieu et en Brionnais*, Montbrison 1892, plate. - Kingsley Porter, *Romanesque Sculpture...*, Vol. II, plate 1.
Beauvais: Kingsley Porter, *Romanesque Sculpture...*, Vol. X, plate 1411.

8] L. Bréhier, *Les origines de la sculpture romane*, in *Revue des Deux-Mondes*, 15th August 1912, pp. 870-901.

La Cathédrale de Clermont au Xe siècle et sa statue d'or de la Vierge, in *La Renaissance de l'Art Français*, April 1924, pp. 205-210.

8a] *Miracula sancte Fidis*, L. I, chap. CXII, edited by A. Bouillet, pp. 46-49.

V. Mortet, *Recueil de Textes relatifs à l'Histoire de l'Architecture...*, *XIe-XIIe siècles*, Paris 1911, pp. 47-49.

9] Paul Deschamps, article quoted, pp. 21-32. In this article we see that stucco was used for the decoration of buildings not only in the early Middle Ages but also during the Romanesque period. Its origin dates from long before the Middle Ages. M. J. Carcopino has recently drawn attention to its occurrence at Rome in the first century of the Christian era on stucco-relief figures for the decoration of interiors. It was used in much more remote regions in Afghanistan, during the first centuries of the Christian era, as has been revealed by the recent excavations at Hadda. From the second to the fifth century of our era and especially in the third century Greco-Buddhist art produced statues in stucco of an exquisitely artistic character. An entire room of the Musée Guimet is filled with heads and small figures in stucco coming from Hadda. See J. Hackin, *Les fouilles de Hadda*, in *Revue des Arts Asiatiques*, new series, No. 2, fifth year, pp. 66-76, figure.

10] Lasteyrie, *op. cit.*, p. 195, figure 172.

G. Bouet, *L'église de Germigny-des-Prés*, in *Bulletin Monumental*, 1868.

Abbé Prévost, *La Basilique de Théodulfe et la paroisse de Germigny-des-Prés*, Orleans 1889.

11] Josef Garber, *Die karolingische St. Benediktkirche in Mals*, Innsbruck 1915; cf. Paul Deschamps, article quoted, pp. 25-28.

12] *Bulletin* of the Société Nationale des Antiquaires de France, 1906, pp. 324-329, and 1911, pp. 274-280; *Memoirs* of the Société Nationale des Antiquaires de France, Vol. LXXII, 1912, pp. 226-243.

13] C. Cecchelli, *Il Tempietto longobardo di Cividale del Friuli*, in *Dedalo*, third year, part 12, May 1923, pp. 735-760.

Other archaeologists assign these figures in Cividale to the eleventh century; cf. Toesca, *Storia dell'Arte Italiana*, 1924, Vol. III, p. 793.

Kingsley Porter, *Spanish Romanesque Sculpture*, Paris, Pegasus Press, 1928, Vol. I, pp. 14-15 and note 93.

14] *Vita S. Angilberti auct. Anschero*, c. 7, in *Acta Sanctorum ordinis sancti Benedicti*, IV, I, p. 127.

15] R. R., *Luoghi romiti: San Pietro al monte sopra Civate*, in *Emporium*, Vol. XXXV, No. 208, April 1912, pp. 286-304.

16] Antoni Muñoz, *Pittura Romanica Catalana, I paliotti dipinti dei Musei di Vich e di Barcellona*, Institut d'estudis catalans, 1907, p. 89 ff.
Puig y Cadafalch..., *L'arquitectura romànica a Catalunya*, Vol. II, 1911, pp. 400-405.
J. Folch y Torres, Junta de Museos de Barcelona, *Museo de la Ciudadela. Catálogo de la sección de arte románico*, Barcelona 1926, pp. 21-27, fig.
Paul Deschamps, article quoted, pp. 90-92, plate.

17] L. Demaison, *L'église Saint-Remi de Reims*, in *Congrès archéologique de France*, held at Rheims in 1911, pp. 66, 79, 81, 82.

18] Paul Deschamps, in *Bulletin* of the Société des Antiquaires de France, 1924, pp. 206-213.

18a] *Rodulfi Glabri Historiarum...*, l. II, c. IV, § 13, edited by M. Prou, 1886, p. 61.
Victor Mortet, *Recueil de textes relatifs à l'Histoire de l'Architecture...*, *XI-XII siècles*, 1911, text I, p. 4.

18b] *Historia dedicationis basilicae Sancti Remigii...*, *auct. Anselmo*, in Mabillon, *Acta S. S. ordinis S. Benedicti, saec. VI, pars I*, pp. 626-627.
Victor Mortet, *Recueil de Textes relatifs à l'Histoire de l'Architecture...*, *XI-XII siècles*, 1911, p. 40.

19] André Michel, *Histoire de l'Art*, Vol. I, Part 2, pp. 589-590. - Paul Deschamps, *Étude sur la Renaissance de la Sculpture...*, pp. 18-21.

20] Otto Rydbeck, *Lunds Domkyrkas Byggnads historia*, Lund 1923, p. 44, figure 27, and p. 124, figure 101.

21] Deshoulières, in *Bulletin Monumental*, 1910, pp. 291-304, fig.

22] *Memoirs* of the Société Nationale des Antiquaires de France, Vol. XLII, 1881, plate VII.

23] E. Lefèvre-Pontalis, in *Bulletin Monumental*, 1910, fig. p. 282.

24] *Congrès archéologique de France*, held at Avignon in 1909, Vol. I, p. 114 ff., fig.

25] Kingsley Porter, *Romanesque Sculpture of the Pilgrimage Roads*, Vol. VIII, plates 1142-1144.
Paul Deschamps, *Étude sur la Renaissance de la Sculpture...*, fig. p. 64.

26] *Congrès archéologique de France*, held at Moulins and Nevers in 1913, p. 390, drawings.
Camille *Martin*, *L'art roman en France*, first series, plates 43-45.

27] Camille Martin, *L'art roman en France*, first series, plate II.
Marcel Aubert, *L'art français à l'époque romane, architecture et sculpture*, Paris, Morancé, I, 1929, plate 53.

28] *Congrès archéologique de France*, held at Montbrison in 1885, pp. 71-74 and 425 ff., 9 drawings.

29] *Ibid.*, pp. 77-78, no figure.

30] Ém. Bonnet, in *Congrès archéologique de France*, held at Avignon in 1909, Vol. II, p. 251 ff., fig.

31] F. Thiollier, *Vestiges de l'Art roman en Lyonnais*, in *Bulletin archéologique*, 1892, p. 403, plate XXVI.
L. Bégule, *Antiquités et Richesses d'art du département du Rhône*, 1925, p. 132 ff., fig. 169-171, and plates XXVIII and XLIV.

32] *Congrès archéologique de France*, held at Angers and Saumur in 1910, Vol. II, p. 106, photograph.

33] Fig. in Eug. Pépin, *Chinon (collection des petites monographies des grands édifices de la France)*, ed. Laurens, Paris. - Cf. E. Meschin, *Le bas-relief de Saint-Mexme à Chinon*, in quarterly *Bulletin* of the Société archéologique de Touraine, Vol. III, 1914, pp. 278-280.

34] Deshoulières, in *Congrès archéologique de France*, held at Valence and Montélimar, in 1923, pp. 269-282, fig.

35] Reproduced in Victor Terret, *La Sculpture bourguignonne aux XII et XIII siècles... Cluny*, Autun and Paris, 1914, royal quarto, pl. XXXIII-XXXVIII. - Vincent Flipo, *La Cathédrale de Dijon (coll. des petites monographies des grands édifices de France)*, Paris, Laurens, 1928, pp. 20, 21, 23.

36] J. Banchereau, *L'âge de la crypte de Saint-Aignan d'Orléans*, in *Bulletin archéologique*, 1922, pp. 155-163, plates XIV and XV.

37] E. Lefèvre-Pontalis, in *Congrès archéologique de France*, held at Paris in 1919, pp. 330-333, plate.

38] Camille Martin, *L'art roman en France*, first series, plates 2, 4, 5, 10.
Marcel Aubert, *L'art français à l'époque romane, architecture et sculpture*, Paris, Morancé, 1929, I, plates 53-60.

39] E. Lefèvre-Pontalis, in *Congrès archéologique de France*, held at Angers and Saumur in 1910, Vol. II, pp. 124-145, plate.

40] R. de Lasteryie, *L'Architecture... à l'époque romane*, pp. 199, 204, 205, plates 187-188.
Kingsley Porter, *Romanesque Sculpture...*, Vol. IV, plates 327-332.

41] Louis de Bonnefoy, *Épigraphie Roussillonnaise* in *Bulletin* of the Société agricole, scientifique et litt. des Pyrénées-Orientales from 1856 to 1868, No. 222.

André Michel, *Histoire de l'Art*, Vol. I, Part II, pp. 596-597.

J.-A. Brutails, *Notes sur l'Art religieux en Roussillon*, in *Bulletin archéologique*, 1893, p. 336, plate XXII.

Joan Sacs, *L'Orfebreria i la llinda de Sant Genis les Fonts*, in *Revista de Catalunya*, Vol. III, No. 15, September 1925, pp. 276-289.

42] Enlart, *Manuel d'Archéologie française*, I, *Architecture religieuse*, second edition, Part I, Paris, A. Picard, 1919, p. 204, plate.

J. Baum, *L'Architecture Romane en France*, plate 136.

43] Paul Deschamps, *Tables d'Autel exécutées dans le Midi de la France au Xe et au XIe siècle*, in *Mélanges d'Histoire du Moyen Age offerts à M. Ferdinand Lot*, Paris, E. Champion, 1925, pp. 137-168, plate.

44] Abbé Bouillet, *Sainte-Foy de Conques, Saint-Sernin de Toulouse, Saint-Jacques de Compostelle*, in *Memoirs* of the Soc. Nat. des Antiquaires de France, sixth series, Vol. III, 1892, pp. 117-128.

45] Anthyme Saint-Paul, *L'église Saint-Sernin de Toulouse*, in *Album des Monuments et de l'Art ancien du Midi de la France*, Toulouse, Privat, Vol. I, 1897, pp. 73-94, plate.

Paul Deschamps, *L'autel roman de Saint-Sernin de Toulouse et les sculptures du Cloître de Moissac*, in *Bulletin archéologique*, 1923, pp. 239-250, plates XIX-XXI. Casts of two fragments of this altar are in the Musée du Trocadéro.

46] C. Douais, *Mélanges sur Saint-Sernin de Toulouse*, Part I: *Vie de Saint Raymond, chanoine, et la construction de l'Église Saint-Sernin, 1080-1118*, Toulouse, Privat, 1894. Canon Auriol, in *Bulletin de la Soc. archéol. du Midi*, No. 44, pp. 63-71.

47] Antoine Noguier, *Histoire Tolosaine*, 1556.

48] Catel, *Histoire des Comtes de Toulouse*, Toulouse, 1623, folio.

49] Casts of three of these figures are at the Trocadéro. Dimensions of the figures of the apostles: breadth of the arch, 2 ft. 5½ inches; height of the arch, 5 ft. 7 inches; height of the figure, 4 ft. 8¾ inches.

49a] M. Raymond Rey observes that these marguerites are also to be found on the Miégeville door on the south side of the church, on the south transept door of Ste.-Foy at Conques and on the Goldsmiths' Door at Santiago de Compostela; see *Quelques survivances antiques dans la Sculpture romane méridionale*, in *Gazette des Beaux-Arts*, September-October 1928, pp. 173-191.

49b] A young American investigator, Mr. Meyer Shapiro, of Columbia University, New York, who is preparing a work on the Romanesque sculptures of

Moissac, was good enough to inform us that he has reason to think that the Porte des Comtes was executed before 1091 or 1093.

50] Cast in the Trocadéro.

51] Lasteyrie, *L'Architecture... à l'époque romane*, p. 710, fig. 720.

52] There is a cast of this inscription at the Trocadéro. - Cf. Paul Deschamps, *Étude sur la paléographie des inscriptions lapidaires*, in *Bulletin Monumental*, 1929, p. 35 and plate XIV, fig. 28.

53] Casts of the figures of St. Peter and St. Paul are in the Trocadéro.

54] Paul Deschamps, *Étude sur la paléographie des inscriptions lapidaires*, in *Bulletin Monumental*, 1929, plate XI, fig. 23.

55] On the *Chronicle of Aimery de Peyrac* see Jules Marion in *Bibliothèque de l'École de Chartes*, second series, Vol. I, 1849, pp. 89-147.
Paul Deschamps, *L'autel roman de Saint-Sernin de Toulouse et les sculptures du cloître de Moissac*, in *Bulletin archéol.*, 1923, pp. 248-250.
Charles Oursel, *Le rôle et la place de Cluny dans la renaissance de la sculpture en France à l'époque romane*, in *Revue archéologique*, Vol. XVII, pp. 277-282, and *L'Art roman en Bourgogne*, Dijon and Boston 1928, pp. 193-196.

56] *Histoire de l'Art*, Vol. I, second part, p. 617.

57] Article quoted in *Bulletin archéol.*, 1923, p. 246 ff.

58] *L'Art religieux du XIIe siècle...*, second edition, 1924, p. 4, note 1.

59] *L'Abbaye de Moissac*, in *Album des Monuments et de l'Art ancien du Midi de la France*, Toulouse 1893, pp. 49-53.

60] *L'Abbaye et les Cloîtres de Moissac*, Paris 1897.

61] *L'Abbaye de Moissac*, in *Coll. des petites monographies des grands édifices de la France*, Paris, Laurens, n. d.

62] There is a cast of the doorway in the Trocadéro.

63] *Op. cit.*, p. 4 ff.

63a] The decoration of this lintel appears to have been imitated from a carvimg in the museum at Cahors which is a remarkable specimen of decoration work. The carving comes from St.-Sernin at Thézel (Lot); cf. Raymond Rey, *Quelques survivances antiques dans la Sculpture romane méridionale*, in *Gazette des Beaux-Arts*, September-October 1928, pp. 180-181, plate.

63b] Worthy of mention, on account of its iconographic peculiarities, is a Romanesque tympanum the subject of which (like that of Moissac) is taken from a manuscript of the Apocalypse. This is the tympanum of Lalande-de-Cubzac (Gironde), in which we see the Son of Man appearing to St. John. A sword projects from the mouth of the Saviour who holds in his right hand a circle enclosing seven stars; near him are the seven candlesticks and seven arcades symbolizing the seven churches (see Mâle, *op. cit.*, p. 14, fig. 7, p. 12).

64] *Op. cit.*, p. 4, note 1.

65] *Op. cit.*, p. 618.

66] Émile Mâle, *op. cit.*, pp. 379-382, fig. 218.
Cast at the Trocadéro.

67] A cast of a part of these fragments is in the Trocadéro.

68] E. Lefèvre-Pontalis, in *Bulletin Monumental*, 1914, pp. 58-87, plate.

69] Emile Mâle, *L'art religieux du XIIe siècle*, pp. 176-180, 407-408, fig. 137.

70] Raymond Rey, *La Cathédrale de Toulouse*, in *Coll. des petites monographies des grands édifices de la France*, Paris, Laurens, 1929, p. 23, plate.

71] J. de Lahondès, *L'église Saint-Étienne, Cathédrale de Toulouse*, Toulouse, 1890, octavo, plate. - *Les Monuments de Toulouse*, Toulouse, 1920, plate.
Raymond Rey, *La Cathédrale de Toulouse*, 1929, pp. 26-29, plate.
Otto Grautoff, *Der Meister Gilabertus*, in *Repertorium für Kunstwissenschaft*, XXXVII, pp. 81-86.
Casts of two of the figures of Apostles are in the Trocadéro.

72] Émile Mâle, *Les Chapiteaux romans du Musée de Toulouse et l'École Toulousaine du XIIe siècle...*, in *Revue archéologique*, Vol. XX, 1892, plate. - *L'Art religieux du XIIe siècle*, pp. 107-108, pp. 238-242, plates 163-166.

73] Cast at the Trocadéro.

74] Émile Mâle, *Les Chapiteaux romans du Musée de Toulouse...*, article quoted, plate.
L'Art religieux au XIIe siècle, plates 85, 96, 112.

75] Casts of these two capitals are at the Trocadéro.

76] René Fage, *Le Tympan de l'Église de Collonges*, extract from the *Bulletin* of the Soc. sientif., hist. et archéol. de la Corrèze, Brive 1923, plate.

77] Émile Mâle, *L'art religieux du XIIe siècle*, plate 80, p. 94 and pp. 398-399.
Raymond Rey, *La Cathédrale de Cahors et les origines de l'architecture à coupoles de l'Aquitaine*, Cahors 1925, p. 18, note 2, and pp. 104-121.
C. Enlart, *Les Églises à coupoles de l'Aquitaine et de Chypre à propos d'un livre récent*, in *Gazette des Beaux-Arts*, March 1926, pp. 130-132.

78] Kingsley Porter, *op. cit.*, Vol. IV, plates 431-433.

79] *Congrès archéologique de France*, held at Agen and Auch in 1901, plate on page 8.

80] Magdeleine Ferry, *Les Portes romanes des Églises du Sud-Ouest de la France*, in *Positions des thèses soutenues à l'École des Chartes par les élèves de la promotion de 1928*, Paris 1928, pp. 43-48.
Mlle Ferry is preparing a series of articles on Romanesque art in this part of France, which has been little studied hitherto. See especially: *Étude sur les portes des églises romanes du département de Lot-et-Garonne*, in *Revue de l'Agenais*, 1929.

81] Bertaux, in *Histoire de l'Art*, published under the direction of André Michel, Vol. II, part I (1906), pp. 220-273, and especially pp. 249-255.
Émile Mâle, *L'Art religieux du XIIe siècle*, pp. 293-294, plates 181, 298 and 301.
Paul Deschamps, *Notes sur la sculpture romane en Languedoc et dans le Nord de l'Espagne*, in *Bulletin Monumental*, 1923, pp. 305-351, plate.
On the sculptures in San Isidoro at León, see Gómez Moreno, *Provincia de León, Catálogo Monumental de España*, Madrid, Ministerio de Instrucción Pública, 1925, two volumes in octavo. - G. Gaillard, *Notes sur les dates des sculptures de Compostelle et de Léon*, in *Gazette des Beaux-Arts*, June 1929, pp. 341-378.

82] On Silos, see below, note 343.

83] C. Enlart, *L'Église Abbatiale de Sant'Antimo en Toscane*, in *Revue de l'Art chrétien*, 1913, January-February.

84] See page 14, note 35 and plate 3.

85] Kinsgley Porter, *Romanesque Sculpture of the Pilgrimage Roads*, Vol. II, plate 3.

86] Kingsley Porter, *ibid.*, Vol. II, plate 107.

87] F. Thiollier, *L'Art roman à Charlieu et en Brionnais*, Montbrison 1892, quarto.
F. and N. Thiollier, *Art et Archéologie dans le département de la Loire*, St.-Étienne 1898, octavo.
J. Virey, *L'Architecture romane dans l'ancien diocèse de Mâcon*, Paris 1892, octavo, pp. 214-222.
A. Rhein, in *Congrès archéologique de France*, held at Moulins and Nevers in 1913, p. 242 ff.
Victor Terret, *La Sculpture Bourguignonne...*, *Cluny*, plate XXVII.
Kingsley Porter, *op. cit.*, plate 4.
Gottfried von Lücken, *Burgundische Skulpturen des XI. und XII. Jahrhunderts*, in *Jahrbuch für Kunstwissenschaft*, Leipzig 1923, plate 29.

88] E. Jeannez, *L'Église et le Prieuré d'Anzy-le-Duc*, in F. Thiollier, *L'Art roman à Charlieu et en Brionnais*, Montbrison 1892, quarto, pp. 73-80.
A. Rhein, in *Congrès archéologique de France*, held at Moulins and Nevers in 1913, pp. 242-291, plate.

Jean Vallery-Radot, *Les analogies des églises de Saint-Fortunat de Charlieu et d'Anzy-le-Duc*, in *Bulletin Monumental*, 1929, pp. 243-267.

Paul Deschamps, in *Gazette des Beaux-Arts*, July-August 1922, pp. 73-74.

G. von Lücken, article quoted, plates 27 and 28.

89] Deshoulières, in *Congrès archéologique de France*, held at Moulins and Nevers in 1913, plate following page 190.

90] *Millénaire de Cluny, Congrès d'histoire et d'archéologie*, Mâcon 1910, 2 volumes in octavo. - F.-L. Bruel, *Cluni (910-1910), Album historique et archéologique*, Mâcon 1910, quarto. - Jean Virey, in *Congrès archéologique de France*, held at Moulins and Nevers in 1913, pp. 73-86.

Jean Virey, *L'Abbaye de Cluny*, in *Coll. des petites monographies des grands édifices de France*, Paris, Laurens, n. d., 111 pages.

Victor Terret, *La Sculpture bourguignonne aux XIIe et XIIIe siècles*, *Cluny*, Autun and Paris, 1914, royal quarto.

90a] Paul Deschamps, *Tables d'autel de marbre exécutées dans le Midi de la France au Xe et XIe siècles*, in *Mélanges d'Histoire du Moyen Age offerts à M. Ferdinand Lot*, Paris, ed. Champion, 1925, pp. 156-158, plate IV.

91] Émile Mâle, *L'Art religieux du XIIe siècle*, pp. 386-390.

92] After each of his visits to Cluny Mr. Conant publishes the results of his excavations. See *Bulletin Monumental*, 1928, pp. 55-64; 1929, pp. 109-123. - *Speculum*, Vol. IV, No. 1, Jan. 1929, No. 2, April 1929, No. 3, June 1929, No. 5, Jan. 1930.

93] Dr. Pouzet, *Notes sur les chapiteaux de l'Abbaye de Cluny*, in *Revue de l'Art Chrétien*, 1912, pp. 1-17 and 104-110, plate.

V. Terret, *La Sculpture Bourguignonne aux XIIe et XIIIe siècles*, *Cluny*, pp. 142-152 and plates XLV-LVI.

Émile Mâle, *Études sur l'art de l'époque romane*, in *Revue de Paris*, 1921, pp. 495-496, and *l'Art religieux du XIIe siècle*, pp. 319-321, 388, fig. 186-188.

On the dating of the capitals preserved in the museum see Kingsley Porter, *La Sculpture du XIIe siècle en Bourgogne*, in *Gazette des Beaux-Arts*, 1920, second series, pp. 73-94.

Paul Deschamps, *Notes sur la sculpture romane en Bourgogne*, in *Gazette des Beaux-Arts*, 1922, second series, pp. 61-80.

Charles Oursel, *Le rôle et la place de Cluny dans la Renaissance de la Sculpture en France à l'époque romane d'après quelques études et travaux récents*, in *Revue Archéologique*, 1923, I (Vol. XVII), pp. 255-289.

Paul Deschamps, *Les Débuts de la Sculpture romane en Languedoc et en Bourgogne*, a reply to M. C. Oursel, in *Revue Archéologique*, Vol. XIX, 1924, pp. 163-173. M. Oursel has reproduced the above-mentioned article, with corrections and additions, in his book: *L'Art roman de Bourgogne* (1928), chapter V: *la Sculpture*, pp. 167-207.

Kenneth John Conant, articles quoted above, note 92.

Louis Bréhier, *Questions d'art roman bourguignon*, in *Revue archéologique*, 1929, pp. 311-316. - We intend to deal with this question again very shortly in an article which will appear in the *Revue de l'Art*.

Casts of these capitals are in the Trocadéro.

94] Paul Deschamps, *Notes sur la Sculpture romane en Bourgogne*, in *Gazette des Beaux-Arts*, 1922, second series, pp. 61-80.

95] *Histoire de l'Art*, I, part II, p. 638.

95a] Denise Jalabert, *La Sculpture Romane*, Paris, Stock, n. d., duodecimo, p. 55.

95b] *Apologia ad Guillelmum, Sancti Theodorici Remensis abbatem*, in *Sancti Bernardi opera*, edited by Mabillon, edition 4a (Gaume), Vol. I, part 1 (1839), col. 1242-1244 (cf. 1690 edition col. 538-540. - Migne, *Patr. lat.*, vol. CLXXXII, col. 914-916):

Ceterum in claustris coram legentibus fratribus quid facit ridicula monstruositas, mira quaedam deformis formositas ac formosa deformitas? Quid ibi immundae simiae? Quid feri leones? Quid monstruosi centauri? Quid semihomines? Quid maculosae tigrides? Quid milites pugnantes? Quid venatores tubicinantes? Videas sub uno capite multa corpora, et rursus in uno corpore capita multa. Cernitur hinc in quadrupede cauda serpentis, illinc in pisce caput quadrupedis. Ibi bestia praefert equum, capram trahens retro dimidiam; hic cornutum animal equum gestat posterius. Tam multa denique, tamque mira diversarum formarum ubique varietas apparet ut magis legere libeat in marmoribus quam in codicibus, totumque diem occupare singula ista mirando quam in lege Dei meditando. Proh Deo! si non pudet ineptiarum, cur vel non piget expensarum?

96] Victor Terret, *La Sculpture Bourguignonne aux XIIe et XIIIe siècles: Autun*. Autun 1925, 2 vols., royal quarto, 129 pages and 78 plates; 61 pages and 87 plates.

97] Vicomte P. de Truchis, in *Congrès archéologique de France*, held at Avallon in 1907, pp. 103-118, plate.

V. Terret, *La Sculpture Bourguignonne...*, *Cluny*. Autun and Paris 1914, plates 24 and 26.

Kingsley Porter, *Romanesque Sculpture...*, Vol. II, plates 52-62.

98] Charles Porée, in *Congrès archéologique de France*, held at Avallon in 1907, pp. 24-43.

Charles Porée, *L'Abbaye de Vézelay* (*Coll. des Petites Monographies des grands édifices de la France*), Paris, Laurens, n. d., 96 pages, fig.

M. l'Abbé Victor Terret is preparing for publication two volumes in royal quarto on Vézelay, which will form a continuation of his *Études sur la Sculpture Bourguignonne, Cluny* (1 Vol.) and *Autun* (2 Vols.).

99] Charles Porée, *L'Abbaye de Vézelay*, p. 15.

100] Certain authors are of the opinion that the main part of the sculptural decoration at Vézelay should be dated between about 1104 and about 1132 (see Ch. Oursel, *L'Art roman de Bourgogne*, 1928, p. 182). We have insisted (*Notes sur la sculpture romane en Bourgogne*, in *Gazette des Beaux-Arts*, 1922, July-August) on the importance which must be attached to the fire of 1120. In addition to this our colleague and friend, M. Jean Vallery-Radot, has drawn our attention to the fact that Renaud de Semur, who was abbot of Vézelay from 1106 to 1128, is described in his epitaph as *reparator monasterii Vezeliacensis*. See J. Vallery-Radot, *Églises romanes de France, Filiation et échange d'influences*, La Renaissance du livre (in course of publication); and his *Analogies des Églises de Saint-Fortunat de Charlieu et d'Anzy-le-Duc*, in *Bulletin Monumental*, 1929, pp. 265-266. Further, it is generally considered that the consecration mentioned as having taken place in 1132 referred only to the narthex; M. Vallery-Radot accepts the hypothesis advanced by a German savant, M. Paul Franke, who thinks that the *ecclesia peregrinorum* consecrated in that year was not merely the narthex, but the entire church of Ste.-Madeleine, which was frequented by numerous pilgrims.

101] Émile Mâle, *L'Art religieux du XIIe siècle*, pp. 326-332.

102] Charles Porée, in *Congrès archéologique de France*, held at Avallon in 1907, pp. 3-10, plate.
Kingsley Porter, *Romanesque Sculpture...*, Vol. II, plates 137-141.
Jules Roussel, *op. cit.*, plate 3.
A cast of the right doorway of the façade is in the Trocadéro.

103] Ed. Jeannez, in F. Thiollier, *L'Art roman à Charlieu et en Brionnais*, Montbrison 1892.
Lasteyrie, *L'Architecture... à l'époque romane*, p. 667, fig. 682.
A. Rhein, in *Congrès archéologique de France*, held at Moulins and Nevers in 1913, p. 290.
Émile Mâle, *L'Art religieux du XIIe siècle*, p. 431, fig. 247.
Kingsley Porter, *op. cit.*, Vol. II, plate 95.
J. Vallery-Radot, *Les Analogies des églises de Saint-Fortunat de Charlieu et Anzy-le-Duc*, in *Bulletin Monumental*, 1929, pp. 243-267.
V. Terret, *La Sculpture Bourguignonne, Cluny*, plate XXXII.
G. von Lücken, article quoted, plate 31.

104] F. Thiollier, *L'Art roman à Charlieu et en Brionnais*, Montbrison 1892.
Lasteyrie, *L'Architecture... à l'époque romane*, p. 668, fig. 683.
Émile Mâle, *L'Art religieux du XII siècle...*, p. 429, fig. 246.
Kingsley Porter, *Romanesque Sculpture...*, Vol. II, plates 93-94.
G. von Lücken, article quoted, plate 32.

105] Christiane Malo, *Les Églises romanes dans l'ancien diocèse de Chalon-sur-Saône*, thesis presented at the École des Chartes in 1929.

106] Émile Mâle, *L'Art religieux du XIIe siècle*, p. 92, fig. 78.
Kingsley Porter, *Romanesque Sculpture...*, Vol. II, plates 104-105.
V. Terret, *La Sculpture Bourguignonne aux XIIe et XIIIe siècles, Cluny*, plate 29.
A. Mayeux, *Le Tympan du Portail de Montceaux-l'Étoile*, in *Bulletin Monumental*, 1921, pp. 239-244, plate.
G. von Lücken, article quoted, plate 39.

107] Kingsley Porter, in *Fogg Museum Notes*, 1922, I, pp. 2 and 23. - *Romanesque Sculpture of the pilgrimage roads*, Vol. I, pp. 114-115; Vol. II, plates 62-66.
G. Sanoner, *Iconographie de la Bible...*, in *Bulletin Monumental*, 1921, pp. 218-219.

107a] Marcel Aubert, in *Bulletin des Musées*, 1929, and the same author's: *Un Chapiteau roman de Moutier-Saint-Jean (Côte-d'Or)*, in *Monuments et Mémoires* published by the Académie des Inscriptions et Belles-Lettres (Fondation Piot), Vol. XXX, 1929, plate.

108] Kingsley Porter, *Romanesque Sculpture...*, Vol. II, plates 84 and 85.
G. von Lücken, article quoted, plates 37 and 38.

109] Émile Mâle, *L'Art religieux du XIIe siècle*, p. 91, fig. 77.
V. Terret, *La Sculpture Bourguignonne aux XIIe et XIIIe siècles, Cluny*, plate 29.
Kingsley Porter, *Romanesque Sculpture...*, Vol. II, plate 96.
G. von Lücken, article quoted, plate 29.

110] F. Thiollier, *L'Art roman à Charlieu et en Brionnais*, pp. 73-80, plate.
Congrès archéologique de France, held at Moulins and Nevers in 1913, pl., p. 290.
Émile Mâle, *L'Art religieux du XIIe siècle*, p. 35, fig. 35.
Kingsley Porter, *Romanesque Sculpture*, Vol. II, plates 97-99.

111] *Catalogue* of the Musée de la Commission des Antiquités du Département de la Côte-d'Or, Dijon 1894, quarto, No. 1138, pp. 184-185 and plate XVIII.
Lasteyrie, *L'Architecture religieuse à l'époque romane*, pp. 674-676.
Émile Mâle, *L'Art religieux du XIIe siècle*, pp. 114, 419.
V. Terret, *La Sculpture Bourguignonne..., Cluny*, pp. 124-125 and plate XL.
V. Flipo, *La Cathédrale de Dijon*, (*Coll. des petites Monographies des grands édifices de la France*, 1928, fig. p. 31.
Kingsley Porter, *op. cit.*, Vol. II, pl. 136.- G. von Lücken, article quoted, pl. 45.

112] See note 111.

There is a reproduction of this tympanum in the catalogue of the Musée de la Commission des Antiquités de la Côte-d'Or, No. 1139, plate XVIII.

V. Terret, *La Sculpture Bourguignonne...*, *Cluny*, plate XLI.

Kingsley Porter, *op. cit.*, Vol. II, plate 135.

Paul Deschamps, *Étude sur la Paléographie des Inscriptions Lapidaires...*, in *Bulletin Monumental*, 1929, plate XXV, fig. 48. See also Émile Mâle, *L'Art religieux du XIIe siècle*, p. 388.

G. von Lücken, article quoted, plate 45.

113] Paul Deschamps, in *Bulletin Monumental*, 1922, p. 383.

114] F. Thiollier, *op. cit.*, plate.

Lasteyrie, *L'Architecture... à l'époque romane*, p. 673, fig. 688.

A. Rhein, in *Congrès archéologique de France*, held at Moulins and Nevers in 1913, fig. pp. 248-251.

Émile Mâle, *L'Art religieux du XII siècle*, pp. 420-429, fig. 241.

Kingsley Porter, *Romanesque Sculpture...*, Vol. II, plates 108-110.

G. von Lücken, article quoted, plate 42.

Cast in the Trocadéro.

114a] For this information we are indebted to Dr. Vitaut, president of the Société des Amis de Charlieu.

114b] *Art et Archéologie dans le Département de la Loire* (1898), p. 43.

115] Lasteyrie, *L'Architecture à l'époque romane*, p. 675, fig. 689.

Kingsley Porter, *Romanesque Sculpture*, Vol. II, plate 111.

G. von Lücken, article quoted, plate 43.

116] Émile Mâle, *L'Art religieux du XIIe siècle*, pp. 77, 114, 419, 420 and fig. 240.

117] Lasteyrie, *L'Architecture à l'époque romane*, p. 588, fig. 586.

V. Terret, *La Sculpture Bourguignonne aux XIIe et XIIIe siècles...*, *Cluny*, plate XXXI.

Émile Mâle, *L'Art religieux du XIIe siècle*, pp. 206-207, fig. 149.

Kingsley Porter, *Romanesque Sculpture...*, Vol. II, plate 143.

118] Kingsley Porter, *Romanesque Sculpture...*, Vol. II, plate 146.

G. von Lücken, article quoted, plate 39.

119] V. Terret, *La Sculpture Bourguignonne aux XIIe et XIIIe siècles...*, *Cluny*, plate 17.

Kingsley Porter, *Romanesque Sculpture...*, Vol. II, plates 86-91.

120] Jacques Meurgey, *Étude archéologique sur Saint-André de Bagé* (Extract from the *Mémoirs* of the Soc. des Arts et des Sciences de Tournus, Vol. XXIX, 1929, 12 pages, 14 plates).

121] J. de Font-Réaulx, in *Congrès archéologique de France*, held at Valence and Montélimar in 1923, fig. pp. 149 and 151.

122] V. Terret, *La Sculpture Bourguignonne aux XIIe et XIIIe siècles...*, Cluny, plate 16.
Louis Serbat, in *Congrès archéologique de France*, held at Moulins and Nevers in
1913, pp. 374-400.

123] Lasteyrie, *Études sur la Sculpture Française au Moyen Age*, in *Monuments et Mémoires* published by the Académie des Inscriptions et Belles-Lettres (Fondation Piot), Vol. VIII, 1902, plate 4, fig. 1 and 2.

124] F. Thiollier, *Les débris du Tombeau de saint Lazare*, in *Bulletin archéologique*, 1894,
pp. 445-457, plate.
Lasteyrie, article quoted, plate X.
V. Terret, *La Sculpture Bourguignonne...*, *Autun*, Vol. II, plates 82 and 83.
Kingsley Porter, *Romanesque Sculpture...*, Vol. II, plates 147-149.
Paul Vitry, *Un fragment du tombeau de saint Lazare d'Autun au Musée du Louvre*,
in *Monuments et Mémoires* published by the Académie des Inscriptions et
Belles-Lettres (Fondation Piot), Vol. XVI, 1923, p. 165 ff.
Marcel Aubert, *Une nouvelle sculpture bourguignonne au Musée du Louvre*, in *Bul-
letin Monumental*, 1924, pp. 127-132, fig.

125] F. Thiollier, *Vestiges de l'Art roman en Lyonnais*, in *Bulletin archéologique*, 1892,
pp. 396-411, fig. and plates 25-27. - Dr. J. Birot, *Les Chapiteaux des pilastres de
Saint-Martin-d'Ainay à Lyon*, in *Congrès archéologique de France*, held at Avallon
in 1907, pp. 527-536, fig.

126] J. Vallery-Radot, *Influences Irlandaises dans la Sculpture*, in the *Bulletin* of the
Soc. Nat. des Antiquaires de France, 1922, pp. 158-159. - *La Sculpture Fran-
çaise du XIIe siècle et les Influences Irlandaises*, in *Revue de la Sculpture Française*,
May 1924, pp. 335-344, fig.

127] L. Bégule, *L'église Saint-Maurice, ancienne cathédrale de Vienne*, Lyons 1914,
plate 13 and fig. 67, 160-162.

128] L. Bégule, *op. cit.*, fig. 163.

129] L. Bégule, *Antiquités et richesses d'Art du Département du Rhône*, 1925, p. 75, fig. 90.

130] J. David, *Les Routes de l'Art roman, notes sur la sculpture chrétienne au XIIe siècle
dans la vallée du Rhône*, Grenoble 1924.

131] *Congrès archéologique de France*, held at Valence and Montélimar in 1923,
p. 244, fig.
Lasteyrie, *L'Architecture... à l'époque romane*, p. 665, fig. 670.
Kingsley Porter, *Romanesque Sculpture...*, Vol. VIII, plates 1187-1189.

132] N. Thiollier, *L'Architecture religieuse à l'époque romane dans l'ancien diocèse du Puy*, Le Puy 1900, p. 60 ff.
N. Thiollier, in *Congrès archéologique de France*, held at Valence and Montélimar in 1923, pp. 128-145, plate.
Kingsley Porter, *Romanesque Sculpture*, Vol. VIII, plate 1186.

133] Kingsley Porter, *Romanesque Sculpture*, Vol. VIII, plate 1185.

134] F. Thiollier, *Vestiges de l'Art roman en Lyonnais*, in *Bulletin Archéologique*, 1892, pp. 408 and 411, plate XXVII.

135] Émile Mâle, *op. cit.*, pp. 388-390 and 430, fig. 224.
Kingsley Porter, *Romanesque Sculpture*, Vol. VIII, plates 1149-1152.

136] See above, note 127, plate 48.

137] L. Bégule, *L'église Saint-Maurice, ancienne cathédrale de Vienne*, Lyons 1914, p. 106, fig. 125.

138] L. Bégule, *op. cit.*, fig. 127, 129, 130.
Casts at the Trocadéro.

139] L. Bégule, *op. cit.*, fig. 132, 134-154, 156-158.

140] L. Bégule, *op. cit.*, fig. 131.

141] Lasteyrie, *Études sur la Sculpture... au moyen âge*, in *Monuments et Mémoires* published by the Académie des Inscriptions et Belles-Lettres (Fondation Piot), Vol. VIII, 1902, pp. 127-130, fig. 33.
Kingsley Porter, *Romanesque Sculpture...*, Vol. IX, plates 1334-1338.

142] F. de Mély, in *Revue Archéologique*, 1908, I, pp. 254-264.
Lasteyrie, *L'Architecture à l'époque romane*, pp. 684-685, fig. 696.
L. Bégule, *Antiquités et Richesses d'Art du Département du Rhône*, Lyons 1925, royal quarto, pp. 50-53.
Kingsley Porter, *Romanesque Sculpture...*, Vol. II, plates 12-16.

143] Ch. Perrat, *L'Autel d'Avenas, la Légende de Ganelon et les expéditions de Louis VII en Bourgogne (1166-1172)*, in *Bulletin historique et archéologique du diocèse de Lyon*, 1927 and 1929.

144] Louis Bréhier, *Les Origines de la Sculpture romane*, in *Revue des Deux-Mondes*, 1912, August 15th, pp. 870-901.
Les Origines de l'Architecture romane, II: *La naissance de la Sculpture Monumentale*, in *Revue de l'Art*, 1920, pp. 263-280.
La Cathédrale de Clermont au Xe siècle et sa statue d'or de la Vierge, in *Renaissance de l'Art français*, 1924, April, pp. 205-210, fig.

144a] Marcel Aubert, communication in the *Bulletin* of the Soc. Nat. des Antiquaires de France, 1928, pp. 116-118.

145] On the commencements of sculpture in Auvergne see: Roger Grand, *Recherches sur l'Art roman à Aurillac*, fig., in *Revue de la Haute-Auvergne*, 1901.
Louis Bréhier, *Les Origines de l'Architecture romane*, II: *La naissance de la Sculpture Monumentale*, in *Revue de l'Art*, 1920, pp. 263-280, 10 fig., 1 plate.

146] Louis Bréhier, *Les Origines de l'Art roman auvergnat*, I: *L'œuvre des Chapitres*, II:
L'œuvre des Monastères, in *Revue Mabillon*, 1923.

147] Works cited above, and *L'Homme dans la Sculpture Romane*, Paris, Librairie de
France, n. d., quarto, 44 pages, 10 figures and LII plates.

148] L. Bréhier, *L'Homme dans la Sculpture romane*, p. 28, fig. 9.

149] L. Bréhier, *Les Chapiteaux historiés de Notre-Dame-du-Port*, in *Revue de l'Art chrétien*, 1912, pp. 248-262 and 339-350, fig.
Marcel Aubert, in *Congrès archéologique de France*, held at Clermont-Ferrand in
1924, pp. 48-56.
Kingsley Porter, *op. cit.*, Vol. VIII, plates 1167-1184.

150] Abbé G. Rochias, *Les Chapiteaux de l'Église de Saint-Nectaire*, in *Bulletin Monumental*, 1929, 32 pages, 22 figures.
L. Bréhier, *Le Martyre de Saint Sébastien sur un chapiteau de Saint-Nectaire*, in *Revue
d'Auvergne*, October-December, 1921.
Deshoulières, in *Congrès archéologique de France*, held at Clermont-Ferrand in
1924, pp. 265-286, fig.
Kingsley Porter, *op. cit.*, Vol. VIII, plates 1190-1204.

151] Jules Roussel, *La Sculpture Française, époque romane*, plate 45.
Cast at the Trocadéro.

152] Camille Martin, *L'Art roman en France*, third series, plates 10-16.
Kingsley Porter, *op. cit.*, Vol. VIII, plates 1212-1214.
Ch. Terrasse, in *Congrès archéologique de France*, held at Clermont-Ferrand in
1924, pp. 80-100.

153] Deshoulières, in *Congrès archéologique de France*, held at Clermont-Ferrand in
1924, pp. 144-154, fig.

154] E. Lefèvre-Pontalis, *Les dates de Saint-Julien de Brioude*, in *Congrès archéologique
de France*, held at Le Puy in 1904, pp. 542-555, numerous illustrations of the
capitals.

155] Deshoulières, in *Congrès archéologique de France*, held at Clermont-Ferrand in
1924, pp. 251-262, fig.

156] Louis Bréhier, *Les Chapiteaux du Chevet de Saint-Pierre de Blesle*, extract from the *Almanach de Brioude*, 1929, 20 pages, 4 plates.

157] Abbé Luzuy, in *Congrès archéologique de France*, held at Moulins and Nevers in 1913, pp. 124-138, fig.
Kingsley Porter, *op. cit.*, Vol. VIII, plate 1223.
Jean Verrier, *Les Églises romanes d'Auvergne*, in *Beaux-Arts*, second year, No. 15, August 1st 1924, fig. p. 232.

158] Kingsley Porter, *op. cit.*, Vol. VIII, plate 1139.

159] Kingsley Porter, *op. cit.*, Vol. VIII, plate 1250.

160] L. Bégule, *Les incrustations décoratives des Cathédrales de Lyon et de Vienne*, 1905, p. 33, fig. 59.

161] There is a cast at the Trocadéro.

162] Taylor and Nodier, *Voyage pittoresque et romantique à travers la France, Auvergne*, 1831, Vol. II, plate CLII.
N. Thiollier, in *Congrès archéologique de France*, held at Le Puy in 1904, pp. 77-78.
Paul Deschamps, in the *Bulletin* of the Soc. Nat. des Antiquaires de France, 1924, pp. 206-213.

163] Abbé Joseph H. M. Clément, *Essai archéologique et historique sur l'Église Sainte-Croix de Saint-Pourçain-sur-Sioule...*, Moulins 1907.

164] Canon Clément, *L'Église d'Autry-Issard*, in the *Bulletin* of the Soc. d'émulation du Bourbonnais, 1909.
Kingsley Porter, *op. cit.*, Vol. VIII, plate 1141.

165] E. Lefèvre-Pontalis, in *Congrès archéologique de France*, held at Moulins and Nevers in 1913, pp. 224-226, fig.
Kingsley Porter, *op. cit.*, Vol. VIII, plate 1251.

166] Jean Hubert and Jacques Barge, *Le Prieuré de Ruffec-en-Berry*, in *Bulletin Monumental*, 1929, pp. 205-241.

167] Ad. de Rochemonteix, *Les Églises romanes de la Haute-Auvergne*, Paris 1902, quarto.
Louis Bréhier, *La Sculpture romane en Haute-Auvergne* (lecture delivered before the Société de la Haute-Auvergne at Aurillac, February 3rd 1924), Aurillac 1926, 22 pages, 17 figures.

168] René Fage, *L'Église de la Graulière*, in *Bulletin Monumental*, 1909, pl. p. 92.

169] On the Cahors sculptures, see above, note 77.

170] Émile Mâle, *L'Art religieux du XIIe siècle*, pp. 92, 398-399, and fig. 228.
Kingsley Porter, *op. cit.*, Vol. VIII, plates 1246-1249.

171] A. Mayeux, *Le Tympan de Collonges*, in the *Bulletin* of the Soc. scientifique et archéologique de la Corrèze, Brive 1923, pp. 164-178.
René Fage, *Le Tympan de l'Église de Collonges*, in the *Bulletin* of the Soc. scientifique et archéologique de la Corrèze, Brive 1923, pp. 209-219, plate.

172] René Fage, *L'Église de Saint-Chamant et son tympan sculpté*, in the *Bulletin* of the Soc. scientifique et archéologique de la Corrèze, 1924. - See also the same author's: *Clochers à hourds du Bas-Limousin*, in *Bulletin Monumental*, 1907, pp. 79-82.
Kingsley Porter, *op. cit.*, Vol. VIII, plate 1276.

172a] René Fage, *L'Église de Lubersac*, in *Bulletin Monumental*, 1912, pp. 38-58, fig.

173] *Chronique de Maleu, Chanoine de Saint-Junien*, died in 1322, published for the first time by M. L'Abbé Arbellot, Saint-Junien and Paris 1847, octavo, 116 pages.
Abbé Arbellot, *Notice sur le tombeau de Saint-Junien*, Limoges 1847, 24 pages, 3 plates.
Prosper Mérimée, *Notes d'un voyage en Auvergne*, Paris 1838, p. 109.
R. de Lasteyrie, *L'Architecture en France à l'époque romane*, pp. 666-667, fig. 681.
René Fage, in *Bulletin Monumental*, 1906, pp. 113-128, fig., and *Congrès archéologique de France*, held at Limoges in 1921, pp. 214-236, fig.
Kingsley Porter, *Romanesque Sculpture...*, Vol. I, p. 155, and Vol. IV, plates 450-452.
Paul Deschamps, *Les Inscriptions du Tombeau de Saint-Junien et la date de ses sculptures*, in *Monuments et Mémoires* published by the Académie des Inscriptions et Belles-Lettres (Fondation Piot), 1929, Vol. XXIX, plates VIII and IX.

174] A. Bouillet and L. Serrières, *Sainte Foy, Vierge et Martyre*, Rodez, E. Carrère, 1900, folio, XII + 782 pages, 6 plates and numerous illustrations.

175] Victor Mortet, *Recueil de Textes relatifs à l'histoire de l'architecture..., XIe et XIIe siècles*, Paris 1911, text No. XXVIII, pp. 105-106, from the *Liber miraculorum sancte Fidis*, l. IV, published by Abbé Bouillet (1897).

176] Kingsley Porter, *op. cit.*, Vol. IV, plate 386.

177] Kingsley Porter, *op. cit.*, Vol. IV, plates 390-391.

178] Kingsley Porter, *op. cit.*, Vol. IV, plate 387.

179] Paul Deschamps, *Étude sur la paléographie des Inscriptions lapidaires de la fin de l'époque Mérovingienne aux dernières années du XIIe siècle*, in *Bulletin Monumental*, 1929, plate XV, fig. 29.

180] Kingsley Porter, *op. cit.*, Vol. IV, plates 392-401.

181] Émile Mâle, *L'Art religieux du XIIe siècle*, pp. 410-416, fig. 235.
Louis Bréhier, *L'École romane de Sculpture auvergnate et le Portail de Conques-en-Rouergue*, in *Actes du Congrès d'Histoire de l'Art*, Paris 1924, Vol. III, pp. 464-478.

181a] Émile Mâle, *L'Art religeux du XIIe siècle*, pp. 415-416.
Louis Saltet, *Perse et Conques*, in the *Bulletin* of the Société Archéologique du Midi de la France, No. 46, 1924, pp. 72-92, 3 plates. - This author believes on the contrary, that the sculpture at Perse is the prototype of Conques.

182] The same is true of architecture. In the last period of his teaching Eugène Lefèvre-Pontalis included a "School of the Lower Valley of the Loire" in his classification of the Romanesque schools of architecture.
Cf. Deshoulières, *La Théorie d'Eugène Lefèvre-Pontalis sur les écoles romanes* in *Bulletin Monumental*, 1923, p. 242 ff.

183] Deshoulières, in *Congrès archéologique de France*, held at Moulins and Nevers in 1913, pp. 24-43, fig.

184] See above, p. 43 and note 116.

185] Deshoulières, in *Congrès archéologique de France*, held at Moulins and Nevers in 1913, plate on p. 214. - *Souvigny et Bourbon-l'Archambault*, in *Collection des Petites Monographies des grands édifices de la France*, Paris, Laurens, n. d., pp. 61-63 and fig.
Émile Mâle, *L'Art religieux du XIIe siècle...*, pp. 323-325 and fig. 189.
Jules Roussel, *La Sculpture Française, époque romane*, plate 32.
Cast in the Trocadéro.

186] *Congrès archéologique de France*, held at Moulins and Nevers in 1913, p. 366.
Victor Terret, *La Sculpture Bourguignonne aux XIIe et XIIIe siècles, Cluny*, plate XV.
Émile Mâle, *L'Art religieux du XIIe siècle*, pp. 424-425 and fig. 244.
Kingsley Porter, *op. cit.*, Vol. II, plates 126-133.

187] Lasteyrie, *Études sur la Sculpture Française au Moyen âge*, p. 27 and plate IV.
Louis Serbat, in *Congrès archéologique de France*, held at Moulins and Nevers in 1913, pp. 374-400, fig.
Camille Martin, *L'Art roman en France*, first series, plates 36-46.
Mme Lefrançois-Pillion, in *Beaux-Arts*, July 15th 1924, pp. 212-214, fig.
Kingsley Porter, *op. cit.*, Vol. II, plates 115-123.
Jules Roussel, *La Sculpture Française, époque romane*, plates 6 and 29.

188] Kingsley Porter, *op. cit.*, Vol. II, plates 112-114.
Jules Roussel, *La Sculpture Française, époque romane*, plate 7.
G. von Lücken, article quoted, plate 47.

189] Jean Hubert, *L'Abbatiale Notre-Dame de Déols*, in *Bulletin Monumental*, 1927, pp. 5-66, plate on p. 48.

190] Deshoulières, *Le Tympan de l'Église Saint-Pierre-le-Puellier*, in *Memoirs* of the Société des Antiquaires du Centre, Vol. 38, Bourges 1919, 11 pages, plate.
Émile Mâle, *L'Art religieux du XIIe siècle*, p. 435, fig. 251.
Kingsley Porter, *op. cit.*, Vol. VIII, plate 1262.

191] Abbé de Roffignac, *Le Tympan de la Porte de Saint-Ursin de Bourges, son caractère religieux*, in *Memoirs* of the Société des Antiquaires du Centre, Vol. XXXVI, 1913, pp. 47-67.
Jules Roussel, *La Sculpture française, époque romane*, plates 32 and 36.
Marcel Aubert, *L'Art français à l'époque romane, architecture et sculpture*, I (1929), plate 16.
Cast at the Trocadéro.

192] H. Focillon, *Apôtres et Jongleurs, étude de mouvement*, in *Gazette des Beaux-Arts*, January 1929, p. 25 and fig. on page 23.

193] Deshoulières, in *Congrès archéologique de France*, held at Moulins and Nevers in 1913, pp. 174-182, fig.

193a] Deshoulières, *ibid.*, p. 49.

194] Lefèvre-Pontalis, in *Congrès archéologique de France*, held at Moulins and Nevers in 1913, p. 292 ff.

195] Deshoulières, *Les Églises romanes du Berri*, in *Bulletin Monumental*, 1909, pp. 469-492, plate and figure.

196] Marcel Aubert, *L'Église Abbatiale de Selles-sur-Cher*, in *Bulletin Monumental*, 1913, pp. 387-403, plate and figure.
Congrès archéologique de France, held at Blois in 1925, pp. 203-214, plate and fig.
Kingsley Porter, *op. cit.*, Vol. VII, plates 1077-1082.
Marcel Aubert, *L'Art français à l'époque romane*, I, plate 52.

197] Deshoulières, in *Congrès archéologique de France*, held at Blois in 1925, pp. 378-410, plate and figure.
Camille Martin, *L'Art roman en France*, second series, plates 13-18.

198] M. Aubert, in *Congrès archéologique de France*, held at Blois in 1925, figure on p. 237.

199] Deshoulières, in *Congrès archéologique de France*, held at Blois in 1925, figure on p. 450.

200] M. Deshoulières had already noticed this; cf. his *Nouvelles remarques sur les Églises romanes du Berri*, in *Bulletin Monumental*, 1922, pp. 22-23, fig.

201] E. Lefèvre-Pontalis, *L'Église de La Celle-Bruère*, in *Bulletin Monumental*, 1910, pp. 272-284, fig.

202] La Celle-Bruère: figure in *Bulletin Monumental*, 1909, p. 492.

203] Deshoulières, in *Bulletin Monumental*, 1922, p. 25.

204] Émile Mâle, *L'Art religieux du XIIe siècle*, pp. 355-356.

205] Camille Martin, *L'Art roman en France*, third series, plates 51-58.
Kingsley Porter, *op. cit.*, Vol. VII, plates 904-905.

206] Kingsley Porter, *op. cit.*, Vol. II, plates 82-83.

207] Kingsley Porter, *op. cit.*, Vol. VII, plates 1100-1107.

208] J. Vallery-Radot, *Loches*, in *Coll. des Petites Monographies des grands édifices de la France*, 1926, pp. 65-82, fig.
Camille Martin, *L'Art roman en France*, third series, plates 17-22.
Kingsley Porter, *op. cit.*, Vol. VII, plates 1108-1119.

209] Abbé Rocher, *Histoire de l'Abbaye de Saint-Benoît-sur-Loire*, Orleans 1865.
L. Delisle, *Vie de Gauzlin, Abbé de Fleuri*, in *Memoirs* of the Soc. archéologique de l'Orléanais, Vol. II, 1853, pp. 257-322.
M. Prou and A. Vidier, *Recueil des Chartes de Saint-Benoît-sur-Loire*, Vol. I, 1900.

210] Jean Malo-Renault, *Les Sculpteurs Romans de Saint-Benoît-sur-Loire*, in *Revue de l'Art*, 1927, pp. 209-222 and 319-322.

211] V. Mortet, *Recueil de textes relatifs à l'Histoire de l'Architecture..., XIe-XIIe siècles* (Paris 1911), Text No. VII, pp. 33-34.

212] *Miracula Sancti Benedicti*, book VIII, chap. XXV and XXVI, in V. Mortet, *Recueil de Textes relatifs à l'Histoire de l'Architecture..., XIe-XIIe siècles* (Paris 1911), Text No. II, p. 11 and note 2.

213] Camille Martin, *op. cit.*, first series, plates 1-10.
Kingsley Porter, *op. cit.*, Vol. X, plates 1414-1420.
Marcel Aubert, *L'Art français à l'époque romane, Architecture et Sculpture*, Morancé edition, I, 1929, plates 53-60.

214] Selles-sur-Cher, articles by M. Aubert quoted above, note 196.
Kingsley Porter, *op. cit.*, Vol. VII, plates 1074-1082.
St.-Benoît, Camille Martin, *op. cit.*, first series, plate 10.
St.-Aignan, *Congrès archéologique de France*, held at Blois in 1925, p. 388, fig.

215] St.-Benoît, Camille Martin, *op. cit.*, first series, plate 5.
St.-Aignan, Camille Martin, *op. cit.*, second series, plate 16.

216] St.-Benoît, Kingsley Porter, *op. cit.*, Vol. X, plate 1420.
J. Roussel, *op. cit.*, plate 29.
There is a cast of this capital in the Trocadéro.
St.-Aignan, *Congrès archéologique de France*, held at Blois in 1925, p. 389.

217] St.-Benoît, Camille Martin, *op. cit.*, first series, plate 6.
Émile Mâle, *L'Art religieux du XIIe siècle*, p. 336 and note 4, fig. 195.
St.-Aignan, Camille Martin, *op. cit.*, second series, plate 17.

218] Baroness Brincard intends to publish very shortly an abundantly illustrated book entitled *"Cunault et les chapiteaux romans de l'Anjou"*.

219] Lasteyrie, *L'Architecture à l'époque romane...*, p. 630, fig. 640.
Kingsley Porter, *Romanesque Sculpture...*, Vol. VII, plate 923.
A. Rhein, in *Congrès archéologique de France*, held at Angers and Saumur in 1910, Vol. I, pp. 48-61, plate and fig.

220] Camille Martin, *op. cit.*, first series, plates 66-67.

221] Camille Martin, *op. cit.*, plates 64-65.
Dr. Lesueur, *L'Église Abbatiale Saint-Lomer de Blois*, in *Bulletin Monumental*, 1923, pp. 36-65, plates.
L'Église et l'Abbaye bénédictine de Saint-Lomer de Blois, Blois 1925, pl. and fig. See also the same author's: *Saint-Lomer*, in *Congrès archéologique de France*, held at Blois in 1925, pp. 93-124.

222] André Michel, *Histoire de l'Art*, Vol. I, part 2, p. 657, fig. 368.
Lasteyrie, *L'Architecture à l'époque romane*, p. 355, fig. 375.
Canon Urseau, in *Congrès archéologique de France*, held at Angers and Saumur in 1910, Vol. I, pp. 218-221, plate.
Kingsley Porter, *op. cit.*, Vol. VII, plates 965-972 and 1069, 1070.

223] J.-A. Brutails, *Les Vieilles Églises de la Gironde*, Bordeaux 1912, pp. 282-284.

224] J.-A. Brutails, *op. cit.*, pp. 8-13 and plate II.
Kingsley Porter, *op. cit.*, Vol. VII, plates 920-921.

225] Kingsley Porter, *op. cit.*, Vol. VII, plates 1041-1044.

226] Magdeleine Ferry, *Les Portes romanes des Églises du Sud-Ouest de la France*, in *Positions des thèses soutenues à l'École des Chartes en* 1928, p. 44.
Kingsley Porter, *op. cit.*, Vol. VIII, plates 926-928.

227] On the Mimizan portal, see G. Beaurain, *Le Portail de l'Église de Mimizan étudié dans ses rapports avec l'histoire du costume et du mobilier au moyen âge*, Dax, octavo, n. d., 58 pages, plates and figures.

228] On Romanesque sculpture in the department of the Basses-Pyrénées (apse of the cathedral of Lescar, church of Ste.-Croix and porch of the church of Ste.-Marie at Oloron, the portal of Morlaas, and the ruins of the abbey church of St.-Pé) see Lanore, *Notice historique et archéologique sur l'Église Notre-Dame de Lescar*, Paris 1903.

229] Ch. Dangibeaud, *L'École de Sculpture romane saintongeaise*, in *Bulletin archéologique*, 1910, pp. 22-49 and plates III-XVI.
Deshoulières, *Les façades des Églises romanes charentaises*, in *Congrès archéologique de France*, held at Angoulême in 1912, Vol. II, pp. 180-194, plate.

J. George and Alexis Guérin-Boutaud, *Les Églises romanes de l'ancien diocèse d'Angoulême*, Paris 1928, royal octavo, 347 pages, 303 figures, 1 plan.

L. Bréhier, *L'Art roman Auvergnat et l'École Saintongeaise*, in *Revue d'Auvergne*, 1917, pp. 1-3.

230] Paul Deschamps, *Étude sur la renaissance de la sculpture en France à l'époque romane*, in *Bulletin Monumental*, 1925, pp. 78-81.

231] Dom Martin, *La Religion des Gaulois*, Paris 1727, Vol. I, p. 346 ff., fig., and Joseph de Malafosse, *Les colonnes gallo-romaines de l'Église Notre-Dame de la Daurade*, in *Album des Monuments de l'Art ancien du Midi de la France*, Vol. I, 1897, p. 106, fig.

232] Émile Mâle, *L'Art religieux du XIIe siècle...*, pp. 248-251, fig. 162. - *Représentation de Constantin à Châteauneuf-sur-Charente*, in *Congrès archéologique de France*, held at Angoulême in 1912, Vol. I, p. 396, Vol. II, plate on p. 186; Kingsley Porter, *op. cit.*, Vol. VII, plate 1008; at Surgères and Aubeterre, Kingsley Porter, *op. cit.*, Vol. VII, plates 1093, 1097; at Parthenay-le-Vieux, *Congrès Archéologique de France*, held at Poitiers in 1903, plate on p. 48.

233] Émile Mâle, *L'Art religieux du XIIIe siècle en France*, fifth edition, p. 100 ff. - *L'Art religieux du XIIe siècle en France*, second edition, pp. 439-441.

Ch. Dangibeaud, article quoted, plates III, XIII, XV.

Paul Deschamps, *Le Combat des Vertus et des Vices sur les portails romans de la Saintonge et du Poitou*, in *Congrès archéologique de France*, held at Angoulême in 1912, Vol. II, pp. 309-324, fig.

234] Lasteyrie, *Étude archéologique sur l'Église Saint-Pierre d'Aulnay*, in *Gazette Archéologique*, 1886, p. 277.

E. Lefèvre-Pontalis, in *Congrès archéologique de France*, held at Angoulême in 1912, pp. 95-111, plate and fig. - See also *Recueil de la Commission des Arts et Monuments de la Charente-Inférieure*, Vol. XX, 1927.

J. Roussel, *La Sculpture Française, époque romane*, plates 9, 10 (casts of one of the doorways and one of the windows are in the Trocadéro).

Kinglsey Porter, *op. cit.*, Vol. VII, plates 979-986.

Camille Martin, *L'Art roman en France*, third series, plates 69-79.

M. Dangibeaud has recently made a study of the portal of the church at Nuaillé-sur-Boutonne, which is related to the art of Aulnay (*Bulletin archéologique*, 1926, pp. 39-48, plate 6).

235] Émile Mâle, *L'Art religieux du XIIe siècle*, pp. 148-149.

236] *Les Occupations des Mois dans l'iconographie du moyen âge*, by J. Le Sénécal, in *Bulletin* of the Soc. des Antiquaires de Normandie, Vol. XXXV, 1921, 1922, 1923, 218 pages, 17 full-page plates.

237] A. Rhein, in *Congrès archéologique de France*, held at Angers and Saumur in 1910, Vol. I, pp. 108-119, plate and fig.

Elisa Maillard, in Memoirs of the Société des Antiquaires de l'Ouest, Vol. V, 1920, p. 365 ff.

La façade de l'Église Saint-Jouin-de-Marnes en Poitou, in *Gazette des Beaux-Arts*, pp. 137-150, fig.

J. Roussel, *op. cit.*, plates 28 and 33.

Kingsley Porter, *op. cit.*, plates 946-950.

Casts at the Trocadéro.

238] André Michel, *Les Sculptures de l'ancienne façade de Notre-Dame de la Couldre à Parthenay*, in *Monuments et Mémoires*, published by the Académie des Inscriptions et Belles-Lettres (Fondation Piot), Vol. XXII, 1918, pp. 180-195, pl. 18 and fig.

Elisa Maillard, *La question des Sculptures de Parthenay au Musée du Louvre*, in *Revue archéologique*, 1925, pp. 330-334.

E. Lefèvre-Pontalis, in *Bulletin Monumental*, 1922, pp. 427-428, fig. - Marcel Aubert, *Deux chapiteaux de Notre-Dame de la Couldre au Musée du Louvre*, in *Bulletin Monumental*, 1926, pp. 186-187 fig.

239] Émile Mâle, *L'Art religieux du XIIe siècle...*, pp. 141-147, fig. 119.

Congrès archéologique de France, held at Angoulême in 1912, Vol. I, pp. 279-290, plate and fig.

Kingsley Porter, *op. cit.*, Vol. VII, plates 951-962.

240] L. Serbat, in *Congrès archéologique de France*, held at Angoulême in 1912, Vol. I, pp. 4-27, plate and fig. - J. de la Martinière, *La consécration de la cathédrale d'Angoulême en 1128*, in *Bulletins et Mémoires* of the Société archéologique et historique de la Charente, 1916.

Kingsley Porter, *op. cit.*, Vol. VII, plates 929-940.

J. Roussel, *op. cit.*, plates 5, 6, 36.

Casts at the Trocadéro.

240a] Émile Mâle, *L'Art religieux du XIIe siècle*, pp. 399-402, fig. 229, 230.

240b] *Congrès archéologique de France*, held at Angoulême in 1912, p. 76, fig.

Kingsley Porter, *op. cit.*, Vol. VII, plates 944, 945.

241] J. Roussel, plate 9. Cast at the Trocadéro.

241a] J. Roussel, plate 10. Cast at the Trocadéro.

241b] *Bulletin archéologique*, 1926, pp. 39-48, plate VI.

242] A. Rhein, in *Congrès archéologique de France*, held at Angoulême in 1912, Vol. I, pp. 205-207.

242a] J. Roussel, *op. cit.*, plate 41. Cast at the Trocadéro.

242b] J. Roussel, *op. cit.*, plate 5. - Vitry and Brière, *Documents de Sculpture française*, plate XXI. - Cast at the Trocadéro.

243] E. Lefèvre-Pontalis, in *Congrès archéologique de France*, held at Angoulême in 1912, Vol. I, pp. 79-86.

243a] There is a cast of the portal in the Trocadéro.

243b] At St.-Hilaire-le-Grand (bas-reliefs reproduced in *Congrès archéologique de France*, held at Poitiers in 1903, plate on p. 216; same plate in Congress held at Angoulême in 1912, Vol. I, plate on p. 312); at St.-Jean-de-Montierneuf, Ste.-Radegonde, and St.-Porchaire (see volumes of Congresses held at Poitiers in 1903 and at Angoulême in 1912).

244] E. Lefèvre-Pontalis, in *Congrès archéologique de France*, held at Paris in 1919, fig. on pp. 330-333.

244a] Other capitals from Ste.-Geneviève are preserved in the courtyard of the École des Beaux-Arts; reproduced in Marcel Aubert, *L'Art français à l'époque romane*, I, Paris, Morancé, 1929, plate 13.

244b] This statue is now in the museum at Boulogne-sur-Mer.
See C. Enlart, *L'Église du Wast-en-Boulonnais et son portail arabe*, in *Gazette des Beaux-Arts*, August 1927, pp. 1-11, 2 figures.

245] Lasteyrie, *L'Architecture... à l'époque romane*, p. 691, fig. 700.
Kingsley Porter, *op. cit.*, Vol. X, fig. 1485-1486.

246] Abbé Sainsot, *Le Tympan du portail de Mervilliers*, in *Congrès archéologique de France*, held at Chartres in 1900, pp. 97-119, plate.

247] Émile Mâle, *L'Art religieux du XIIe siècle*, pp. 176-180.

248] Marcel Aubert, *French Sculpture at the Beginning of the Gothic period 1140-1225*, The Pegasus Press, Paris, 1929.
M. Aubert's new work will deal with this question. Useful information will also be found in G. Fleury, *Études sur les Portails imagés du XIIe siècle*, Mamers 1904, royal quarto, 296 pages, 65 fig.

249] C. Enlart, *Étude sur quelques fonts baptismaux du Nord de la France*, in *Bulletin Archéologique du Comité des Travaux Historiques*, 1890, pp. 46-73, fig. - *Manuel d'Archéologie Française*, I: *Architecture Religieuse*, part 2, 1920, pp. 878-902.
R. de Lasteyrie, *L'Architecture religieuse en France à l'époque romane*, pp. 697-709, fig.

250] Wierre-Effroy, cast at the Trocadéro; reproduced in J. Roussel, *op. cit.*, plate 48.

251] Sélincourt, cast at the Trocadéro. Reproduced in J. Roussel, *op. cit.*, plate 48.

252] Vermand, cast at the Trocadéro. Reproduced in J. Roussel, *op. cit.*, plate 48.

253] On the exportation of materials in this region see also: Paul Parent, *Les Caractères régionaux de l'Architecture dans le Nord de la France (Flandre et Artois)*, in *Revue du Nord*, XII, No. 49, February 1927, p. 5 ff.

254] *Acta SS. ord. Sancti Benedicti*, VIII, 526.

255] *Willelmi chronica Andrensis*, edited by J. Heller, in *Monumenta Germ. hist., Scriptores XXIV*, p. 724.

256] "Formas quoque ad lapides formandos his qui convenerant sculptoribus tradit...". Victor Mortet, *Recueil de Textes..., XIe-XIIe siècles*, pp. 211-212.

257] René Fage, *La Décoration géométrique dans l'École romane de Normandie*, in *Congrès archéologique de France*, held at Caen in 1908, Vol. II, pp. 615-633, fig. Denise Jalabert, *L'art normand au moyen âge*, Paris, La Renaissance du Livre (in course of publication).

258] Deshoulières, *L'Église de Graville-Sainte-Honorine (Seine-Inférieure)*, in *Congrès archéologique de France*, held at Rouen in 1926, pp. 508-530, fig.

259] Louis-Marie Michon, *L'Abbaye de St.-Georges-de-Boscherville*, in *Congrès archéologique de France*, held at Rouen in 1926, pp. 531-549, fig.

260] Abbé Le Mâle, *Un bas-relief roman découvert à Meuvaines*, in the *Bulletin* of the Société des Antiquaires de Normandie, 1916, Vol. XXXI, pp. 365-366, plate. Georges Huard, *L'Art en Normandie*, Paris, Les Beaux-Arts, 1928, plate CII, fig. 199.

261] Bayeux: J. Vallery-Radot, *La Cathédrale de Bayeux (Petites Monographies des grands édifices de la France)*, Paris, H. Laurens, n. d., 120 pages and fig. Rucqueville: same volume, pp. 100, 101.

262] J. Vallery-Radot, *op. cit.*
Jules Roussel, *La Sculpture Française, époque romane*, plate 35.
Marcel Aubert, *L'Art Français à l'époque romane*, I, plates 36 and 37.
Casts of three of the bas-reliefs are in the Trocadéro.

263] Jean Vallery-Radot, *La Sculpture française du XIIe siècle et les influences irlandaises*, in *Revue de l'Art*, May 1924, pp. 334-335, fig.; by the same author, *La Cathédrale de Bayeux*, p. 45, fig.

264] Roger Grand, *Mélanges d'archéologie bretonne*, 1921, p. 95 ff.

265] Roger Grand, *L'Église de Merlévenez (Morbihan)*, in *Bulletin Monumental*, 1927, p. 91 ff.

266] Roger Grand, *Saint-Gildas-de-Rhuis*, in *Mélanges d'archéologie bretonne*, Nantes and Paris 1921, pp. 95-117 and especially pp. 109-113.

267] Georges Durand, *Églises romanes des Vosges*, Paris, 1913, quarto, p. 96.

268] Marcel Aubert, *L'Art Français à l'époque romane*, Vol. I, plate 21.

269] Georges Durand, *op. cit.*, p. 375, fig. 284.

270] Georges Durand, *op. cit.*, pp. 266-273, fig. 201-204.
Lasteyrie, *L'Architecture... à l'époque romane*, p. 360, fig. 380.

271] Lasteyrie, *Études sur la sculpture française au moyen âge*, pp. 118-127 and fig. 29-31. - *L'Architecture... à l'époque romane*, p. 652, fig. 664-667.
Émile Mâle, *L'Art religieux du XIIe siècle*, p. 114 and fig. 100.
Kingsley Porter, *op. cit.*, Vol. IX, plates 1292-1298.

272] Émile Mâle, *L'Art religieux du XIIe siècle*, pp. 126-139.

273] Lasteyrie, article quoted, p. 125, fig. 32. - Kingsley Porter, *op. cit.*, Vol. IX, plate 1299.

274] Millin, *Voyage dans les Départements du Midi*, Vol. III, p. 434.

275] Lasteyrie, article quoted, plate XXII.
Kingsley Porter, *op. cit.*, Vol. IX, plate 1386.

276] Kingsley Porter, *Lombard architecture*, Atlas, plate 164.

277] Vöge, *Die Anfänge des monumentalen Stiles im Mittelalter*, Strasburg 1894, octavo. M. Richard Hamann has recently returned to the theory maintained by Vöge as to the priority of the school of Provence; see especially R. Hamann, *Deutsche und französische Kunst im Mittelalter*, I: *Südfranzösische Protorenaissance und ihre Ausbreitung in Deutschland*, Kunstgeschichtliches Seminar, Marburg a. Lahn, 1923.

277a] A. Marignan, *L'École de sculpture en Provence, du XIIe au XIIIe siècle*, Paris 1899, octavo.

278] R. de Lasteyrie, *Études sur la Sculpture française au moyen âge*, 145 pages and 22 plates, in *Monuments et Mémoires* published by the Académie des Inscriptions et Belles-Lettres (Fondation Piot), Vol. VIII, 1902.

279] L. H. Labande, *Étude sur St.-Trophime d'Arles*, in *Bulletin Monumental*, 1904, pp. 31 and 38, and *Congrès archéologique de France*, held at Avignon in 1909, Vol. I, p. 223.

280] Lasteyrie, article quoted, p. 96.

281] Augustin Fliche, *Aigues-Mortes et St.-Gilles (Petites Monographies des grands édifices de la France)*, Paris, Laurens, n. d.

282] There is a cast of the façade in the Trocadéro.

283] Émile Mâle, *L'Architecture et la Sculpture en Lombardie à l'époque romane*, in *Gazette des Beaux-Arts*, 1918, pp. 44-46.

284] There is a cast of this statue in the Trocadéro.

285] This slab is now preserved in the Musée Borély at Marseilles. There is a cast of it at the Trocadéro.
J. Roussel, *op. cit.*, plate 33.
Kingsley Porter, *Romanesque Sculpture...*, Vol. IX, plate 1278.
Paul Deschamps, *Étude sur la paléographie des Inscriptions Lapidaires*, *Bulletin Monumental*, 1929, plate IX, fig. 19.

286] Lasteyrie, *Études sur la Sculpture française au moyen âge*, pp. 116-118.
Kingsley Porter, *op. cit.*, Vol. IX, plates 1378-1383.

287] L. H. Labande, *L'Église de Notre-Dame-des-Doms d'Avignon, des origines au XIIIe siècle*, in *Bulletin archéologique*, 1906, pp. 282-365, plates LXIV-LXXXII.

288] Kingsley Porter, *op. cit.*, Vol. IX, plate 1341.

289] L. H. Labande, article quoted, plate LXXVI.
Lasteyrie, *L'Architecture... à l'époque romane*, p. 361, fig. 642.
Kingsley Porter, *op. cit.*, Vol. I, p. 166, and Vol. IX, plates 1342, 1343.

290] L. H. Labande, article quoted in *Bulletin archéologique*, 1906, p. 311, note 1; and Victor Mortet, *Recueil de Textes relatifs à l'Histoire de l'Architecture...*, *XIe et XIIe siècles*, Paris, A. Picard, 1911, Text No. CXII, pp. 305-308.

291] Text of 1156, L. H. Labande, article quoted, p. 359, note 2; and Victor Mortet and Paul Deschamps, *Recueil de Textes relatifs à l'Histoire de l'Architecture*, *XIIe-XIIIe siècles*, Paris, A. Picard, 1929, Text No. XXXVII, pp. 96-97.

292] Lasteyrie, *L'Architecture... à l'époque romane*, p. 651, fig. 663.
Congrès archéologique de France, held at Avignon in 1909, Vol. I, pp. 259-262, fig.

293] Jules Baum, *op. cit.*, plates 31 and 32.

294] Fernand Benoit, *L'Abbaye de Montmajour*, in *Coll. des Petites Monographies des grands édifices de la France*, Paris, Laurens, 1928, p. 52 ff.

295] *Congrès archéologique de France*, held at Avignon in 1909, Vol. I, pp. 253-258.

296] *Ibid.*, pp. 262-273.

297] Jules Baum, *op. cit.*, plates 29 and 30.

298] Kingsley Porter, *op. cit.*, Vol. VIII,. plate 1230.

299] Émile Bonnet, *Antiquités et Monuments du Département de l'Hérault*, Montpellier 1905, royal octavo, 558 pages, 12 full-page plates, 72 illustrations.

300] See p. 15 and note 43.

301] Émile Bonnet, *op. cit.*, p. 376, fig.
Lasteyrie, *Études sur la Sculpture Française...*, p. 77, fig. 20.
Kingsley Porter, *op. cit.*, Vol. IX, plate 1384.

302] J. Sahuc, *L'Art roman à Saint-Pons de Thomières*, Montpellier 1908, p. 74, fig.
Émile Bonnet, *op. cit.*, p. 379, fig.
Émile Mâle, *L'Art religieux du XIIe siècle*, pp. 131-132, fig. 111.
Kingsley Porter, *op. cit.*, Vol. VII, plates 1265-1274. See also the same author
in his *Romanesque Capitals*, in *Fogg Museum Notes*, 1922, I.

303] André Michel, *Histoire de l'Art*, Vol. I, part 2, pp. 630-631, fig. 350.

304] *Congrès archéologique de France*, held at Carcassonne and Perpignan in 1906,
pp. 54-56, 3 plates.
Kingsley Porter, *Romanesque Sculpture...*, Vol. IX, plate 1404.

305] Émile Bonnet, *op. cit.*, p. 380, fig.
Émile Bonnet, *L'Église Abbatiale de Saint-Guilhem-le-Désert*, in *Congrès archéolo-
gique de France*, held at Carcassonne and Perpignan in 1906, pp. 384-440,
plates on pp. 422, 424, 426.
Lasteyrie, *Études sur la Sculpture Française...*, p. 131, fig. 34.
A. Joubin, *Quelques aspects archéologiques du Languedoc méditerranéen*, in *Revue
archéologique*, 1920, p. 83.
Kingsley Porter, *op. cit.*, Vol. IX, plates 1397-1403.
Richard Hamann, *Ein unbekannter Figurenzyklus in St.-Guilhem-le-Désert* in *Mar-
burger Jahrbuch für Kunstwissenschaft*, Vol. II, 1926, pp. 71-89, pl. XXV-XXXVI.

306] J.-A. Brutails, *Notes sur l'Art religieux en Roussillon*, in *Bulletin Archéologique*, 1893,
pp. 329-404, fig.

307] J. Puig y Cadafalch, A. de Falguera y Sivilla, J. Goday y Casals, *L'Arquitectura romànica a Catalunya*, Vol. III, 1918.

307a] See p. 15.

308] Lasteyrie, *L'Architecture... à l'époque romane*, p. 638, fig. 650.
Congrès archéologique de France, held at Carcassonne and Perpignan in 1906,
plate on page 130.
Kingsley Porter, *op. cit.*, Vol. V, plate 518.

309] Émile Mâle, *op. cit.*, p. 432, fig. 248.

310] *Congrès archéologique de France*, held at Carcassonne and Perpignan in 1906,
pp. 148-152, plate.
Kingsley Porter, *op. cit.*, Vol. V, plates 556-559.

311] J.-A. Brutails, *Notes sur l'Église de Serrabone*, in *Congrès archéologique de France*, held at Carcassonne and Perpignan in 1906, pp. 515-517, plate.

312] A. Mayeux, *Saint-Jean-le-Vieux à Perpignan*, in *Bulletin Monumental*, 1913, plate on p. 96.

313] Arles-sur-Tech: J.-A. Brutails, *Église Notre-Dame d'Arles-sur-Tech*, in *Album des Monuments et de l'Art ancien du Midi de la France*, Toulouse 1893, pp. 70-72, drawing.
Kingsley Porter, *op. cit.*, Vol. V, plate 627.
Elne: J.-A. Brutails, *Notes sur l'Art religieux en Roussillon*, in *Bulletin Archéologique*, 1893, p. 384 and plate XXVIII.
Congrès archéologique de France, held at Carcassonne and Perpignan in 1906, plate on p. 146.
Kingsley Porter, *op. cit.*, Vol. V, plates 623-626.

314] J.-A. Brutails, *Monographie de la Cathédrale et du Cloître d'Elne*, Perpignan 1887, 91 pages, plates (extract from the 28th *Bulletin* of the Société agricole, scientifique et littéraire des Pyrénées-Orientales).
Congrès archéologique de France, held at Carcassonne and Perpignan in 1906, pp. 135-147, plate.
Puig y Cadafalch..., *op. cit.*, Vol. III, pp. 275-286, fig.
Kingsley Porter, *op. cit.*, Vol. V, plates 611-614.

315] Same congress, plate on p. 130.

316] Puig y Cadafalch..., *op. cit.*, Vol. III, pp. 253-274, fig.

317] Puig y Cadafalch..., *op. cit.*, Vol. III, pp. 227-246, fig.

318] Puig y Cadafalch..., *op. cit.*, Vol. III, pp. 246-253, fig.
Kingsley Porter, *op. cit.*, Vol. V, plate 599.

319] Puig y Cadafalch..., *op. cit.*, Vol. III, pp. 479-494, fig.
Kingsley Porter, *op. cit.*, Vol. V, plates 607-610.

320] Puig y Cadafalch..., *op. cit.*, Vol. III, pp. 494-498.

321] Puig y Cadafalch..., *op. cit.*, Vol. III, pp. 324-331, fig.
Kingsley Porter, *op. cit.*, Vol. V, plates 594, 595.

322] Puig y Cadafalch..., *op. cit.*, Vol. III, pp. 287-300, fig.

323] Puig y Cadafalch..., *op. cit.*, Vol. III, pp. 301-308, fig.

324] Puig y Cadafalch..., *op. cit.*, Vol. III, pp. 385-392, fig.

325] Puig y Cadafalch..., *op. cit.*, Vol. III, pp. 814-848, fig.
Kingsley Porter, *op. cit.*, Vol. V, plates 560-594.

326] Puig y Cadafalch..., *op. cit.*, Vol. III, pp. 814-848, fig.
Puig y Cadafalch, on the Ripoll portal, in *Bulletin Monumental*, 1925, pp. 303-320, fig.
Émile Mâle, *L'Art religieux du XIIe siècle*, p. 38.

327] Louis Bréhier, *Les chapiteaux du chevet de Saint-Pierre de Blesle* (extract from the *Almanach de Brioude*, 1929, 20 pages, 4 plates).

328] Magdeleine Ferry, *Les Portes romanes des Églises du Sud-Ouest de la France*, in *Position des Thèses soutenues à l'École des Chartes par les élèves de la Promotion de 1928*, Paris 1928, pp. 43-48.

329] Abbé S. Daugé, *Inventaire des Chrismes du Département du Gers* (extract from the *Bulletin* of the Société Archéologique du Gers, Auch 1916). On the Christian monograms in Spain, see Torrés Balbas, *La escultura románica aragonese y el crismon de los timpanos de las iglesias de la región pireneica*, in *Arch. de arte y arqueología*, 1926.

330] André Michel, *La Sculpture romane, Histoire de l'Art*, Vol. I, part 2, p. 633, fig. 353.

331] Puig y Cadafalch..., *op. cit.*, Vol. III, pp. 315-318, fig.
Kingsley Porter, *op. cit.*, Vol. V, plate 551.

332] Paul Lafond, *Notice sur l'Église de Sévignac (Basses-Pyrénées)*, in *Bulletin archéologique*, 1893, pp. 15-21, plate IX.

332a] Camille Martin, *Saint-Pierre, ancienne cathédrale de Genève*, Geneva 1911, folio.

333] Émile Bertaux; *La Sculpture en Italie de 1070 à 1260*, in *Histoire de l'Art*, Vol. I, part 2, pp. 670-708, fig.

334] Émile Bertaux, *La Sculpture chrétienne en Espagne des origines au XIVe siècle*, in *Histoire de l'Art*, Vol. II, part I (1906), pp. 214-273, fig.

335] Émile Mâle, *L'Architecture et la Sculpture en Lombardie à l'époque romane, à propos d'un livre récent*, in *Gazette des Beaux-Arts*, January-March 1918, pp. 35-46, fig.
L'Art religieux du XIIe siècle, p. 145.
See also the same author's: *Les influences du Drame liturgique sur la Sculpture romane*, in *Revue de l'Art Ancien et Moderne*, 1907, Vol. XXII, pp. 81-92.

336] Paul Deschamps, *La légende Arturienne à la Cathédrale de Modène et l'École Lombarde de Sculpture romane*, in *Monuments et Mémoires* published by the Académie des Inscription et Belles-Lettres (Fondation Piot), Vol. XXVIII, 1926.

337] Émile Mâle, article quoted, *Gazette des Beaux-Arts*, p. 43.
Reproduced in Kingsley Porter, *Lombard Architecture*, 1915, Vol. IV, Atlas, plate 145, fig. 4.
Pietro Toesca, *Storia dell'Arte italiana*, Vol. I, p. 771.

338] Paul Deschamps, *Notes sur la Sculpture romane en Languedoc et dans le Nord de l'Espagne*, in *Bulletin Monumental*, 1923, pp. 305-351.
See also Émile Mâle, *L'Art religieux du XIIe siècle*, pp. 288-303.

339] Émile Mâle, *L'Art religieux du XIIe siècle*, pp. 293-294, fig. 181.

340] G. Gaillard, *Notes sur la date des Sculptures de Compostelle et de Léon*, in *Gazette des Beaux-Arts*, June 1929, pp. 341-378.

341] Manuel Gómez Moreno, *Provincia de León, Catálogo Monumental de España*, Madrid, Ministerio de Instrucción Pública, 1925, 1926, 1 volume of text and 1 volume of plates, octavo.

342] Kingsley Porter, *Pilgrimage Sculpture*, in *American Journal of Archaeology*, Vol. XXVI, 1922, pp. 1-53. - *Romanesque Sculpture of the Pilgrimage Roads*, Vol. I, pp. 44-58. - *Spanish Romanesque Sculpture*, Vol. I, pp. 74 ff., plates 35-42.

343] On Silos, see Émile Bertaux, *Santo Domingo de Silos*, in *Gazette des Beaux-Arts*, July 1906, pp. 27-44, fig., and in *Histoire de l'Art*, published under the direction of André Michel, Vol. II, part I (1906), pp. 220-228.
Dom Roulin, *Les Églises de l'Abbaye de Silos*, in *Revue de l'Art Chrétien*, 1908, pp. 289-299; and *Les cloîtres de l'Abbaye de Silos*, *ibid.*, 1909, pp. 75-76, 166-174, 358-368, and 1910, pp. 1-12, fig.
D. Serapio Huici, *Marfiles de San Millán de la Cogolla y Escultura de Santo Domingo de Silos*, Madrid, Calpe, 1928, 40 pages, 15 illustrations of Silos.
Don Francisco Anton y Casaseca, *Las influencias hispano-arabes en el arte occidental de los siglos XI y XII, discurso leido por el autor*, Real Academia de Bellas Artes, Valladolid 1926, 52 pages.
Georges Gaillard, *Notes sur la date des Sculptures de Compostelle et de Léon*, in *Gazette des Beaux-Arts*, June 1929. Casts of two sculptured slabs from Silos are at the Trocadéro, and represent the Pentecost and the Pilgrims of Emmaus.

344] Paul Deschamps, *Notes sur la Sculpture romane en Languedoc et dans le Nord de l'Espagne*, in *Bulletin Monumental*, 1923, pp. 305-351.
See also G. Gaillard, article quoted.

345] G. Gaillard, *Notes sur les Tympans aragonais*, in *Bulletin Hispanique*, Vol. XXX, No. 3, July-September 1928, pp. 193-203, 6 illustrations.

346] Fathers Vincent and F. M. Abel, *Jérusalem*, Vol. II: *Jérusalem nouvelle*, Paris, Gabalda, 1926, plate XXVI.

347] C. Enlart, *Les Monuments des Croisés dans le Royaume de Jérusalem, Architecture religieuse et civile*, Paris, Geuthner, 1927-1929, Vol. II, pp. 165-170 and Atlas, plates 18 and 101.

348] C. Enlart, *op. cit.*, plate 100.

349] Fathers Vincent and Abel, *op. cit.*, plate XXIII.
C. Enlart, *op. cit.*, Vol. II, p. 164 and fig. 303, plate 99.

350] Fathers Vincent and Abel, *op. cit.*, plates 16 and 18.
C. Enlart, *op. cit.*, Vol. II, pp. 157-159, and plate 96, fig. 293.

351] L. Bégule, *L'Église Saint-Maurice de Vienne*, p. 116, fig. 136.

352] C. Enlart, *op. cit.*, Vol. II, pp. 211-213 and 217.

353] C. Enlart, *op. cit.*, Vol. II, plate 115 bis, fig. 359.

354] Fathers Vincent and Abel, *op. cit.*, pp. 587-595, fig. 238, plate LIX.
C. Enlart, *op. cit.*, Vol. II, pp. 202-204.

355] Fathers Vincent and Abel, *op. cit.*, plates 40-42.
C. Enlart, *op. cit.*, Vol. II, pp. 256-257, fig. 332.

356] Carl Watzinger and Karl Wulzinger, *Damaskus, die antike Stadt*, Berlin and Leipzig 1921, royal quarto, pp. 110-111, fig. 82-85.
C. Enlart, *op. cit.*, Vol. I, pp. 127-128, Vol. II, pp. 101-102, and plate 194, fig. 386-388.
Paul Deschamps, in *Bulletin des Musées de France*, first year, No. 11, November 1929, pp. 243-245.

357] V. Terret, *La Sculpture Bourguignonne aux XIIe et XIIIe siècles, Autun* (Autun 1925), Vol. II, plate XXVII.
C. Enlart, *op. cit.*, plate 194, fig. 389.

358] Cdt. Gendronneau, *Un cavalier Constantin à Saint-Trophime d'Arles*, in *Nouvelle Revue du Midi*, Nîmes 1925.
C. Enlart, *op. cit.*, plate 194, fig. 390-391.

359] Fathers Vincent and Abel, *op. cit.*, plate LXXXVII.
C. Enlart, *op. cit.*, pp. 263-264, plate 195.

360] C. Enlart, *op. cit.*, plate 195, fig. 585.
Cast at the Trocadéro.

361] Father Prosper Viaud, *Nazareth*, Paris, A. Picard, 1910, royal octavo, pp. 55-57 and 149-163, fig.
R. de Lasteyrie, Letter in the above-mentioned work, pp. 167-168.
Father Germer-Durand, *La Sculpture franque en Palestine, Conférences de Saint-Étienne*, 1911, p. 143.
Pietro Egidi, *I capitelli romanici di Nazaret*, in *Dedalo*, Milan and Rome 1921, part XII, fig.
C. Enlart, *op. cit.*, Vol. II, pp. 294, 302-307, fig. and plates 131-133.
Casts of these capitals are in the Trocadéro.

362] Published in the *Survey of Western Palestine*, Vol. I, p. 398. - Described by Father Germer-Durand in his *Sculpture franque en Palestine, Conférences de Saint-Étienne*, 1911, p. 247.
C. Enlart, *op. cit.*, pp. 303, 307-308, and sketch on plate 136.
Cast at the Trocadéro.

363] We have not been able to study here the question of floral and foliated decoration. We hope that the book which Mlle Denise Jalabert is preparing on ornamental sculpture in the twelfth century will shortly be published.

GEOGRAPHICAL INDEX

152

PLATES 1-96

I

2

A. VIENNE. Musée St.-Pierre
Choir-screen panel with interlaces.
CAROLINGIAN PERIOD
Photo E. Lefèvre-Pontalis

B. FLAVIGNY (Côte-d'Or). Abbey Church of St.-Pierre
Gallery of the crypt: Pillar with interlaces.
IX CENTURY
Photo Archives d'Art et d'Histoire

C. ANGERS. Church of St.-Martin
Choir-screen panel with interlaces.
CAROLINGIAN PERIOD
Photo E. Lefèvre-Pontalis

D. BESSUÉJOULS (Aveyron)
Capital with interlaces.
XI CENTURY
Photo Archives d'Art et d'Histoire

E. CELLEFROUIN (Charente)
Capital at the crossing of the transept.
ROMANESQUE PERIOD
Photo E. Lefèvre-Pontalis

F. BESSUÉJOULS (Aveyron)
Lintel with interlaces.
XI CENTURY
Photo Archives d'Art et d'Histoire

F

A

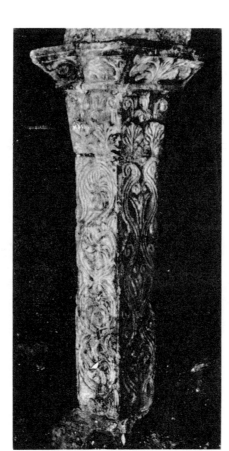

B

C

D

E

3

4

A. ST.-GENIS-DES-FONTAINES (Pyrénées-Orientales)
Lintel of the doorway.
1020-1021
Photo Archives d'Art et d'Histoire

B.-C. ST.-ANDRÉ-DE-SORÈDE (Pyrénées-Orientales)
B. Lintel of the doorway.
C. Bas-relief (now beneath window of the façade).
BEGINNING OF XI CENTURY
Photo Archives d'Art et d'Histoire

5

A.-C. ST. BENOÎT-SUR-LOIRE (Loiret)
Capitals of the porch:
A. Christ in Majesty.
B. The Flight into Egypt.
LATTER HALF OF XI CENTURY
Photo Archives d'Art et d'Histoire

D. LE RONCERAY D'ANGERS (Maine-et-Loire)
Capital.
LATTER HALF OF XI CENTURY
Photo E. Lefèvre-Pontalis

6

A.-C. TOULOUSE. CHURCH OF ST.-SERNIN
Panels from the table of the high altar.
ABOUT 1096
Photo C. Lassalle

D. LAVAUR (TARN)
Panel from the table of the altar.
END OF XI OR BEGINNING
OF XII CENTURY (?)
Photo Archives d'Art et d'Histoire

E.-F. TOULOUSE. CHURCH OF ST.-SERNIN
Bas-reliefs now in the ambulatory of the choir.
END OF XI CENTURY
Photo Meyer Shapiro

7

TOULOUSE. Church of St.-Sernin

A.-D. Marble bas-reliefs now in the ambulatory of the choir.

END OF XI CENTURY

A.-C. *Photo C. Lassalle*

D. *Photo Archives d'Art et d'Histoire*

8

TOULOUSE. Church of St.-Sernin
A.-E. Capitals of the choir and transept.
END OF XI CENTURY
A., B., D., E. *Photo C. Lassalle*
C. *Photo Meyer Shapiro*

F. Capital of the Miégeville door.
END OF XI OR EARLY YEARS OF XII CENTURY
Photo C. Lassalle

9

TOULOUSE. Church of St.-Sernin

Tympanum of the Miégeville Door: The Ascension of Christ.

END OF XI OR EARLY YEARS OF XII CENTURY
Photo R. Hamann

10

TOULOUSE. Church of St.-Sernin
Details of the Miégeville Door:
A. Base of the statue of St. James.
B. Base of the statue of St. Peter.
BEGINNING OF XII CENTURY (?)
Photo R. Hamann

II

12

CAPITALS AND ABACI IN THE STYLE OF TOULOUSE
FIRST HALF OF XII CENTURY

A. TOULOUSE. Church of St.-Sernin
West façade (after the cast in the Trocadéro Museum).
Photo Archives d'Art et d'Histoire

B. ST.-GAUDENS. (Haute-Garonne)
(After the cast in the Trocadéro Museum)
Photo Archives d'Art et d'Histoire

C. SANTIAGO DE COMPOSTELA
Goldsmiths' Door.
Photo E. Lefèvre-Pontalis

D. SANT'ANTIMO (Tuscany)
Photo C. Enlart

13

MOISSAC. Abbey Church of St.-Pierre
Bas-reliefs of the cloister pillars:
A. St. Paul and St. Peter.
Photo E. Lefèvre-Pontalis

B. St. Bartholomew.
Photo Paul Deschamps
ABOUT 1100

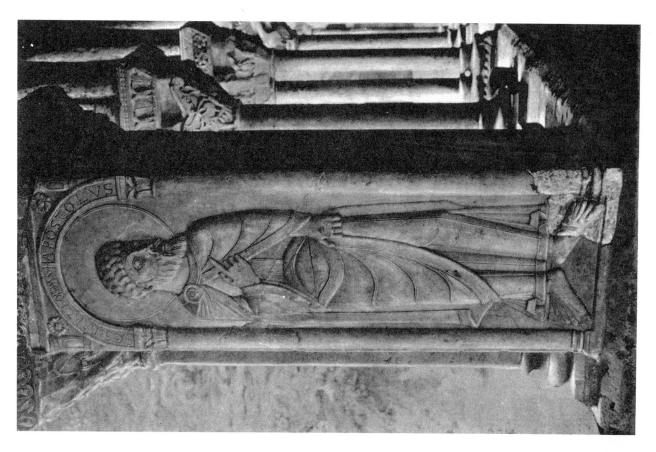

14

MOISSAC. Abbey Church of St.-Pierre
Bas-reliefs of the cloister pillars:
St. James and St. John.
ABOUT 1100
Photo E. Lefèvre-Pontalis

15

MOISSAC. Abbey Church of St.-Pierre
A.-B. Capitals in the cloister.
ABOUT 1100
A. *Photo E. Lefèvre-Pontalis*
B. *Photo C. Lassalle*

16

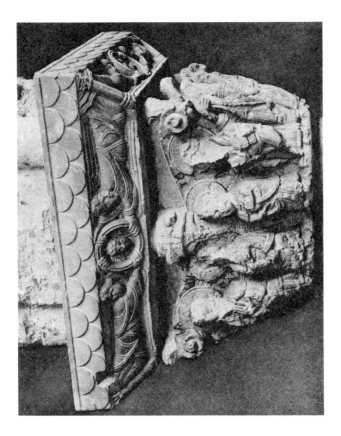 

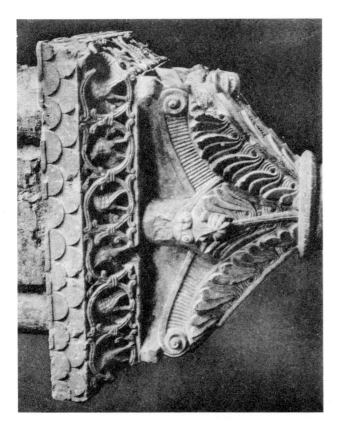 

17

MOISSAC. Abbey Church of St.-Pierre
Tympanum of the doorway (after the cast in the Trocadéro).
BETWEEN 1100 AND 1135
Photo Archives d'Art et d'Histoire

18

MOISSAC. Abbey Church of St.-Pierre
Pier of the doorway (after the cast in the Trocadéro).

BETWEEN 1100 AND 1135

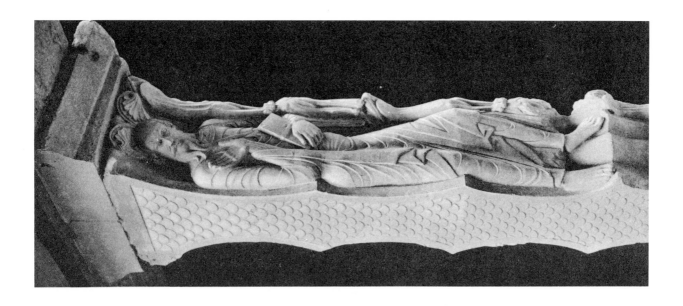

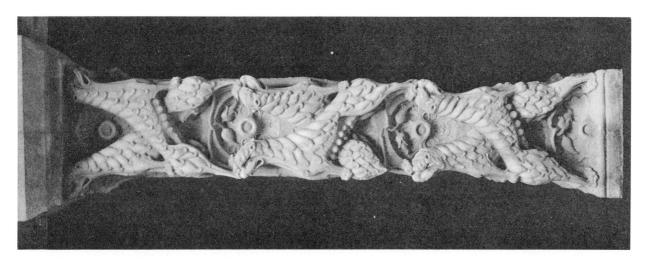

19

MOISSAC. Abbey Church of St.-Pierre

A.-B. Details of the bas-reliefs on the projection of the doorway.

MIDDLE OF XII CENTURY

Photo E. Lefèvre-Pontalis

20

CARENNAC (Lot)
Tympanum of the doorway.
FIRST HALF OF XII CENTURY
Photo E. Lefèvre-Pontalis

2I

SOUILLAC (Lot)

Pier of the doorway (after the cast in the Trocadéro).

FIRST HALF OF XII CENTURY

22

A. SOUILLAC (Lot)
Detail of an abutment of the doorway: The Prophet Isaiah.
FIRST HALF OF XII CENTURY
Photo E. Lefèvre-Pontalis

B. RODEZ. Musée de la Société des Lettres d'Aveyron
God in Majesty.
FIRST HALF OF XII CENTURY
Photo B. de Gauléjac

23

BEAULIEU (Corrèze)
Central portion of the tympanum.
SECOND QUARTER OF XII CENTURY
Photo E. Lefèvre-Pontalis

24

BEAULIEU (Corrèze)
A.-B. Carvings on a pier of the doorway.
SECOND QUARTER OF XII CENTURY
Photo E. Lefèvre-Pontalis

25

TOULOUSE. Musée des Augustins

Carvings from the door of the chapter-house of the cathedral
of St.-Étienne.

FIRST HALF OF XII CENTURY

Photo R. Gaubert Père

26

CAPITALS
FIRST HALF OF XII CENTURY

A. ST.-GAUDENS (HAUTE-GARONNE)
Photo Heuzé

B. HAGETMAU (LANDES)
Photo E. Lefèvre-Pontalis

C.-D. LESCAR (BASSES-PYRÉNÉES)
Photo E. Lefèvre-Pontalis

27

CAPITALS
FIRST HALF OF XII CENTURY

A. LESCAR (Basses-Pyrénées)
Photo Heuzé

B.-C. CASTELNAU-RIVIÈRE-BASSE (Hautes-Pyrénées)
Photo Archives d'Art et d'Histoire

28

CATUS (Lot)

Capital: Delivery of the keys to St. Peter.

FIRST HALF OF XII CENTURY

Photo E. Lefèvre-Pontalis

29

TOULOUSE. Musée des Augustins
Capitals from the cloister of the cathedral of St.-Étienne:
A. Herod and Salome.
Photo R. Hamann

B. The Wise Virgins.
Photo C. Lassalle
MIDDLE OF XII CENTURY

TOULOUSE. Musée des Augustins
Capital from the church of La Daurade: A bear-hunt
(after the cast in the Trocadéro).
END OF XII CENTURY
Photo Archives d'Art et d'Histoire

31

A. CHARLIEU (Loire)
Tympanum of the doorway.
ABOUT 1094
Photo Heuzé

B. NEUILLY-EN-DONJON (Allier)
Tympanum of the doorway.
BEGINNING OF XII CENTURY
Photo Archives d'Art et d'Histoire

32

A. ANZY-LE-DUC (Saône-et-Loire). Priory Church
Capital.
END OF XI CENTURY
Photo Heuzé

B. CHARLIEU (Loire). Priory Church of St.-Fortunat
Capital (the same as at Anzy-le-Duc).
END OF XI CENTURY
Photo Coll. V. Terret

33

CLUNY (Saône-et-Loire). Musée Ochier
Capital from the abbey church of St.-Pierre:
A.-B. Adam and Eve.
AFTER 1088: END OF XI OR FIRST YEARS OF XII CENTURY
Photo Giraudon (Coll. Dr. Pouzet)

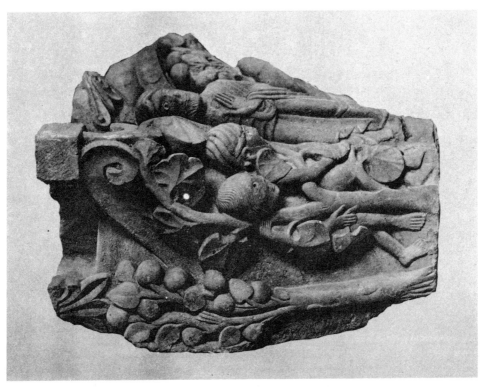

34

AUTUN. Cathedral of St.-Lazare
Centre portion of the tympanum of the main doorway.
ABOUT 1120 (?)
Photo E. Lefèvre-Pontalis

AUTUN. V. Terret Collection
Fragment of the lintel of a lateral doorway of the cathedral:
A.-B. Eve.
Photo R. Hamann

36

AUTUN. Cathedral of St.-Lazare
Capitals:

A. Stoning of St. Stephen.
Photo E. Lefèvre-Pontalis

B. Flight into Egypt.
Photo E. Lefèvre-Pontalis

C. Apparition to St. Mary Magdalen.
Photo Heuzé

D. The body of St. Vincent protected by eagles.
Photo Coll. V. Terret

FIRST HALF OF XII CENTURY

37

VÉZELAY. Abbey Church of Ste.-Madeleine
Tympanum of the doorway of the nave
(after the cast in the Trocadéro).
ABOUT 1130
Photo Archives d'Art et d'Histoire ·

38

VÉZELAY. Abbey Church of Ste.-Madeleine

Capitals:

A. Miracle of St. Benedict.
Photo E. Lefèvre-Pontalis

B. Moses and the golden calf.
Photo E. Lefèvre-Pontalis

C. The Building of the Ark.

D. St. Paul grinding the corn of the ancient Law into the fine
flour of the Gospel.
Photo E. Lefèvre-Pontalis

BETWEEN 1120 AND 1138

39

CAPITALS
FIRST HALF OF XII CENTURY

A. SAULIEU (Côte-d'Or). Church of St.-Andoche
Christ appearing to St. Mary Magdalen.

B.-C. CHALON-SUR-SAÔNE. Church of St.-Vincent
B. Christ appearing to St. Mary Magdalen.
C. Capital decorated with foliage.

D. ANZY-LE-DUC (Saône-et-Loire)
Capital ornamented with birds and foliage.
Photo Heuzé

40

CAPITALS
FIRST HALF OF XII CENTURY

A. MOUTIER-ST.-JEAN (Côte-d'Or)
Vintage Scene (now in the Louvre).
Photo Archives d'Art et d'Histoire

B. CAMBRIDGE (Mass.). Fogg Museum
Cain and Abel make their offerings.
Photo E. Lefèvre-Pontalis

C.-D. ROMANS (Isère). Church of St.-Barnard
Capitals from the nave (cast in the museum at Valence):
C. Annunciation.
D. The weighing of souls.
Photo E. Lefèvre-Pontalis

41

42

CLUNY. Musée Ochier
Capital from the choir of the abbey church of St.-Pierre:
Spring.
SECOND QUARTER OF XII CENTURY
Photo Giraudon (Coll. Dr. Pouzet)

43

CLUNY. Musée Ochier

Capitals from the choir of the Abbey Church of St.-Pierre:

A. One of the liberal arts (?).

Photo Archives d'Art et d'Histoire

B. The first tone of music.

Photo Giraudon (Coll. Dr. Pouzet)

SECOND QUARTER OF XII CENTURY

44

CLUNY. Musée Ochier

Capitals from the choir of the abbey church of St.-Pierre:

A. The third tone of music.
Photo Archives d'Art et d'Histoire

B. The fourth tone of music.
Photo Giraudon (Coll. Dr. Pouzet)

SECOND QUARTER OF XII CENTURY

45

46

PARAY-LE-MONIAL. Museum
Tympanum from the church of Anzy-le-Duc
(cast in the Trocadéro Museum).

LATTER HALF OF XII CENTURY
Photo Archives d'Art et d'Histoire

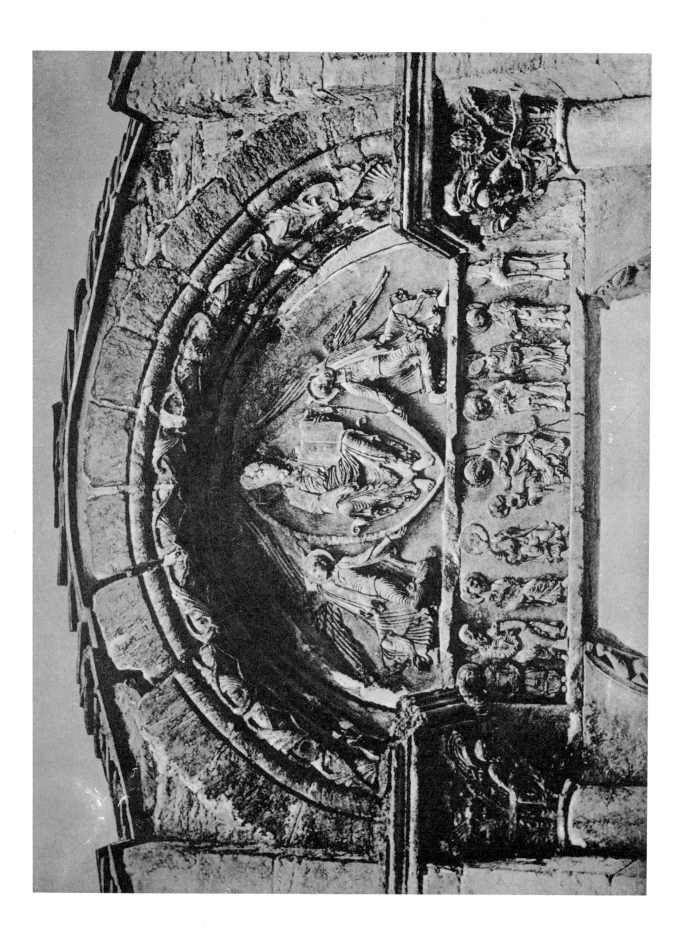

47

A. CHARLIEU (Loire). Church of St.-Fortunat
Tympanum of a small door at the side of the entrance at the
front of the porch. Lintel: The sacrifice of the Ancient Law.
Tympanum: The Marriage at Cana.
Archivolt: The Transfiguration
(cast in the Trocadéro Museum).

MIDDLE OR THIRD QUARTER OF XII CENTURY
Photo Archives d'Art et d'Histoire

B. ST.-JULIEN-DE-JONZY (Saône-et-Loire)
Tympanum: Christ in Majesty.
On the lintel: The Last Supper.

MIDDLE OR THIRD QUARTER OF XII CENTURY
Photo Heuzé

48

A. VIENNE. Cathedral of St.-Maurice
Statue of St. Paul.
Photo C. Didier, St.-Romain-Gal (Rhône)

B. VIENNE. Musée St.-Pierre
Tympanum of a doorway of the church of St.-Pierre.
Bas-relief: St. Peter.
Photo E. Lefèvre-Pontalis

C. VIENNE. Cathedral of St.-Maurice
Statue of a saint.
FIRST HALF OF XII CENTURY
Photo L. Bégule

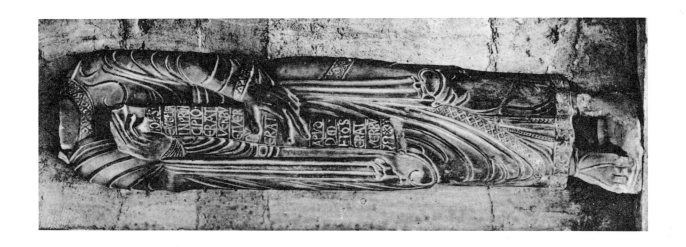

49

A.-B. VIENNE. Church of St.-André-le-Bas
Capitals (cast of the Trocadéro Museum):
A. Samson and the lion.
B. Job an object of disgust to his family.
ABOUT 1152
Photo Martin-Sabon (Archives d'Art et d'Histoire)

C.-D. VIENNE. Cathedral of St.-Maurice
Capitals:
C. The Holy Women at the Tomb.
D. David and Goliath.
Photo L. Bégule

50

THINES (Ardèche)
Statues on the abutments of the doorway.
LATTER HALF OF TWELFTH CENTURY
Photo E. Lefèvre-Pontalis

51

AVENAS (Rhône)

Altar:

A. Lateral panel.

B. Front.

ABOUT 1166

Photo Dr. Loison

52

CAPITALS
FIRST HALF OF XII CENTURY

A.-C. MOZAT (Puy-de-Dôme)
A.-B. Figure capitals.
Photo E. Lefèvre-Pontalis

C. Annunciation
(cast of the Trocadéro Museum).
Photo Archives d'Art et d'Histoire

D. VOLVIC (Puy-de-Dôme)
Angels.
Photo E. Lefèvre-Pontalis

53

CAPITALS
FIRST HALF OF XII CENTURY

A.-B. CLERMONT-FERRAND. Notre-Dame-du-Port

A. Combat between Virtues and Vices
(cast in the Trocadéro Museum).
Photo Neurdein

B. Annunciation.
Photo Archives d'Art et d'Histoire

C.-D. ST.-NECTAIRE (Puy-de-Dôme)
C. Miracle of the loaves.
Photo Archives d'Art et d'Histoire

D. The Guardians of the Sepulchre.
Photo E. Lefèvre-Pontalis

54

ISSOIRE. Church of St.-Paul
Capitals:
A. The Last Supper.
B. The Bearing of the Cross
(cast in the museum at Clermont).
FIRST HALF OF XII CENTURY
Photo E. Lefèvre-Pontalis

55

MAURIAC (Cantal)

Tympanum.

FIRST HALF OF XII CENTURY

Photo E. Lefèvre-Pontalis

56

ST.-JUNIEN (Haute-Vienne)
Tomb of St. Junien (northern face).

LAST QUARTER OF XII CENTURY
Photo P. Lafontan

57

CONQUES. Church of Ste.-Foy
Central portion of the tympanum: The Last Judgement.
SECOND QUARTER OR MIDDLE OF XII CENTURY
Photo E. Lefèvre-Pontalis

58

BOURGES. Church of St.-Ursin

Detail of the tympanum: Fables of Aesop and hunting-scenes.

BEGINNING OF XII CENTURY

Photo E. Lefèvre-Pontalis

59

ST.-RÉVÉRIEN (Nièvre)
Seraph.

MIDDLE OF XII CENTURY
Photo E. Lefèvre-Pontalis

60

ST.-GENOU (Indre)

A.-B. Capitals.

FIRST HALF OF XII CENTURY

Photo E. Lefèvre-Pontalis

61

LA BERTHENOUX (Indre)

A.-D. Capitals.

FIRST HALF OF XII CENTURY

Photo E. Lefèvre-Pontalis

62

CAPITALS
FIRST HALF OF XII CENTURY

A.-B. ST.-GENOU (Indre)
C. NEUVY-ST.-SÉPULCRE (Indre)
Photo E. Lefèvre-Pontalis

63

CAPITALS

FIRST HALF AND MIDDLE OF XII CENTURY

A. ST.-PIERRE-LE-MOUTIER (NIÈVRE)
Photo Heuzé

B. BOMMIERS (INDRE)
Sacrifice of Isaac.
Photo E. Lefèvre-Pontalis

C.-D. GARGILESSE (INDRE)
Photo E. Lefèvre-Pontalis

64

ST.-BENOÎT-SUR-LOIRE (Loiret)

A.-C. Capitals of the choir, transept and nave.
Photo E. Lefèvre-Pontalis

D. (Cast in the Trocadéro Museum).
Photo Giraudon
END OF XI AND FIRST HALF OF XII CENTURY

65

ST.-AIGNAN (LOIR-ET-CHER)

Capitals:

A. Centaur shooting an arrow at a stag.

B. Flight into Egypt.

C. The Beast of the Apocalypse.
Photo E. Lefèvre-Pontalis

D. Sirens.
Photo Dr. Loison

FIRST HALF OF XII CENTURY

66

L'ILE-BOUCHARD (INDRE-ET-LOIRE)
Capitals:
A. Annunciation, Visitation and Adoration of the Magi.
Photo Heuzé

B. Entry into Jerusalem.
Photo E. Lefèvre-Pontalis

C. The Announcement to the Shepherds.
Photo Heuzé

D. Decorative capital.
Photo Heuzé
FIRST HALF OF XII CENTURY

67

CAPITALS

A.-B. FONTEVRAULT (Maine-et-Loire)

THIRD QUARTER OF XII CENTURY

A. *Photo E. Lefèvre-Pontalis*
B. *Photo Archives d'Art et d'Histoire*

C. CUNAULT (Maine-et-Loire)

MIDDLE OF XII CENTURY
Photo Coll. Baronne Brincard

68

CHAUVIGNY (Vienne)

A.-D. Capitals:

A. Announcement to the Shepherds.

FIRST HALF OF XII CENTURY

A.,B. *Photo E. Lefèvre-Pontalis*
C.,D. *Photo Archives d'Art et d'Histoire*

69

ANGOULÊME. Cathedral of St.-Pierre

A. Western façade. Frieze: A scene of combat
(cast in the Trocadéro Museum).
Photo Giraudon

B. Western façade. Tympanum of a blind bay:
The Apostles going out to preach the Gospel.
Photo E. Lefèvre-Pontalis

C. Frieze of the Apse
(cast in the Trocadéro Museum).
FIRST HALF OF XII CENTURY

70

A. AULNAY (Charente-Inférieure). Church of St.-Pierre
Window in the apse.
THIRD QUARTER OF XII CENTURY
Photo Archives d'Art et d'Histoire

B. ST.-SULPICE-D'ARNOULT (Charente-Inférieure)
West Door.
MIDDLE OF XII CENTURY
Photo Archives d'Art et d'Histoire

71

PÉRIGNAC (Charente-Inférieure)
Detail of the west front.
MIDDLE OF XII CENTURY
Photo Archives d'Art et d'Histoire

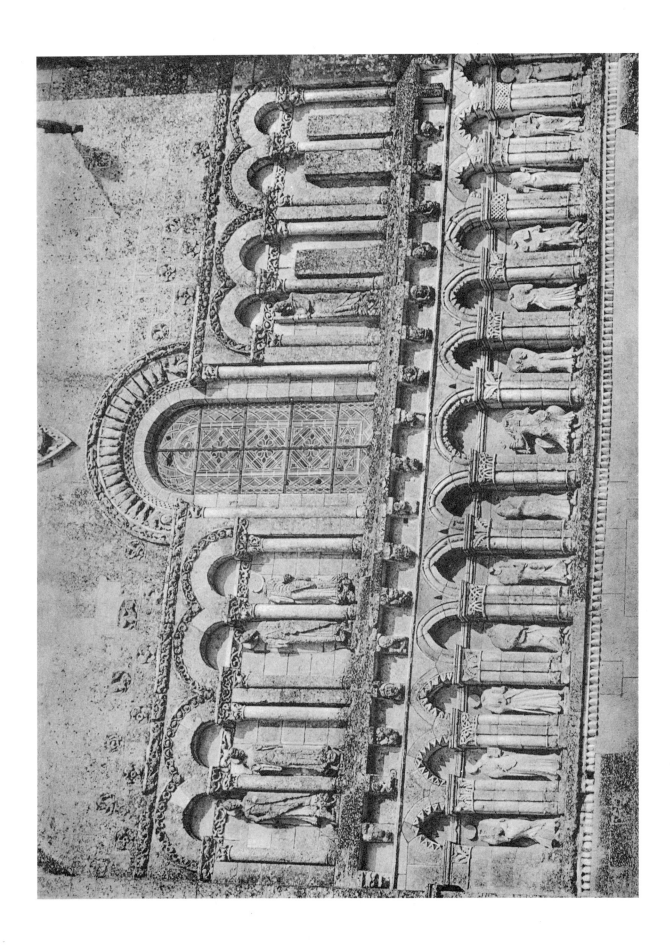

72

AULNAY (Charente-Inférieure). Church of St.-Pierre
Detail of the arch-rims on the west door.
THIRD QUARTER OF XII CENTURY
Photo E. Lefèvre-Pontalis

73

AULNAY (Charente-Inférieure). Church of St.-Pierre

A. Samson and Delilah.
Photo Archives d'Art et d'Histoire

B. The Murder of Abel.
Photo Archives d'Art et d'Histoire

C. Monsters.
Photo Martin-Sabon

D. Elephants.
Photo E. Lefèvre-Pontalis

THIRD QUARTER OF XII CENTURY

74

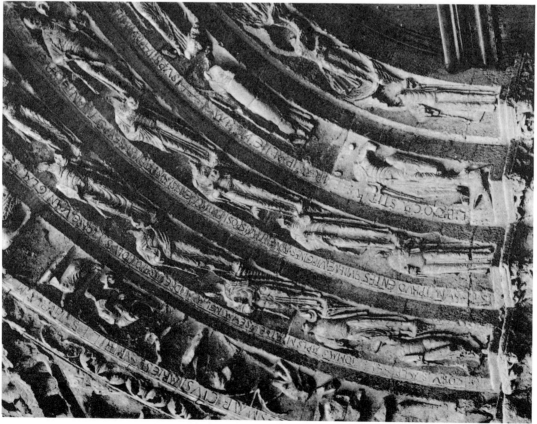

75

CIVRAY (Vienne)
Detail of the arch-rims.
THIRD QUARTER OF XII CENTURY
Photo E. Lefèvre-Pontalis

76

ST.-MICHEL-D'ENTRAIGUES (Charente)
St. Michael slaying the dragon.

ABOUT 1137
Photo E. Lefèvre-Pontalis

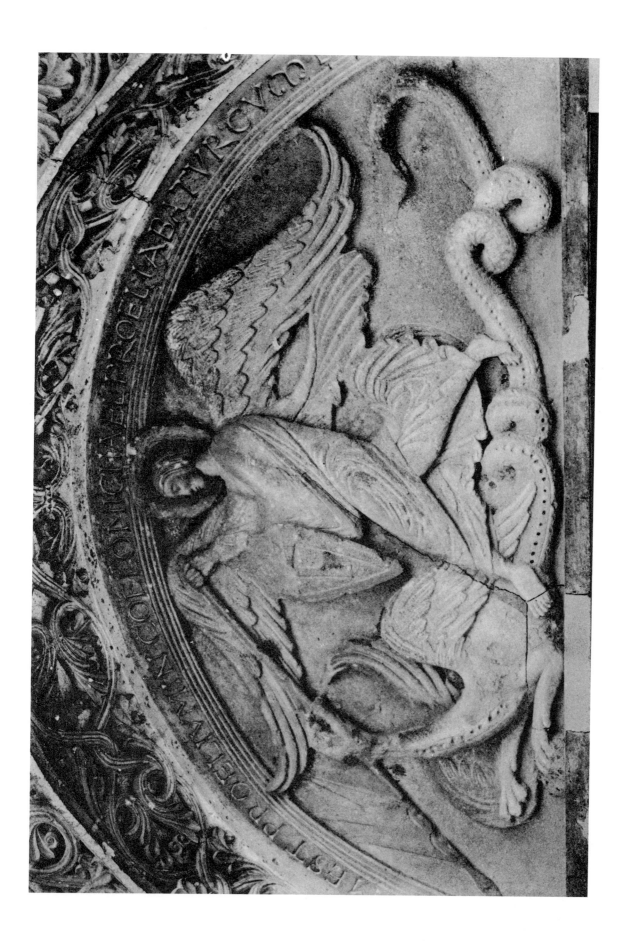

77

POITIERS. Church of Notre-Dame-la-Grande
Detail of the façade.

MIDDLE OF XII CENTURY

Photo Archives d'Art et d'Histoire

78

BAYEUX. Cathedral
Sculptures in the nave
(cast in the Trocadéro Museum).
MIDDLE OF XII CENTURY

79

RUCQUEVILLE (Calvados)

A.-D. Capitals with figures:
c. Flight into Egypt.
D. Incredulity of St. Thomas.

BEGINNING OF XII CENTURY
Photo Archives d'Art et d'Histoire

80

ST.-GILLES-DU-GARD
Façade:
A. St. Michael slaying the dragon.
B. St. James the Less and St. Paul.
LATTER HALF OF XII CENTURY
Photo R. Hamann

81

ST.-GILLES-DU-GARD
Façade: Details.
LATTER HALF OF XII CENTURY
Photo R. Hamann

82

ST.-GILLES-DU-GARD
Frieze of the Façade:

A. Christ purges the Temple.
B. Arrest of Christ in the Garden of Olives.

LAST QUARTER OF XII CENTURY
Photo E. Lefèvre-Pontalis

83

ARLES. Church of St.-Trophime
Doorway: Details.
LAST QUARTER OF XII CENTURY
Photo E. Lefèvre-Pontalis

84

ARLES. CLOISTER OF ST.-TROPHIME
North-west pillar: St. Peter, St. Trophime and St. John.
Bas-relief in two tiers:
Two sellers of spices, the Holy Women.

ABOUT 1180-1190
Photo E. Lefèvre-Pontalis

85

A. ARLES. CLOISTER OF ST.-TROPHIME
Capitals.
END OF XII CENTURY
Photo Archives d'Art et d'Histoire

B.-C. CAMBRIDGE (MASS.). FOGG MUSEUM
Capitals from Notre-Dame-des-Doms at Avignon:
B. Samson and Delilah.
C. Samson pulling down the pillars of the Temple.
LATTER HALF OF XII CENTURY
Photo Fogg Museum

86

87

A.-B. ST.-GUILHEM-LE-DÉSERT (Hérault)
A. Fragment imitated from the antique.
B. Virgin and Child.
Photo R. Hamann

C.-D. MONTPELLIER. Musée Archéologique
Bas-reliefs from St.-Guilhem-le-Désert (Hérault).
Photo Oudot de Dainville and G. Aubes

88

ELNE

Cloister of the Cathedral.

LAST QUARTER OF XII CENTURY

Photo E. Lefèvre-Pontalis

89

GERONA (Catalonia). Cathedral
Bas-relief on a pillar of the cloister.
LATTER HALF OF XII CENTURY
Photo Arxiu Mas

90

A. CUIXA. ABBEY OF ST.-MICHEL
Bas-reliefs now on the doorway of the abbot's lodge.
Photo Archives d'Art et d'Histoire

B. BOULE D'AMONT (PYRÉNÉES-ORIENTALES)
ABBEY OF SERRABONE
Porch.
LATTER HALF OF XII CENTURY
Photo Archives d'Art et d'Histoire

91

92

BOULE D'AMONT (Pyrénées-Orientales)
Abbey of Serrabone
A.-C. Capitals of the porch.
LATTER HALF OF XII CENTURY
Photo Archives d'Art et d'Histoire

93

A. CORNEILLA-DE-CONFLENT (Pyrénées-Orientales)
Tympanum.
LATTER HALF OF XII CENTURY
Photo Archives d'Art et d'Histoire

B. BOULE D'AMONT (Pyrénées-Orientales)
ABBEY OF SERRABONE
Capital of the porch.
LATTER HALF OF XII CENTURY
Photo Archives d'Art et d'Histoire

94

PAMPLONA (Navarre)

A. Decorative capital.
B. The Kiss of Judas.
C. The Entombment.

LATTER HALF OF XII CENTURY
Photo G. Gaillard

95

NAZARETH. Basilica of the Annunciation
Capitals supposed to have belonged to the doorway:

A. Apparition of Christ to St. Thomas.
B. The Raising of Tabitha.
c. Legend of St. James the Greater.
D. Legend of St. Matthew.

BEFORE 1187

96

JERUSALEM. Museum of the Greek Patriarchate
Heads found at Nazareth, probably destined for the Basilica
of the Annunciation.

BEFORE 1187
Photo R. P. Savignac